THE ADOLESCENT
JOURNEY

THE ADOLESCENT JOURNEY

DEVELOPMENT, IDENTITY FORMATION, AND PSYCHOTHERAPY

Marsha H. Levy-Warren, Ph.D.

A JASON ARONSON BOOK

ROWMAN & LITTLEFIELD PUBLISHERS, INC.
Lanham • Boulder • New York • Toronto • Oxford

The author gratefully acknowledges permission to reprint the lyrics from "When I Grow Up to Be a Man," copyright © 1992, Irving Music, Inc. (BMI). All rights reserved. International copyright reserved. Used by permission.

A JASON ARONSON BOOK

ROWMAN & LITTLEFIELD PUBLISHERS, INC.

Published in the United States of America
by Rowman & Littlefield Publishers, Inc.
A wholly owned subsidary of The Rowman & Littlefield Publishing Group, Inc.
4501 Forbes Boulevard, Suite 200, Lanham, Maryland 20706
www.rowmanlittlefield.com

PO Box 317
Oxford
OX2 9RU, UK

Copyright © 1996 by Marsha H. Levy-Warren
First Rowman & Littlefield Edition 2004

British Library Cataloguing in Publication Information Available

Library of Congress Cataloging-in-Publication Data

Levy-Warren, Marsha.
    The adolescent journey : development, identity formation, and psychotherapy / Marsha Levy-Warren.
        p. cm.
    Includes bibliographical references and index.
    ISBN 1-56821-546-0 (hc : alk.paper) / ISBN 0-7657-0285-1 (pb : alk. paper)
    1. Adolescent psychopathology. 2. Adolescent psychology. I. Title.
    [DNLM: 1. Adolescent Psychology. 2. Psychotherapy—in adolescence. 3. Adolescence. WS463 L668a 1996]
RJ503.L486   1996
616.89'022—dc20
DNLM/DLC
For Library of Congress   96-4642

Printed in the United States of America

♾™ The paper used in this publication meets the minimum requirements of American National Standard for Information Sciences—Permanence of Paper for Printed Library Materials, ANSı/NISO Z39.48-1992.

For Jaj

Contents

Acknowledgments

There are many to whom I wish to express deep gratitude. I think first of the patients who so graciously gave me permission to describe them in this book; the students at Barnard, Princeton, the Institute for Child, Adolescent, and Family Studies (ICAFS), and NYU Postdoctoral Program in Psychoanalysis and Psychotherapy, who kept me alert to both the importance and changing nature of adolescence; and Jason Aronson, M.D., who, by offering to publish this book, gave me the opportunity to share my ideas and experience with readers.

There are people who read specific chapters in their areas of expertise and gave me valuable feedback: my sincere thanks to Katherine Dalsimer, Ph.D., Daniel Levy, M.D., Andrea Marks, M.D., Wendy Olesker, Ph.D., and Ava Siegler, Ph.D. I also thank Carolyn Ellman, Ph.D., Susan Ball Roane, Ph.D., and Dale Ryan, C.S.W., who helped me shape my ideas and presentations by sharing their general reactions.

Donald Kaplan, Ph.D., and Fred Wolkenfeld, Ph.D., teachers, colleagues, and friends, read early drafts of some chapters and parts of chapters. Their counsel on these and other issues was tremendously valued. I miss them both enormously.

To Mary Bralove, friend, compatriot, and reader/editor extraordinaire, I offer my heartfelt gratitude. She has been steadfast, honest, and, at critical moments, supportive. To David Jeandheur, ever-ready to address my computer questions at the drop of a hat, however foolish they may have been—and without even a shade of condescension—my deepest thanks. It is hard to imagine how I could have been able to do this without his help.

I am thankful for the extraordinary support afforded by my dear friends and colleagues, Roslyn and Jerry Meyer and their wonderful children—Rebecca, Michael, and James. I feel deeply fortunate that they are a part of my personal and professional life. Similarly, Abby Adams, Ph.D., has been an invaluable presence in my life in a multitude of ways. I am profoundly grateful for her careful reading of my work and her consistent and longstanding encouragement.

And as for my phenomenal children, Anna and Jonathan, there are no words that can fully describe my feelings. You have offered interest, support, and anecdotes. You have been unbelievably patient, present, and proud. Without your love and sense of humor about my preoccupations during the writing of this book, it may never have been completed. Thank you both: for who you are, for what you have offered me, and for your faith in this project and me.

Last, but far from least, I want to offer my ever-present thanks to my dear husband, Jay, who has read every word I have written, endured every doubt I have experienced, and been present in mind and spirit throughout the writing of this book in ways that cannot possibly be sufficiently described.

I know I have written each word presented, for which I take full responsibility. But I also know that these acknowledgments are very real and the gratitude heartfelt. Each person mentioned has played a role for which I shall always be indebted.

Marsha H. Levy-Warren, Ph.D.

Introduction:
The Adolescent Journey

Adolescence is a developmental phase that spans roughly the ages of 10 to 22. It brings to mind the often-quoted Charles Dickens line: "It was the best of times, it was the worst of times, it was the age of wisdom, it was the age of foolishness. . . ."

Those of us who work or live with adolescents know first-hand the possibilities, problems, challenges, and conflicts that are part of this stage in life. Adolescents are at once impossible to live with and a joy to have around. They are moody, critical, combative, and absent-minded. They are also creative, energetic, and impassioned about the world and their place in it. *The Adolescent Journey: Development, Identity Formation, and Psychotherapy* shows these mercurial creatures in moments of both orneriness and fragility. It depicts the indomitable spirit and youthful excitement that is so much a part of the adolescent experience. It is this spirit that enriches family life and gives so much vitality to the sociocultural world.

The Adolescent Journey is inspired by a profound appreciation of adolescents that spans over twenty years of clinical work and teaching. Its purpose is to deepen health professionals' and parents' awareness of the importance of this developmental phase. Adolescence is a period in life in which critical psychological changes occur. It is a time when character, a person's customary way of being in the world, crystallizes, and identity, the stable sense of who a person is, forms. It is the time that a fundamental psychological issue—achieving an independent identity, rooted in family but reaching out to the world beyond—is confronted and resolved.

Without an adequate resolution of these critical aspects of adolescent development, individuals move into adulthood compromised in their functioning. Their troubles can include difficulties in making commitments in their intimate lives, difficulties in maintaining a sense of confidence and self-esteem, and difficulties in making important life choices about careers, religious beliefs, and morality. In short, adolescent wounds left untreated fester in the psyche. Many unhappy years later, these same issues come into focus as adult patients and their therapists go back to confront unresolved adolescent conflicts.

The Adolescent Journey seeks to give this crucial, but often misunderstood, period its due. It aims to be a comprehensive statement about adolescent development, identity formation, and psychotherapeutic treatment. In this book, I examine adolescence from three different points of view: those of the individual, the family, and the sociocultural world. Of course, it is possible to write from any one of these perspectives, but I feel a single viewpoint is inadequate. No adolescent goes through this developmental period in isolation, no family sets itself apart from an individual going through adolescence, and every adolescent's experience is colored by the historical and cultural period in which it occurs. This latter point is particularly important. In *The Adolescent Journey*, I specifically address cultural pressures affecting today's adolescents: the earlier onset of puberty; the rise in the incidence of adolescent eating disorders; the threat of AIDS infection; the danger of alcohol and drug abuse; and increasingly competitive school and work environments.

Cultural issues, in general, are central to adolescent identity formation. How and when adolescents see themselves as separate from their families and how they come to see themselves as members of larger ethnic and cultural groups are major themes in this work. I also explore in depth the connection between physical development and emotional and social growth. I emphasize how this connection develops into adolescent gender and sexual identities, as well as the capacity for emotionally and physically intimate relationships.

This contemporary Freudian view of adolescent development comes from my own thinking, observation, and years of practical experience. I am influenced by the psychoanalytic theory of development, my clinical and supervisory experience, and psychological research findings. Friends, colleagues, students, patients, and my own adolescent children and their friends have all informed my thinking as have numerous books, papers, and research reports. I have tried to be scrupulous in documenting these influences, but apologize in advance for any failure to credit a source properly. The omission is strictly inadvertent.

I am appreciative of certain work that has particularly influenced me. Sigmund Freud noted the personal and social significance of puberty. His "The Transformations of Puberty" (1905a) aptly describes the psychological sea-change represented by this physiological event. He also treated and wrote about three adolescents, Katharina (Breuer and Freud 1895), Dora (1905b), and "the homosexual woman" (1920), but did not grasp the necessity for articulating technical differences in treating this age group. Indeed, his problems in working with both Dora and "the homosexual woman" stemmed in part from his dealing with them as if they were adults rather than late adolescents (Glenn 1978). The case descriptions themselves, however, give us some of our earliest examples of adolescent psychopathology and efforts at clinical intervention.

Anna Freud honed in on adolescence and outlined many important aspects of this period of development. In three seminal papers, "Instinctual Anxiety During Puberty" (1936a), "The Ego and the Id at Puberty" (1936b), and "Adolescence" (1958), she describes both the advance in development and the rise in anxiety at puberty (which Sigmund Freud had suggested in "The Transformations of Puberty"). She discusses how this anxiety derives from the relative difficulty the weakened ego and superego have in contending with the hormonally induced upsurge in the strength of the id. The defenses adolescents form to contend with the anxiety, such as asceticism and intellectualization, do not develop until this time.

Anna Freud worked with both Siegfried Bernfeld (1938) and August Aichhorn (1925) early in the psychoanalytic movement. Bernfeld and Aichhorn distinguished themselves by attempting to treat delinquents with psychoanalytic methods. Their success, relative to others, alerted those who worked with these young adolescents to the importance of early childhood in the etiology of delinquency. Their particular focus was the early symbolic or real loss of significant people in these children's lives, and how these early losses affected the development of their sense of right and wrong and their conscience (i.e., superego development).

With the ideas of the Freuds and Margaret Mahler and her colleagues (Mahler 1968, Mahler et al. 1975) on separation and individuation in early childhood as his foundation, Peter Blos (1962, 1963, 1967, 1968, 1974) wrote extensively on adolescent development. He identified five phases: preadolescence, early adolescence, adolescence proper, late adolescence, and postadolescence. He described a second individuation process, modeled on the one of infancy and early childhood, but characterized by progression and regression, leading to stability in mood and functioning. In this second individuation, adolescents form a mature ego ideal to which they aspire, and modify their intrapsychic structures. He portrays adolescence as a "second chance" (1967), one that permits adolescents to reorganize themselves internally in such a way that prior conflictual resolutions can be re-worked and a better functioning character and personality can be formed. His work is seminal in the psychoanalytic literature on adolescence, and serves as a significant underpinning for this book.

Erik Erikson (1950, 1956, 1959, 1968) is an inspiration to me. His capacity to integrate individual development and influences from the social world throughout the life cycle was extremely important in the development of my own thinking. I, too, try to look at individual development as it occurs in the social world, and weave together the adolescent's developmental needs with the needs of the society in which the adolescent lives.

Louise Kaplan's (1984) book on adolescence, which explicated the adolescent mourning for childhood and narcissistic development during this phase, has been on the syllabus for my college courses on adolescence since the time it was published. Aaron Esman's (1975b, 1983) collections of work on adolescence and his recent book on culture (1990) have also been part of my teaching repertoire in both college and psychoanalytic training courses for many years. I know that they have subtly and directly influenced my work. Katharine Dalsimer's (1986) rendition of female adolescent subphase development, as elaborated through the use of characters from literature, is a wonderfully written book that provided both substantive insight and aesthetic pleasure.

My thinking also has been profoundly influenced by D.W. Winnicott (1958, 1964, 1965, 1967, 1971) and Hans Loewald (1973, 1979, 1980). Their exquisite sensitivity to the unfolding of development, with its ever-growing and changing perceptions, feelings, and integrations, has made me more attuned to the intricate changes that adolescents experience over the course of this phase of life.

In a similar vein, the complexity and thoroughness of Edith Jacobson's (1961, 1964) work on self and identity has been a foundation for my thinking about adolescent identity formation; the particular clinical considerations raised by Kurt Eissler (1950, 1958), Selma Fraiberg (1955), Elizabeth Geleerd (1957), Marjorie Harley (1970), John Meeks (1971), and Judith Mishne (1986) have informed my own practice as well as my thinking about adolescent treatment. Finally, the overall depth and creativity demonstrated in the work on adolescence by Moses and Eglé Laufer (1966, 1968, 1976, 1981, 1984) have focused my attention on many profound and fascinating dimensions of adolescent psychic life.

Work with patients is equally influential in my thinking about adolescence. Cases from my practice and life experience are therefore used throughout the book. In the development and identity formation sections, I use these case studies to illustrate theoretical points. In the psychotherapy section, they are used to demonstrate various treatment issues, including those related to assessment, diagnosis, and technique. In some instances, I quote at length from conversations with a particular patient. These conversations, reconstructed from my clinical notes, try to give the spirit and flavor of the sessions and aim to convey the courage, humor, and honesty of the patients. Their names are changed and certain details altered to protect their identities.

The patients described here, as in the general population of those in psychotherapy, are typically from middle- or upper-class families. I also have drawn from a multitude of experiences, both direct and indirect, with adolescents from less privileged backgrounds: I consulted for many years in inner-city schools in three different cities, and worked and supervised in clinics that served low-income populations. These experiences, and extensive reading and discussions, are integral to my views of development and treatment. I believe both that these views are generally applicable across class and cultural lines, and that it is necessary for clinicians and others who work with adolescents to take family and ethnocultural contexts into account in understanding and treating adolescents.

Chapter One, "Adolescent Development," contrasts the world of a child to that of an adolescent. The chapter demonstrates how our perception of inner and outer worlds expands through the subphases of adolescence. Where children are rooted in their families, adolescents are based in their families but focus much of their attention on the world outside the home. Early adolescents look back at childhood and compare their prior images of themselves to those that they form in the present. They attempt to integrate their bodily changes, new thinking capacities, and transformed relations with parents. Middle adolescents, who primarily live in the present, turn to their contemporaries for aid in their exploration of sexuality, group affiliations, and overall competence. Late adolescents consolidate the images they have of themselves into a cohesive and stable identity, then are able to begin to look toward what the future may hold for them. The chapter ends with a description of the tasks of adolescence: the development of autonomy, competence, and sexual identity.

In *The Adolescent Journey*, I significantly broaden and elaborate Freud's early definition of genitality. He described genitality as the last of the psychosexual stages. It followed the oral, anal, phallic, oedipal, and latency phases. I place particular emphasis on the contribution of each subphase (early, middle, and late) of adolescence to genitality. Chapters Two, Three, and Four explore this expanded concept of genitality. The early adolescent aspects are explored in Chapter Two, and embrace the elements of puberty, masturbation, and the revisiting of the Oedipus complex. The advent of puberty, with its vast attendant physiological changes, creates the necessity for adolescents to contend with newly formed bodies, sensations, and urges. Masturbation contributes to their ability to get to know how these changed bodies work. Growth in stature and the attainment of a reproductive capacity bring the nature of adult sexuality into awareness. Childhood theories about sexuality (i.e., the Oedipus complex) must be revisited and revised in light of adolescents' new knowledge and experience.

Middle adolescence brings with it a necessity for integrating one of the hallmarks of puberty: the change from a child's comparatively sexually ambiguous body shape to the adolescent's unmistakably gendered body shape. The growth in abstract thinking, an important characteristic of the cognitive changes of this developmental phase, permits adolescents to perceive and appreciate the social significance of being female or male. This, in turn, brings into focus what it means to be feminine or masculine and how much a particular adolescent wishes to behave in keeping with sex-role stereotypes. Chapter Three examines adolescent gender and sexual identity, with particular focus on the role of the world of peers in the identity transformations of this time.

When adolescents begin to develop greater objectivity about parents who were, in childhood, comparatively unquestioned authorities, they undergo a shift in their moral and ethical beliefs. They explore different ideas about what is right or wrong, and what is good or bad. They can begin to see that the world exists with many shades of gray, rather than the black and white of childhood days.

Profound questions about spirituality, justice, and the nature of belief systems abound in their thoughts and conversations. This results in the formation of a personally derived moral and ethical code. The code becomes an aspect of the mature ego ideal, a set of ideas about who and what the late adolescent wishes to be. Chapter Four describes the development and function of a mature ego ideal. Once formed, this component of identity allows the adolescent to regulate self-esteem internally, based upon the degree to which actions in the world are in keeping with the set of aspirations that the mature ego ideal represents. This chapter also explores the nature and synthesis of adult identifications and the way they coalesce into a sense of "I."

Adolescence is the period of time in which the sociocultural world becomes more comprehensible; past, present, and future more clearly delineated; and the foundations of identity better articulated. As they move out of their families, adolescents temporarily lose the sense of belonging that gives them a sense of place in the world. In early adolescence, they turn to their best friends to derive a sense of belonging. In middle adolescence, they look to various group identifications at first, then to steady boyfriends and girlfriends. In late adolescence, they become conscious of their ethnocultural origins and chosen affiliations to achieve a larger sense of belonging. Chapter Five, "Mature Ethnocultural Identity," explores the evolution of ethnocultural identity and some of the ramifications of interferences in its development.

Adolescents' issues about autonomy, and parents' frustrations with and fears about their children, can create enormous difficulties for therapists. Establishing whether to see the adolescent alone or with the parents or family, payment routines, frequency of sessions, parent contact paradigms, and cancellation policies are but a few of the many elements constituting a viable structure for adolescent treatment. What therapists are hoping to accomplish, how they communicate with their adolescent patients, how they can expect treatment to end, and what kind of post-termination contact is best are the subjects of Chapter Six, "Adolescent Treatment: Beginning, Middle, and End." This chapter explores relevant developmental issues, family concerns, and treatment pitfalls, and offers both clinical anecdotes and practical suggestions for envisioning and structuring the clinical situation.

Deciphering the roots of psychopathology requires consideration of when in a person's life symptoms develop. The same symptoms, erupting at different points in life, may have quite different meanings. Chapter Seven, "Considering Subphase: Early vs. Late Adolescent Outbreak of Bulimia," uses the example of the outbreak of bulimia in two cases, one in which the symptoms appeared in early adolescence and one in late adolescence, to illustrate the significance of timing in evaluating the meaning of bulimia in patients' lives and in the context of the flow of adolescent development.

Chapters Eight, Nine, and Ten present three extensive case studies, one in each of the subphases. Chapter Eight, "Frozen at the Brink: An Early Adolescent's Wish Not to See," presents the case of a girl who steadfastly refused to observe and accept the changes that were taking place in her body, in her family, and among her peers. Her strong wish was to remain a child. The adolescent view of the world that was now available to her was frightening and sad. Her parents lived together, but were estranged. Her friends were changing rapidly, as exemplified by their different social activities and their questioning of adult authority, but this early adolescent did not feel the desire to join them. She was frozen at the brink of adolescence.

Chapter Nine describes a middle adolescent who broke into a department store to prove to his friends that he was not a wimp. He "did not care" about what his mother, father, or the school authorities thought about his actions; he only hoped that he would not get caught in the act. The court mandated psychotherapy. This chapter, "Inside Out: A Middle Adolescent's Wish to Stay at Home," describes a middle adolescent's underlying wish to remain at home with his parents rather than venturing out with his friends, and how treatment ultimately aided him in moving out into his peer group. The central issue of the treatment was how much this patient was able to focus on himself and his life outside the home, rather than on his parents.

Chapter Ten, "Going Through the Motions: A Late Adolescent's Wish to Wait," describes a young woman who came to treatment at the age of a late adolescent, but with primary issues that made her seem much more like someone in the throes of early adolescence. Her early traumatic history and multiply symptomatic presenting picture led to a decision to undertake a psychoanalysis. The first five years of this ten-year treatment were focused on moving this young woman from early adolescence to late adolescence, with particular attention placed on the development of her genitality. The physical traumata of her early life made adolescent integration of pubertal changes especially difficult. The psychoanalytic treatment outlined in this chapter establishes links between these early traumata and interferences in her adolescent development.

Forming a more mature relationship with parents requires that adolescents be able to see them more objectively. Where once they were idealized, parents are now alternately de-idealized and appreciated for who they actually are and have been to and for their adolescents. If the parents undergo a divorce, thus throwing their own lives into flux, adolescents often have to struggle more in their attempts to keep who their parents are in focus. This may inhibit their ability to shift their attention away from defining themselves through their parents' reactions and toward more self-derived conceptions of who they are. Similarly, if adolescents are thrust into dependent situations such as those that arise in cases of severe illness or physical disability, at the same time as their body images are changing and they are taking over caretaking functions from their parents, there may be a disruption in the developmental process of establishing bodily responsibility. Adolescents also must come to grasp the symbolic and real meaning of death. If, because of life circumstances, they are forced to confront these issues before they are ready, the usual adolescent process may well go awry. Chapter Eleven, "Developmental Disruptions: Transcultural Movement, Divorce, Death, Infirmity, and Adoption," describes these potential stumbling blocks and others by interweaving case examples and developmental theory.

The epilogue, "The Journey Continues: Adolescence and Adult Life," discusses the ways in which the issues of adolescence appear in adulthood. Waves of nostalgia, creative spurts, and rushes of emotion are often instances of recaptured adolescent experience in the form of adult memories or reenactments. How characteristics of adolescence are typically carried into adult life, what effect having adolescent children has on parents, how adult experiences (such as menopause) resonate with adolescence, and the role adolescence has in the life cycle are considered.

I hope that those who read *The Adolescent Journey* will come to appreciate the profound impact adolescence has on our lives. I hope that those who live with adolescents will come to see them with greater respect and understanding, and thus will find it easier to react to them with greater tolerance; that those who work clinically with adults will come to recognize more readily when adolescent issues arise with their patients; and that those who work with this age group will come to share my enthusiasm and wonder in seeing them change from day to day. Finally, I hope that this book will inspire a return to adolescence: to the deep questioning of ourselves and our world that is the hallmark of this remarkable time of life.

1

Development

1

Adolescent Development

Hold every moment sacred. Give each clarity and meaning, each the weight of thine awareness, each its true and due fulfillment.

Thomas Mann, *The Beloved Returns*

There is perhaps no other developmental phase more hotly debated and more misunderstood than adolescence. Many perceive it as a single, undifferentiated block of time, a period in which the child undergoes a metamorphosis and emerges as an adult. The significant transitions and difficulties that make up the texture of the phase are often glossed over. My view is that adolescence is more aptly described in three separate subphases, each distinguished by dominant issues, problems, and resolutions for the adolescents themselves, their parents, and the sociocultural world in which they live. Early adolescents, for example, are predominantly concerned with loosening dependencies upon parents while making the transition out of childhood. Middle adolescents are preoccupied with establishing themselves among their peers. By late adolescence, the most important task is that of moving out into the world in a manner that feels self-defined.

Adolescence is a phase of life that can be and is described by others in a variety of ways. It can be examined chronologically, for it involves physiological and cognitive maturational processes. It can be described psychologically, for it involves internal processes of change in each individual. It also can be discussed from the perspective of its reverberations in the social and cultural worlds, for it is during this time of life that socialization into the role of the adult takes place. This chapter describes each of them and the interactions among them. The perspective I take is that no one of these dimensions of adolescence is dominant. Each is key, and each must be taken into account when looking at the adolescent process. Ultimately, each adolescent must be aware of and integrate all of them.

Those who think and write about adolescence also come from different theoretical and practical orientations. This chapter, indeed this book, puts forth a view that integrates psychoanalytic theory and practice and psychological research findings about this developmental phase. What follows is a distillation of the conclusions drawn from these orientations, with special attention to those issues that I view as dominant in the adolescent process, both for the adolescents themselves and for the adults they become.

Children's roots are in their families' homes. Needs and wants are met at home, ideas of right and wrong are established at home, and a sense of basic goodness and worth grows out of the ways in which families respond to and appreciate their children at home. The view children have of the world, though not simple, is clear, defined, and, in adequate families, secure (Mahler et al. 1975, Winnicott 1971). Children feel small in a world that is divided between the big and the small, and feel safe knowing that those who are big care for those who are small.

Families thus provide the lenses through which children see the world. The arrival of adolescence in children's lives is a change in focus. Their view of themselves, their parents, and the world shifts enormously. Suddenly the world of big and small is not so clearly delineated: where once they knew they were small, now they see themselves as growing big . . . and bigger. The values of their parents, once held so unquestioningly, are now compared (sometimes unfavorably) to the views and values of others whose opinions may seem more important or wiser. Even the sense of comfort once enjoyed at home may come only intermittently. Children's stable sense of themselves and their families often feels thrown into relative disorder.

While adolescents' roots, like those of children, are in the home, their overriding attention during this later phase of development turns to the world outside the home. They must find their ways in that world, using the lenses of their families but also refining them in keeping with their personal experiences. The refinements come particularly in the dimensions of identity (genitality and ethnicity) that have their foundation in the family life of childhood but develop social and cultural meanings during adolescence. (See Chapters Two, Three, and Four for an extensive discussion of the components of genitality, and Chapter Five for a fuller discussion of ethnocultural identity).

In the context of this move into the world outside the family home, childhood comes to be seen as an experience of the past. Adolescents speak wistfully of childhood experiences, look at old pictures, and ask parents to recount stories of days long past. They begin to realize that there simply is no going back. The growth process is unidirectional (Katan 1951).

Until this phase of life, children are comparatively unaware of the passage of time. It is a developmental advance for them to take note of time passing. It is with the beginning of adolescence that children become aware that a part of their lives is actually over. This often evokes their first feelings of loss, and, at times, nostalgia (Jacobson 1961, Kaplan 1984).

It is not uncommon for adolescents to begin to keep diaries to stave off the feelings of emptiness and loss that characterize this time (Dalsimer 1986). The feelings can include the loss of a continuous sense of self. Bach (1994) suggests that diaries permit adolescents to mark the many variations in their moods and sense of self, thus providing them with a way to maintain continuity of self at a time when this is often quite difficult.

In the course of development, there is ever-increasing complexity in children's perceptions of themselves and their environments. They are able to take in more and more of the world as they mature. It is because of this greater complexity that adolescents experience feelings such as nostalgia and loss in relation to childhood, for they are able to distinguish between what they are now and what they were then and to realize that the ways of the past must remain part of the history they are now forming.

This is the process of adolescent differentiation, which involves seeing the world in more and more highly complex ways. Adolescent differentiation includes shifts in the perception of time, thinking capabilities, bodily definition, and social and cultural awareness. There is a substantial transformation of the sense of self, one which leads to greater autonomy and a specific, realistic appraisal and integration of capacities in all spheres of an adolescent's life: physiological, cognitive, psychological, and social.

THE PHYSIOLOGICAL CHANGES OF PUBERTY

The arrival of pubescence heralds the major shifts of adolescence. "Pubescence" derives from the Latin word *pubescere*, which means "to grow hairy." The hairless bodies of children begin to change, and both children and parents have reactions. They know that these changes signal the beginning of a larger set of changes that move the child into adulthood. Pubescence is the process of puberty, the formal beginning of adolescence; to be pubescent is to have reached puberty. "Puberty" comes from the Latin word *pubertas*, or "the age of manhood," "adolescence" from the Latin word *adolescere*, or "to grow up." The physiological changes initiate the adolescent process, while a psychological sense of consolidation of identity ends the process.

The rate, timing, and nature of puberty is mostly determined by potentials established genetically. There is some evidence, however, that birth weight, nutrition, and general health affect the way these

potentials emerge. Rose Frisch (1983), a noted researcher on
menarche (i.e., first menstruation), suggests, for example, that
menarche is reached by girls now at an earlier age than was the case
in previous centuries because children are heavier today, and
menarche occurs when girls reach a critical weight. With careful
nutrition and adequate health practices becoming the norm, there
is some evidence that this downward trend is stabilizing (Wyshak
and Frisch 1982).

Once begun, however, the pubertal process unfolds in a way that
is largely predetermined: the hypothalamus secretes gonadotropin-
releasing hormone (GnRH), which stimulates the anterior pituitary.
The pituitary then produces growth stimulating hormone (which
effects a growth spurt) and gonadotropins, which stimulate the
gonads (sexual glands). These sexual glands are the ovaries (which
produce estrogen and progesterone) in females and the testes
(which produce testosterone) in males. Gonad stimulation leads to
genital growth and the development of secondary sex characteristics. These hormonal changes result in the obvious signs of puberty,
such as the growth of pubic and axillary hair, deepening of the
voice, growth of facial, chest, leg, and forearm hair in boys, and
growth of breasts and widening of the hips in girls. This is also the
time when boys begin to produce live sperm and girls reach their
menarche (Ford and Beach 1951, Katchadourian 1977, Stoltz and
Stoltz 1951).

In contemporary Western society, it is normative for the age of
menarche to be 12½ (for girls), and the age of live sperm pro-
duction to be 14½ (for boys). A two-year range in either direction is
considered to be normal. In general, then, girls reach puberty two
years earlier than boys (Brooks-Gunn and Warren 1985). The
average age of puberty also has dropped about four months every
ten years for the last several decades (Tanner 1962, 1978).

This is a fact with enormous social significance. It means, for
example, that some girls must contend with the realization that they
can produce children when they are in fifth and sixth grades! It is
difficult for girls this age and younger to feel prepared for such a
change, and difficult for boys to feel they are contemporaries of
their female counterparts during this time. A girl at the earlier end

of the normal range for reaching puberty is only 10½. For a girl this age to feel "ready" to take care of the essential bodily needs that menstruation entails, and to integrate the social and psychological meanings of this event in her life and in her cultural surrounds, requires an exceptional degree of emotional maturity. More and more girls have had to face this challenge in the last several decades.

The rapid rate at which pubertal changes take place, especially in the first few years, are reminiscent of the first years of life, but affect adolescents in a manner that is more conscious—perhaps even more self-conscious—than was true during the earlier growth period. Adolescents may feel that their bodily changes run at a pace and in a manner that is different from any other sense that they have of themselves. Emotional maturity may develop more quickly than physiological growth, or physiological maturity may occur before the adolescent feels ready for it. These typical asymmetries have led some theorists to suggest that adolescents' identities are separate from their bodies at this time (Stone and Church 1957).

Freud (1905a) addressed a sexual aspect of the effects of pubertal changes. He believed that these significant physiological changes resulted in surges of sexual feeling that required adolescents to turn away from intimate contact with family members. He described the necessity for upholding the incest taboo: the new sexual tension in contacts with family members leads those involved to maintain greater distance than they had in childhood. While children can turn to their parents for comfort, adolescents must find other sources.

In the physiological sphere, adolescents are attempting to become familiar with their newly changed bodies and how they work, and developing alternative ways of seeking comfort and affection to those that were typical of childhood. They must come to see themselves as having bodies that function in an adult manner, with greater size, strength, and coordination, and a reproductive capacity. All of these physiological changes have an important impact on the ways adolescents perceive themselves, that is, their sense of self.

COGNITIVE CHANGES

Adolescents perceive themselves and the world in ways that dramatically differ from those of children. The shift feels much like one that precedes it: from being a non-reader to being a reader, when incomprehensible groups of letters suddenly become recognizable words, phrases, and sentences. In this instance, however, it is ideas and concepts, the world of abstract thought, that becomes comprehensible in a new way. This is a source of endless fascination, for adolescents now find it possible to think about the thinking process, develop hypotheses, and contemplate the future. The political, philosophical, aesthetic, and spiritual worlds open up at this time in ways not available to children (Levy-Warren 1992). (See the section of Chapter Four on "The Mature Ego Ideal" for a full discussion of how these cognitive changes permit adolescents to form independent ideas, aspirations, and self-reproductions.) Adolescents develop theories about how these worlds should be and then try to validate their hypotheses through careful observation (Leadbeater and Dione 1981, Piaget 1947, 1972).

Bärbel Inhelder and Jean Piaget (1958) emphasize a change in the direction of the thinking process during this developmental period. Children look around and develop theories to explain what they see; adolescents contemplate possibilities, then look out into the world to validate their hypotheses. This is the change from the child's concrete form of thinking to that of the adolescent, that is, formal thinking. Reality becomes secondary to hypothesis. Adolescents are often far more interested in generating theories about how the world *could* work than they are in carefully observing how the world *does* work. The countless heated conversations that echo in the halls of high schools in which adolescents spin out metatheories to explain the history of war over the centuries or the fundamental sources of knowledge over time amply illustrate this cognitive change.

Adolescents can think things through on their own. This cognitive change contributes to a growing sense of autonomy. Adolescents do not have to look to others for explanations. Rather, they can generate and test hypotheses on their own (Ausubel and

Ausubel 1966, Manaster et al. 1977). They are able now to look more
clearly at their inner and outer worlds and note their complexity. It
is possible for them to perceive and accept ambiguities that children
would attempt to simplify, for the cognitive apparatus of children
cannot bear the lack of clarity on which adolescents thrive. This is a
significant component of adolescent differentiation.

Their increased cognitive capacities permit adolescents to see
themselves and the world more clearly. Thus, they are able to see
their parents in a different light (Eisert and Kahle 1986). The
parents of childhood are left to the past. Where once parents were
regarded as all-powerful and all-knowing, they are seen now for the
mere mortals that they are. This is often not a welcome realization
for either adolescents or their parents. Adolescents may feel disappointed or disillusioned; parents may feel hurt or threatened. This
interplay of feelings is an element of the separation process that
characterizes adolescence, one of the important components of
change in the psychological sphere.

DIFFERENTIATION: CHANGE IN THE PSYCHOLOGICAL SPHERE

Separation processes recur in each individual's life. The first such
process occurs in early childhood and is vividly and thoroughly
described by Mahler and her colleagues (1975), as well as a number
of other theorists and researchers (e.g., Kaplan 1984, Pine 1985).
Most fundamentally, it involves the growing awareness in infants and
young children of being distinct people, different from the significant caregivers and siblings who share their worlds.

In adolescence, there is a separation from childhood. Adolescents come to recognize that they are not the same as they used to
be: they look different, feel different, see the world differently, and
interact with others differently. Their parents do not need to play
the same roles in their lives, for adolescents are more capable and
able to be more responsible for themselves. Parental functions in a
number of areas can now be managed by the adolescent, for
example, personal hygiene, eating, sleeping, or being motivated to

do schoolwork. Taking over these functions does not happen immediately upon reaching puberty but occurs over the course of adolescence. The greater sense of autonomy which results is a source of real pride.

In the psychological sphere, the differentiation of adolescence includes both separation and individuation processes (Blos 1962, Kaplan 1984). The first individuation, described by Mahler and her colleagues, entails a gradual evolution of the infant and young child from relative self-focus and containment to awareness of self and others, in more and more complex terms. The development of a sense of object constancy (Fraiberg 1969), the capacity to keep an (internal) image of the primary caregiver, is an important aspect of this individuation process. Once achieved, object constancy permits a young child to feel secure without the actual presence of the caregiver. The internal representation suffices for evoking the comfort once felt in the caregiver's presence.

The constancy that needs to be achieved during the adolescent individuation process (which Blos [1962] refers to as the second individuation process) is in the self-regulation of feelings, urges, and values. Adolescents no longer look to others to determine what they should feel, think, believe, or do. Once this self-regulatory constancy is achieved, mood and self-esteem remain relatively stable. This autonomy of functioning can occur when a disengagement from both significant internalized and external objects has taken place, that is, when adolescents have separated from the significant caregivers of childhood and taken on primary responsibility for themselves. (This involves major transformations in all aspects of identity formation, as elaborated in Chapters Two, Three, Four, and Five.)

In the individuation process, adolescents realistically take into account their specific characteristics, including weaknesses and strengths, and fantasies and observations. Accurate mental representations of body parts, competencies, personality traits, and so on are collected by each adolescent, for the eventual purpose of forming a cohesive image of self. This is the consolidation of the sense of self that characterizes the end of adolescence.

This consolidation process is described in a number of different ways. Max Gitelson (1948), David Beres (1961), and Peter Blos (1968), for example, see adolescence as the most important period for the formation of character, a person's habitual way of dealing in the world and engaging in social interactions (from a psychological point of view). Leo Spiegel (1961) describes adolescence as the period of an "achievement of a firm sense of self" (p. 11), in which constancy is achieved in self-feeling. Erik Erikson (1956, 1959) sees it as the time for establishing an "ego identity," a persistent sameness within oneself and a persistent sharing of some kind of essential character with others. To accomplish this, adolescents must have a "normative crisis," in which there is a period of increased internal conflict, but also potential for real growth; and a "psychosocial moratorium," a time in which adolescents freely experiment in the social world for the purpose of finding a personal niche in that world.

Adolescence was not always regarded as the specific phase of development that theorists such as Gitelson, Blos, and Erikson presume. G. Stanley Hall (1904), the first psychology Ph.D. in America, was the first to name and characterize it as a specific phase. Hall understood adolescence to be a period of life that recapitulates an earlier period in each individual's life and in history. For the individual, adolescence is a period in which the social awakenings of infancy are repeated and extended. Where infants become increasingly aware of their social surroundings in the context of the family, adolescents become increasingly aware of their larger social contexts. His Darwinian leanings led Hall to describe this also in evolutionary terms. He saw it as a time of transition, similar to that which linked the cave-dwelling period to the period of civilization. He also noted that it is a period of *sturm und drang* (storm and stress), in which social relationships are structured and moral values established. Children become adults during adolescence; the precivilized become the civilized. Hall's work was a forerunner to Erikson's "normative crisis."

Ernest Jones (1922) reiterated and elaborated on Hall's ideas about recapitulation, noting that adolescence repeats and expands on both the earlier historical subphases and on earlier psychosexual subphases in each person's life. Others expand on Hall's ideas about adolescence as a separate developmental phase characterized by upheaval.[1] Whether there is psychological upheaval, and, if so, of what type, are issues that have caused much upheaval in psychoanalytic and psychological circles. Battle lines have been drawn between those who downplay the presence of turmoil[2] and those who stress it.[3] There are also those who claim that adolescents who appear to remain relatively calm are at some psychological risk.[4]

The varied points of view are difficult to sort through because the different writers operate in different realms of thought and experience. Many of the psychoanalytic thinkers, for example, are describing unconscious turmoil, which manifests itself in ways that are not necessarily observable by others or would not necessarily be characterized as turmoil by others. The early adolescent male who pierces his ear, the straight-A student who gets a C, the former preppy dresser who starts wearing punk clothing, might all be involved in such turmoil.

Daniel Offer and his associates (1981), the primary proponents of the position that turmoil is insignificant in normal adolescence, still note that there is evidence, especially in early adolescence, of conflicts between parents and their children about dress, routine, curfew, and other issues. What they emphasize is that adolescent "rebellion" (instances of out-and-out defiance between adolescents and their families or society) is not the norm. Offer and his colleagues, whose work was publicized in the popular press, may well

---

1. Some of the most prominent of the psychoanalytic authors who take this position include Blos 1962, 1967, Erikson 1959, A. Freud 1936, 1958, Furman 1973, Geleerd 1961, 1964, Jacobson 1961, 1964, Kaplan 1984, Katan 1951, and Spiegel 1951, 1958.

2. Important representatives of this group are Ausubel 1954, Baittle and Offer 1971, Elkin and Westley 1955, Gesell et al. 1956, Hsu 1961, Offer 1969a,b, Offer and Offer 1975, Offer et al. 1981, and Stone and Church 1957.

3. These writers and researchers include Blos 1962, Deutsch 1967, A. Freud 1958, Geleerd 1961, Jacobson 1961, 1964, Josselyn 1952, 1967, Kiell 1964, Laufer 1966, and Pearson 1958.

4. Some of the psychoanalytic writers and psychological researchers who fall into this group are Douvan and Adelson 1966, A. Freud 1958, Friedenberg 1959, and Keniston 1962.

have had an impact on what parents and others now expect of adolescents. The anticipated adolescent "rebellion" of the sixties and seventies is not what is expected today.

In contrast, I believe that adolescents typically experience turmoil. Adolescents feel different from how they felt as children, and this is unsettling to them (and, often, those around them). Adolescents know that their bodies are changing, sometimes in ways that do not please them. They know that they are more moody, and are unclear about the sources of their moodiness. They know that their feelings about their parents have changed, and this leaves them feeling uneasy. All of these point to inner turmoil being a very real experience for the adolescents themselves. Whether it manifests itself in ways that lead them to take actions that are very different from actions they would have taken before varies from individual to individual. Actions that are a danger to themselves or others, or out of touch with reality, are pathological. There are, however, many nonpathological actions that would have been unusual for them as children, and yet they do them now (and may never again). Smoking cigarettes, wearing only black clothing, getting a tattoo, piercing a nose, choosing someone to date or befriend who is either unacceptable or very different from their families, getting involved in a political event or a religious movement—all of these may be regarded as "rebellious" by others, such as parents or legal authorities, but feel like equalizers for the adolescents. They feel different, and wish their actions in the world to reflect this difference. This is what very real adolescent turmoil looks and feels like. It cannot be dismissed by research that shows that adolescents' values never move very far from those of their parents, and adolescents themselves do not report feeling rebellious.

Therefore, there *is* turmoil, but not the same expectation of out-and-out rebellion between parents and adolescents that was present a few decades ago. The relationship between adolescents and their families, however, was then and remains now an important consideration in the adolescent process. Adolescence is not simply a phase of an individual's life; there is no doubt that it is also a distinct time in the life of a family. Parents and siblings are acutely aware of the changing adolescents and how they shift the balance of interactions in the family. The shape of a given youth's adolescence can also be very much influenced by the reactions of parents and siblings. Adolescents are constantly looking around at parents, siblings, peers, and the larger social world to see what is expected of them and to try to see how they are being seen. They try to filter this into how they see themselves, at the same time as they are trying to develop a sense of themselves that derives from within.

The major change is in the direction of the input. Where once they felt defined by how others saw them and what others (especially their parents) wanted them to be, now they are in the throes of attempting to decide for themselves who and what they want to be, and merely using the external world as a source of data. Where once the ultimate authorities were others, now adolescents are trying to become their own authorities (about themselves).

"This is the best time of your life," claim the parents (and the adolescents light up).

"But what about these pimples?" cry the kids (a mere moment later).

"How does my hair look?" ask the kids.

"Great," says Mom.

"It does not," retort the kids. "How can you even say that? The other kids will laugh their heads off if they see me. I look like a baby."

And so it goes. Adolescents become acutely, self-consciously aware of their bodily changes, the social and cultural significance of those changes, and their parents' (and others') reactions to those changes. The fact that their parents may have very different perceptions and conceptions is factored into how adolescents react to the views of their peers and how they form their own views.

Cultural assumptions about what is attractive, for example, have a major impact on how content adolescents are with how they look. They are far more influenced by the outer world, including peers and cultural assumptions, than they are by the views of their parents. In each aspect of identity, however, adolescents look to their families and their social world to help them in defining personal views and goals.

THE ADOLESCENT SOCIAL WORLD

The social world is a constant source of interest, concern, and speculation during adolescence. Indeed, the social world of peers, cultural norms, and the sociopolitical context virtually preoccupy adolescents. They compare their multitude of changes to those of their peers. To get a grasp on what is expected of them outside the family, they look to cultural norms. To feel a sense of mastery in the world outside the home, they debate about and attempt to develop a deep understanding of their sociopolitical context. Their families and the homes in which they lived as children pale in comparison to the world outside.

The separation process requires that adolescents define themselves in ways that are more self-derived; the individuation process requires that adolescents see, refine, and integrate their personal characteristics. As adolescents become engaged in these differentiation processes, they turn to the world outside the home to gain wisdom and experience. In so doing, they find bases for comparing their upbringing to those of others, as well as situations in which they can test out newly developed capacities in physiological, cognitive, and social realms.

The current social world in America does not provide them, however, with clear indications of when they have reached adulthood (Friedenberg 1959, Hill 1973, Hotaling et al. 1978). The varied legal ages for driving, drinking, voting, marrying without parental assent, financial emancipation, and leaving school are examples of this overarching ambiguity. When adulthood is reached in the view of adults outside the family also varies by geographic location, ethnic background, socioeconomic class, and sex (Epstein and McPartland 1976, Group for the Advancement of Psychiatry 1968).

With such varied social and cultural messages to integrate about the endpoint of adolescence, alternative means to define the consolidation process must be found. Adolescents end up trying to define themselves through an ambiguous psychological state such as a feeling of wholeness, which amounts to the attainment of a relatively stable and cohesive set of self-images (mental representations). Failing this, they resort to seeing adulthood as related to ending high school or college, having a baby, getting a job, or some other act of significance in the social world.

The discussion thus far describes adolescence as if it were a unitary phase of development. This homogenizes a period that is in fact much more complex and uneven. Dividing adolescence into three subphases (early, middle, and late) provides greater precision in exploring the process of development.

Each of the subphases has its own character, including customary ways that adolescents think, feel, and act. Parents react differently to adolescents in their early, middle, or late periods of development. There are also varying social expectations for adolescents in each of the subphases. Relative resolutions of the issues of one subphase permit an adolescent to move on to those of the next. Inadequate resolutions make further development far more difficult for the adolescent to navigate.

THE SUBPHASES OF ADOLESCENCE

Early adolescence begins with pubescence and ends with a slowing of physical growth, accompanied by a shift away from the family and toward the peer group; its age range is (roughly) 10 to 14. Middle adolescence is a peer-oriented time, characterized by a strong focus on establishing sexual identity and a customary way of dealing in the social world; its age range is (approximately) 15 to 18. Late adolescence is the period of refinement and consolidation of identity, in which family, friends, and self are perceived in balanced and complex ways; its endpoint is particularly difficult to assess (especially in American culture), but its range is from 19 to 22 (though, at times, it is more accurate to place it as late as 25).

The subphases are most accurately defined by their characteristics. Using age as a criterion is, at best, a crude measure. Development is most variable in early adolescence. It gradually normalizes as the end of adolescence approaches. As a result, some do not move into late adolescence until quite a bit later than others, making the end of the process most difficult to define.

Early Adolescence

When Anna Freud (1958) describes adolescence as "an interruption of peaceful growth" (p. 267), she is actually writing about early adolescence. When children begin to feel new sensations in their bodies, observe a myriad of physical changes in the mirror that suggest that they are no longer children, and find themselves able to think and understand the world in ways that differ from those of childhood, early adolescence has arrived.

This is the period of greatest variability among adolescents and within each adolescent. Bodily and emotional changes rarely are synchronized, and growth occurs at varied rates: gradual, intermittent, and in spurts. Within the first two years of early adolescence, for example, adolescents can grow as much as eight to twelve inches. In a brief time, then, they shift from being small to being big. This shift is replete with meaning for them and those around them.

Being bigger makes it more difficult for adolescents to turn to their parents in the ways that were available to them as children. There are poignant moments of awareness for both adolescents and their parents, in which it becomes clear that the adolescents seeking physical comfort are too big to sit on their parents' laps or to be held by them in the same ways. This is one of the ways in which early adolescents hover on the cusp between childhood and adolescence.

Adolescents' greater physical strength and competence and their more adult-like appearance place them in a different social world. Eleven-year-olds, for example, can have trouble getting children's tickets for movie theaters, and 12 year-olds may have to go to men's and women's departments to buy clothes that fit.

The growth in cognitive capacities permits early adolescents to think through ideas in a systematic, logical manner, hypothesize, and begin to grasp abstract concepts. This enables them to see and understand more of the complexity of the world. Early adolescents ponder the meaning of life, the passage of time, the nature of death, and other fundamental issues in ways that are markedly different from those of childhood. They also see themselves and their parents differently. They are able to contemplate possibility; therefore, they see what may be missing in a situation or a person rather than simply seeing what is in front of them. They are able to be aware of what their parents may or may not be or have. They often compare their parents to other adults. Children have a tendency to see their parents as greater, more powerful than they actually are; early adolescents' cognitive growth (and their need to leave childhood behind) permits them to see their parents more realistically.

Adolescents of this age have a heightened capacity to see what is actually there rather than what they wish were there, both in relation to themselves and others. Friends seem less than ideal, parents seem less than ideal, and they themselves seem less than ideal. This process of deidealization is a critical one, for it moves early adolescents (psychologically) out of childhood. The wishful views of childhood are shed and the more complex, reality-based views of adolescence take precedence.

The de-idealization process is an aspect of an important shift in narcissism that occurs at this time. Where children look to their parents for definition, appreciation, and love, and, thus, look to them to achieve a sense of (narcissistic) well-being, adolescents' de-idealization of their parents in tandem with their greater capacities to perceive themselves and the world leads them to divest their parents of some of the authority to supply them with a sense of well-being. They must turn to themselves as they had once turned to their parents; they must be able to offer themselves a sense of appreciation and love that gives them a sense of well-being.

This narcissistic shift, so necessary for adolescents' growing autonomy and need for self-definition, often leaves those around them feeling that adolescents are too self-focused. The powerful investment in their parents' love and approval that adolescents had as children was, often, both a source of satisfaction for their parents and a source of security for themselves. It is not easily given up by either.

Adolescents do, however, need to turn their attention to themselves, for the fundamental changes of the adolescent period require them to do so. They need to be able to rely on their own feelings, thoughts, and reactions. They need to be able to have confidence in these internal processes in order to function autonomously. Without this confidence, they will require others to supply their views, their thoughts, and their beliefs. To become more aware of their personal perceptions, they need this period of heightened self-focus, which begins in early adolescence, takes hold in middle adolescence, and resolves in late adolescence. As adolescents mature, their sense of themselves evolves and becomes more comfortably self-determined. By late adolescence, then, their narcissism shifts once again, and their attention is focused more evenly on themselves and others.

Early adolescence also brings a particular concern with sameness and difference: adolescents of this age are especially focused on how they are the same as they used to be, or different; how their families are the same or different from those of their friends; and how their friends are the same or different from them (Selman 1980). When and how they mature becomes an important factor in their choice of friends. Girls and boys who mature early, for example, tend to cluster. Those who mature more slowly are often kept at a distance, or keep others at a distance.

Same-sex peer relationships are of paramount importance at this time.[5] In the face of feeling so much in flux, early adolescents want to know that their friends share similar feelings and experiences. Close relationships with parents are superseded by relationships with best friends.

Best friendships can be transitional experiences (Winnicott 1971) on the way to achieving greater personal autonomy. First, early adolescents begin to see themselves and their parents in a different, more complex and mature light. They feel some sense of loss of the old relationships with their parents and of their childhood bodies and selves. To support their progress toward greater maturity, they seek out those who are going through a similar process. This relieves some of their sense of isolation. Often, early adolescents are inseparable from their friends, and quite exclusive of other peers. The relationships can be temporarily intense and

5. Prominent writers such as Blos 1962, Dalsimer 1986, Deutsch 1944, and Sullivan 1953 emphasize such relationships.

over-idealized, serving the purpose of strengthening their resolve in becoming more independent from their families and more accepting of their changed bodies and selves (Hoffman et al. 1988).

At some point, most early adolescents also change schools. They leave schools organized for children, with single-teacher classrooms, and move to the multiple-teacher, multiple-classroom settings that characterize adolescent school situations (Hamburg 1974). This provides social verification of the metamorphoses adolescents are undergoing. As a result, the school change is usually experienced with both excitement and trepidation, much like other changes of this period.

The early adolescent process begins two years earlier for girls than boys; thus, what they begin (on average) at age 10½, boys begin at age 12½. Girls must acclimate to the reality of becoming bigger, more adult, at an early age. The pressures are very great. In fact, they are overwhelming to some, who fall pray to a host of psychopathological resolutions, such as eating disorders, precocious sexuality, or substance abuse. At the very least, early adolescent girls often struggle with where to focus their attention, for example, their changing bodies, or the ways in which they are now perceived by others. What is most difficult is to remain on an even keel.

Early adolescents attempt to stay on course by defining a place for themselves in their families. Reminiscent of the rapprochement subphase in early childhood, in which toddlers touch base with their caregivers before venturing out to explore the world, early adolescents seek to affirm roots in the family home before moving out into the social world to explore their changed bodies and selves. They redefine themselves in relation to their families first; once redefined, they are able to move out into the now more complex world of friends, social exchanges and situations, and realms of abstract thought.

To parents, early adolescents' redefinitions may be difficult to see or comprehend.

"Comb my hair for me, Mom?" says the early adolescent in the morning.

"Okay if I stay out 'til midnight with my friends?" says the early adolescent that night.

It takes a number of years for this fundamental asynchrony to resettle into greater consonance. Middle adolescence is a step along the way.

Middle Adolescence

While early adolescence is dominated by the need to adjust to vast physiological changes that transform an adolescent's familial and social relationships, middle adolescence is dominated by the need for the now transformed adolescent to feel squarely rooted in peer, school, and social cultures. There is a distinct shift away from the familial home and toward the contemporary world. Best friendships remain significant, but give way to the ascending importance of group allegiances, for example, playing on athletic teams, listening to particular music groups, wearing certain kinds of clothing, or engaging in different social activities.

Early adolescents look back and forth, from childhood to the present. Middle adolescents live very much in the present. They have little interest in childhood and little interest in adulthood. They want to know what and who they are, who else is like them, and who else wants to be with them, and they want to know all of this *now*. This is not an age group known for its patience.

Middle adolescents consolidate the separation process they began in early adolescence. More often than not, they are quite comfortable on their own. They are far more focused on individuation: exploring themselves in ways that give specificity to their self-representations. The middle adolescent credo is best stated in the words of the Delphic Oracle, "Know thyself." They move full tilt into the social world to accomplish just this: they seek to know themselves in as many social situations as possible. They also look inside, through daydreams and fantasies and the writing of diaries, poetry, and stories. This is often a period of great creativity.

A visit to a freshmen or sophomore high school class will readily confirm that adolescents this age constantly seek out stimulation and tension discharge. No one can sit still. Eyes dart around the room, feet tap, hands doodle, arms shoot up, or voices speak out.

These adolescents need and want to test out their bodies and capacities. They also are beginning to know how they look and want to see who is attracted to them.

The narcissistic shift that begins in early adolescence is pervasive during middle adolescence. In order to come to know themselves as fully as possible, adolescents must divest their parents of the importance they once had ("decathect" the mental representations of their parents) and turn their attention to themselves and those who are most like them, that is, their friends. This is an aspect of what Anny Katan (1951) terms *object removal,* the leaving behind of early relationships with parents to make room for those of the present and future. There are new relationships with the parents, but also—and in middle adolescence most importantly—with people outside the family. The first blush of object removal takes place in early adolescence, when adolescents begin to see their parents' shortcomings. By middle adolescence, their full attention is outside the home. At times, this is to the chagrin of their parents, who may find the self and social involvement of their middle adolescents hard to bear.

Adolescents of this age are more keenly aware of what they have left behind. Many write about the mourning process characteristic of this middle period.[6] In disengaging from their parents of childhood, both internally (through decathecting the mental representations of their parents) and externally (by relying less on their parents for direction), middle adolescents are left in a more isolated, lonely state. The moodiness so characteristic of middle adolescence often derives from this mourning process. It takes some time for adolescents to form both new relationships with their parents that fit their changes and new relationships of significance with others.

The new relationships middle adolescents seek out are with their contemporaries, both male and female. They shift. from involving themselves primarily with same-sex peers to having mixed

---

6. Blos 1962, Esman 1990, Kaplan 1984, Katan 1951, and Mishne 1986 emphasize this mourning process.

groups of friends. They also seek out adults who (specifically) are not their parents. Coaches, teachers, and parents of friends become more important as adolescents look for qualities that they can incorporate into their now more conscious formation of self. Characteristically, they both admire and disdain adults with great intensity. Parents may find it difficult when their adolescents express such admiration for other adults. At the same time that they are enthralled with these other adults, middle adolescents are often more distant from their own parents.

During middle adolescence, there is a change from the primacy of group identifications to a more differentiated network of social contacts. This is, for example, the period in which many adolescents have crushes and begin to date. Fantasizing a personal connection with one of these new objects of desire, be it a rock or movie star or a highly popular person at school, is one source of well-being at this age. Having this star stare down at them from the walls of their bedrooms is a comfort to adolescents (who are no longer feeling as comforted by the attentions of their parents). Blos (1962) notes that being "in love" is one of the ways middle adolescents counter the loneliness that arises from the disengagement from their parents (object removal).

After the crush stage, having a girlfriend or boyfriend becomes socially and personally important. At first, social status is often attached to having a steady boyfriend or girlfriend, which is seen as a sign of maturity, including that connected to sexual experimentation. It may seem as if this early dating is more for the experience of dating, and so that others see the middle adolescent as someone who dates, than it is for the experience of getting to know someone else well. Later, having a girlfriend or boyfriend is a way for middle adolescents to refine a sense of intimacy, that is, to get to know both others and themselves in some depth. Phyllis Greenacre (1958) notes that a sense of identity involves feelings of both uniqueness and similarity. These later middle adolescent steady relationships contribute to the dual sources of identity, for adolescents explore their similarities and differences within the relationships with intensity and focus.

Middle adolescents come to know their bodies, feelings, sensations, and dreams. They make better use of the changes in their thought processes, and are more conscious of both their sexual impulses and body parts. They are more familiar with their social worlds and more comfortable with them, and more independent of their families. In sum, they feel self-aware and competent. They move into late adolescence prepared to consolidate this self-awareness and grapple with what the future may hold for them.

Late Adolescence

Early adolescence is dominated by the necessity to contend with vast physiological changes, and middle adolescence by turning inward and outward to explore a changed self. Late adolescence brings with it a need to encompass all that has previously transpired in adolescence. Late adolescents must find ways to contain the more complex psychic structure that early and middle adolescents develop (Jacobson 1964). They need to establish a cohesive and stable set of self-representations that lead to a sense of "me."

Early adolescents look back toward childhood and into the present. Middle adolescents focus on the here and now. Late adolescents live in the present, but have an eye toward the future. They are far more aware of who they are, and want to think through who they want to be in the future and, perhaps, what they want to be doing and with whom. They know adulthood is on the horizon.

The narcissistic shift that characterized both early and middle adolescence is on the wane. Late adolescents are far less preoccupied with themselves and their daydreams, far more calm and focused on the constraints of reality and their personal limitations and aspirations. Their relationships with others are generally less intense, more in keeping with everyday expectations. The crushes and idealizations of the earlier subphases of adolescence give way to relationships that are more reciprocal. This is true not only with friends and adults, but also with their parents.

Late adolescents must consolidate the various aspects of identity that rise to the surface during the preceding subphases. These consolidations mark significant psychological achievements. They occur in three major areas: genitality, ethnocultural identity, and the ego ideal. (Each of these is discussed in detail in subsequent chapters.)

Genitality is the last of the psychosexual stages outlined by Freud (1905a). (It is preceded by the oral, anal, and phallic-oedipal stages). It represents the attainment of a capacity for intimacy in both emotional and physical realms. In order to be intimate, late adolescents must come to terms with the vast physiological changes that have transformed their comparatively sexually undifferentiated children's bodies to those of gendered young adults.

The fact that one is a boy or girl is known by the time of toddlerhood.[7] Even neonates show observable sex differences (Garai and Scheinfeld 1968, Lewis 1972, Moss 1967). The implications of the fact of sex difference, particularly in social, cultural, and ethnic terms, become clear during adolescence. Adolescents must assess the personal meaning of being male or female, and think through how masculine or feminine they are and/or wish to be. They need to appreciate the social implications of the position they assume in relation to these aspects of gender. They also must shift their central focus from their parents' relationship with one another or with them to their relationships in the world outside the family home. Their relationships with their parents remain important, but other relationships are able to be important as well. The oedipal resolutions of childhood, in other words, are revisited and revised in such a way that adolescents are comfortable both with their own sexuality and that of their parents.

Placing themselves in the world involves not only late adolescents' genitality, but also a sense of where they belong and with whom. The move out of the family home, literally and figuratively, engages late adolescents in a personal and social search for roots and group affiliations. Who are they? What are they? Where do they come from? Where do they want to go? These kinds of questions

---

7. There are a number of highly regarded psychoanalytic researchers who have established this early recognition of sex differences, such as Galenson and Roiphe 1976, Olesker 1984, 1990, Roiphe 1968, and Roiphe and Galenson 1981.

abound in their minds and in their conversations with friends and mentors. These adolescents sharpen their views of their cultural surrounds, and their personal ethnic, racial, and religious histories, as part of the process of establishing a distinct sense of who they are and where they belong in a broad sense: their ethnocultural identities. (Chapter Five outlines the development of a sense of ethnocultural identity).

The moral values, aspirations, and beliefs of children are largely determined by how parents respond to them. Children are most motivated by how much love and appreciation they can obtain from parents. Their behavior, self-concepts, values, and beliefs derive from what they perceive their parents want for and from them. The separation and individuation processes of adolescence make this profound, all-encompassing reliance on parents impossible. Adolescents must find ways of acting, thinking, perceiving themselves, and believing that are self-derived. In so doing, they establish a mature ego ideal: a set of self-representations that are reality-based and self-conceived, and which serve as a model for how and who they wish to be (Chapter Four includes a fuller discussion of the mature ego ideal).

In early adolescence, there is an important transition from relying on parents to looking toward others, including themselves, for ways of thinking and being. In middle adolescence, parents are the least important sources for approval; friends, non-parent adults, and the adolescents themselves ascend in importance. Late adolescence is the time of a real turn inward, toward self-determined and realistically assessed aspirations and moral/ethical beliefs. These aspirations and beliefs are what make up the mature ego ideal. The cognitive changes of this period of development contribute substantially to the stronger capacities late adolescents have to see themselves and the world more clearly, and to place themselves in that world.

The major components of the late adolescent consolidation of identity need to be brought together to form a cohesive and stable sense of self. The increased energy needed for this process becomes available to adolescents as a result of the divestment of energy from their parents. Cognitive and emotional growth provide them with the requisite capacities. The separation-individuation processes free adolescents to focus on their own developmental needs. The most significant need is to form an autonomous identity, one which includes attention to the adolescents' competencies and sexual identity. Late adolescence is the subphase in which these monumental integrations take place.

This is the time in adolescents' lives when they often leave their families' homes for the first time without the intention of returning to live on a permanent basis. It is another leave-taking, one which parallels that of early adolescence but has a real-life factor that makes it quite different from the earlier time. The leave-taking of early adolescence is that of childhood for adolescence, and is largely a psychological transformation. The late adolescent leave-taking, a poignant one for both their families and the adolescents themselves, is psychological and physical: not only do adolescents see themselves moving on in terms of their needs for their families, but they are also moving on in terms of the physical presence, the overseeing presence, of their families. Whether or not they feel ready, they venture forth to take care of themselves in a way not previously required of them.

These late adolescents venture forth more adultlike in appearance, affect, and thought process. Compared to early and middle adolescents, they are far more stable, calm, and predictable, both to themselves and those around them. They often struggle with issues of commitment. They struggle with commitment to other people, to principles, to beliefs, and to ideas. Commitment suggests demarcation, which, in turn, suggests limitation. Coming to terms with their particular limitations is often quite difficult for late adolescents. They want to hold onto the possibilities represented by old fantasies of doing anything and everything.

Making choices often carries the same kind of message for late adolescents. They are hyperconscious of the fact that one choice precludes another. If you decide you are going to be a Democrat, you cannot vote in the Republican primary. If you decide you are going to wear your hair long, you are not going to be seen as a preppy. If you decide you are a socialist, you are not going to be seen as someone who will pursue personal gains. If you decide to go out steadily with one person, you cannot be sexually intimate with others.

Late adolescents move into young adulthood with relative clarity about who they are, what they are, what they want, and where they will go. If development until this time has been "good enough," the delineation of these important aspects of identity will be founded in realistic assessments of themselves and the worlds in which they live. Commitments will be established, and choices will be made. They will have come to terms with the fact that other possible commitments and/or other choices will be temporarily put aside or left behind. They will feel good about their commitments and choices, and be reasonably confident in the knowledge of who they wish to be and who they are.

2

Identity Formation

Leaving Home

2

Early Adolescent Genitality: Puberty, Masturbation, and the Oedipus Complex

My father and I used to be pretty tight. . . . The sad truth is my breasts have come between us.

Fourteen-year-old on TV show, "My So-called Life"

The physiological changes of puberty, with their concomitant psychological reverberations, are building blocks of adolescent character and identity formation. Adolescents' customary ways of acting in the world, that is, their characters, are established both by them and by the responses of those around them to their newly changed physical states. Their identities, which are composed of integrated mental images of themselves and others, that is, self and object representations, are re-established to take into account their new physical features, sensations, and thought processes.

Genitality is a concept that embraces all of the physiological and psychological changes that begin with puberty. As I elaborate it in this and the next two chapters, the concept has two important meanings. The first derives from the necessity for integrating the

newly enlarged and sexual functional genitals into the adolescent's
concept of self. Mental representations of the genitals themselves,
the sensations emanating from them, and the capacity for procre-
ation become part of who adolescents perceive themselves to be.
This is an element of the adolescent identity formation process. The
second meaning denotes a way of relating to others that incorporates the attainment of a mature (post-ambivalent) capacity for
emotional and physical intimacy. It emerges in the post-latency stage
of psychosexual development, a phase that is defined (in part) by
the capacity for adult (genital) sexual satisfaction (Freud 1905a).
This is a component of adolescent character formation.

Genitality, in both senses, is difficult to achieve. There are so
many changes taking place in pubertal adolescents, and the changes
come so quickly in individuals who are self-conscious without being
self-aware. Their observing egos have not yet caught up with their
experiencing egos; they feel without being able to conceptually
frame what they are feeling. Their capacities for observing lag
behind their capacities for experiencing in relation to themselves;
also their self-perceptiveness has not yet caught up with their
capacities for being perceptive about other people. It takes most of
adolescence for some measure of synchrony among these ego
functions to be achieved.

To reach the genital stage of development, adolescents must be
able to integrate representations of their functioning genitals with
representations of their overall growth and changed bodies. They
also must develop the capacity to see themselves, in these changed
states, in intimate relationships with others. This is a substantial
accomplishment, and takes all of adolescence to achieve. It engages
both the observing and experiencing ego.

The major components of adolescence that contribute to the
development of genitality are discussed in this and the next two
chapters. This chapter describes those components that arise in
early adolescence: puberty, masturbation, and the revisiting of the
Oedipus complex.

Once puberty is reached, a host of relatively rapid changes take
place in each adolescent. Masturbation aids these early adolescents

in taking over some of the authority and power their primary caregivers had during childhood, particularly the authority to define them physically and the power to comfort them. It also aids them in achieving an awareness of their genital and overall bodily functioning. Questions about sexuality, both theirs and their parents', start to emerge at this time. This results in a resurgence of focus on the issues of the Oedipus complex, all reframed in the context of the now more adult-like adolescent's mind and body.

The bodily changes bring into bold relief for adolescents the social fact of being either female or male, their biological gender. Their greater cognitive capacities lead them to take into account the implications of this distinction. They must then focus on a personal sense of the meaning of the fact, and integrate aspects of femininity and masculinity into their self and object representations, that is, their sense of self. These are the aspects of gender that constitute components of middle adolescent genitality.

Fueled by their new sensations and hormonal surges, middle adolescents march out into the social world to establish their identities as sexual beings among their peers. Their sexual relationships go through a number of transformations over the course of their subphase development, but the bulk of the transformations of sexuality take place during middle and late adolescence.

Late adolescent genitality involves the integration of moral/ ethical values in a number of realms, but especially in the domain of sexuality. This integration requires another sorting through and synthesis of oedipal identifications. The process of revisiting the Oedipus complex that began in early adolescence is renewed and reinvigorated as the adolescent moves toward adulthood.

The evolution of early adolescent genitality begins with the vast changes of puberty, and ends with the integration of the identifications of the adolescent Oedipus complex. This discussion will proceed in the same manner.

PUBERTY

The earliest sense of "me" that children experience is a physical one (Freud 1923, Greenacre 1958). Contact with the caregiver's body through physical ministrations aid the baby and young child in distinguishing where the other person's bodily boundary begins and ends and where "I" begins and ends (Hoffer 1950). This is generalized over time to a more complex sense of "me" and "not-me," in which the developing child stores up images of a physical self in interaction with the world in the process characterized as separation (Jacobson 1964, Mahler 1968, Mahler et al. 1975). Ultimately, young children can differentiate their separateness both from the environment and from other people.

What happens in pubescence and then puberty is that the "I" becomes separate from who the "I" was; there was a child "me" and now there is an adolescent "me." The small "me" gives way to the big "me" (who is about to be bigger).

In this context, psychologically speaking, there is a shift of bodily ownership (Laufer 1968). Where once children's bodies were in the hands of their caregivers, as big(ger) people, adolescents are now supposed to be responsible for their own bodies, bodily processes, and bodily regulation. This is another aspect of the separation process of adolescence.

This shift in bodily ownership is preceded by a process in which children gradually assume greater responsibility for their physical care under the watchful eyes of their caregivers (Adams-Silvan 1995). For example, babies are fed by their caregivers; then they feed themselves the food that their caregivers prepare and watch them eat. Babies first eliminate into diapers and caregivers clean them up; then they are toilet trained and cleaned by caregivers; finally they use toilets and wipe themselves on their own. It is this gradual process of independent physical care that becomes a fully autonomous function during adolescence.

As noted earlier (in Chapter One), adolescents separate from their parents of childhood in part by de-idealizing them, bringing them down to human proportions. They withdraw some of their attention, attachment, and admiration (object libido) from their significant caregivers and invest themselves (and their friends) with greater value and authority (narcissistic libido). This permits them to move away from relying on their parents for self-definition and bodily care, for they are beginning to feel that their parents are less powerful and that both they themselves and their friends are more powerful. With the added sense of power, it becomes more possible to imagine caring for their own bodies. Their prior (magical) belief that only their caregivers knew how to care for them adequately gives way to a belief that they themselves can manage or do even better than their parents had done. Parents are certainly aware that their adolescents begin doubting them in a range of previously unfamiliar ways:

"What makes you think *that*?"
"Where'd you get that from?"
"Don't you think I know myself better than you know me?"
"You think I don't know how to do that? What do you think I am, some kind of baby or something?"

Despite their sometime protestations to the contrary, taking over their own bodily care does not occur overnight. It takes quite a number of years, usually until middle adolescence—but often until late adolescence—for adolescents to become autonomous in aspects of bodily care such as the regulation of their hygiene and eating practices. To parents, the process may seem endless. A young man, 14 years old, stood with his mother at the door of his 12-year-old sister's room. The room was in disarray: clothes strewn everywhere, books piled up, shades drawn in the middle of the day. The exasperated mother started to say something to her daughter but before she could, her son put his hand gently on her shoulder and said, "Don't, Mom. It's okay. She's just shedding childhood." He was right, and this shedding process takes time.

Indeed, it takes a number of years for both the psychological and physiological changes of puberty to evolve. Once the evolution has taken place, adolescents can form a clearer image of who they are in the present and attempt to establish relationships with this more mature sense of self in mind. Though the order of most of these physiological changes is similar (Tanner 1978), the length of time roughly two to four years for both, the advent of puberty is a different experience for boys and girls. First, I will discuss female pubertal experience, then male; this will be followed by a more general discussion that includes both females and males.

Female Puberty

Puberty is the critical organizing experience for girls with regard to their genitals, no less their genitality. Sensations change, the outer parts of their genitals grow, pubic hair appears, and girls feel the flow of menstrual fluid in a way and in places that are different from urination. There is a first awareness of an inner organ, the womb, from feelings such as cramping. There is an opportunity for clarification of early possible confusions about the bodily orifices of urination, defecation, and childbirth (e. g., cloacal theories of child-birth). Even the twinges of ovulation give girls a way of better knowing where their ovaries are, as the flow of vaginal fluid and the use of menstrual tampons can provide an awareness of the vaginal canal (Shopper 1979). Adolescent girls thus are able to develop a more visceral sense and understanding of their reproductive organs.

Judith Kestenberg (1961) writes about menarche as a central experience for girls, one which permits them to feel a sense of order with regard to their previously more diffuse female organs. Eric Plaut and Foster Hutchinson (1986) see puberty as even more important in female development than the oedipal phase (which they *do* see as central for male development). In either case, the significance of this time cannot be overestimated.

Puberty is experienced in a context that is both individual-historical and sociohistorical. Each girl has had a history in which bodily processes have been invested with meaning, and bodily events have been reacted to in a particular atmosphere. (Sociohistorical aspects of gender are a central focus of Chapter Three). The ways in which other physical aspects of development were explained and reacted to form a foundation for these pubertal experiences, for example, how comfortable girls are talking with and asking questions of their caregivers will play a role in how, when, and in what fashion information is exchanged about the particulars of this phase. Sometimes adolescents are more comfortable speaking with a third party, such as a physician or health teacher, than they are with their own mothers, particularly in situations in which there generally has been a high degree of modesty in their homes about physical changes or development. In general, however, mothers are still the most likely sources of information about the changes of this time; two-thirds of adolescent girls with older sisters turn to them for information; most turn to their friends; and only one-fifth turn to their fathers (Brooks-Gunn and Ruble 1986).

Clinicians report, however, that their female patients often describe first menstruation experiences in which they were reluctant to tell their mothers. A fragile sense of autonomy, especially with regard to feminine development, and conflictual familial relationships made them fear telling their mothers. One patient reported, for example, that she was sure her mother "would ruin it for her." Pubertal girls, who are just on the cusp between childhood and adolescence, cannot afford to feel pulled back into an early parent/child relationship with their mothers. Aggressive feelings aid them in keeping their mothers at what feels like a safer distance from them. These feelings may be attributed to their mothers (e.g., "she'll ruin it," or "she'll never understand, she doesn't want me to grow up"), to themselves (e.g., "I can't deal with it, if I tell her it will seem too real"), or to both (e.g., "I don't want to tell her, I can't stand how she treats me like a baby").

In terms of the pubertal changes themselves, first there are the physical components to be considered, for instance, the fact that in menstruation there is an involuntary flow of fluid, which varies in color and in strength of flow. Early experiences with toilet training, accidents that may have occurred at that time, and the atmosphere in which this experience took place all have a potential impact on how a pubertal girl (and often her family members) react in the present. Fantasies often abound in girls, and the relative comfort each girl has in discussing these kinds of matters at home varies tremendously. It is not uncommon for a girl to turn to her friends, some of whom may already have menstruated, to ask questions about what to use, how to use it, or what is going on, but, as previously noted, the physical events most often bring with them a reconnection with mothers around instructions and the necessity for information (Shopper 1979). At the brink of their young womanhood, then, girls are often seeking out their mothers in ways that are very reminiscent of much earlier days. This can make the transition from childhood to young womanhood more difficult.

There is a wide range of emotional reactions to these physical changes. Girls who reach puberty at the younger end of the spectrum may feel ashamed, frightened, or worried about people noticing their "grownup" changes, either because of the telltale signs of menstruation, such as bulky pads, smells, or bloatedness, or other signs of looking older such as breast or hip development (e.g., some girls wear undershirts over their bras). Girls who reach puberty at the older end of the spectrum are often eagerly anticipating the changes; thus, they have fewer fears about being noticed.

Menstruation actually begins rather late in the pubertal process. Breast development, often a focus for both boys and girls of this age, is the earliest sign. It is usually followed by the growth of pubic hair, first downy and light in color, then rough in quality and dark in color. Perspiration and axillary hair develop soon after, along with a spurt of fat (Warren 1983) and nose growth, all of which leave their bodies somewhat disproportionate. They are, therefore, experienced as rather unwelcome. Girls' growth spurts (in height) peak at about the time that menarche arrives. With menstruation comes the most unwelcome component of puberty: acne.

Pubertal girls (through early and middle adolescence) report being particularly unsatisfied with their weights and body types (Simmons and Blyth 1987), and Carol Gilligan (1989) reports a generally lowered self-esteem and disconnectedness in early adolescent girls. These vast changes, many of which leave them feeling ungainly and uncomfortable, are difficult to assimilate. It becomes easier for these girls when their growth rate slows down; their bodies stabilize and they can form a clear image of how they look. Puberty ends for girls with the establishment of regular ovulatory cycles, usually in middle adolescence. At this time, the relative diminution in hormonal surges leaves them with less acne and more proportioned faces and bodies (particularly with respect to the distribution of fat tissue).

This general dissatisfaction with their bodies, cannot, however, be overgeneralized. There are many girls who feel, as Kestenberg (1961) and Ruth Fischer (1991) suggest, real pride in the attainment of womanhood. In early adolescent Anne Frank's (1947) diary, for example, when she writes about getting her period, she notes: "What is happening is wonderful . . . not only what can be seen, but all that's taking place inside. . . . Each time I get a period, and it's only been three times . . . in spite of all the pain, unpleasantness, and nastiness, I have a sweet secret and I long to have it" (p. 117). This is the important shift from girls' having a diffuse sense of an inner space to their having a sense of a valuable set of organs and functions that make them special (Dalsimer 1986, Hart and Sarnoff 1971, Shopper 1979).

The mother of childhood reappears in this context as well, for there is an identification with her as a mother, or at least the pubertal girl is now prompted to see herself as a potential mother. The power that the mother of childhood holds for a girl is then partially shifted over to the now adolescent young woman. Her growing breasts buttress this identification, and are often, then, the source of wonderment, envy, and preoccupation.

It was most often in interaction with the mother of childhood that the girl's earliest sense of bodily definition was achieved. These pubertal young women must now be able to leave that use of the mother behind, achieve full ownership of their bodies, and then move on to share their bodies with someone else.

Male Puberty

Boys are also faced with leaving their mothers behind, but do not have the same pressure to simultaneously identify with their mothers as women. Instead, boys compare themselves with their fathers, with other male adults of significance in their lives, and with themselves as boys (rather than as the young men that they are now becoming).

A boy's growth spurt is usually more dramatic than a girl's; for example, he suddenly is eye to eye with his mother when only some months ago he was small to her being large. This often sets the deidealization process in motion for boys in a paradoxical fashion. On one hand, it is harder for the mother of childhood to loom so large when she is, in fact, smaller! On the other, there is a strong wish to hold on to the fantasy that some powerful person can take care of you. The growing desire to be independent, however, generally prevails over the wish to be childlike. The mother is no longer seen as larger than life, especially as the pubertal boy gets taller and taller.

Boys of this age grow for a longer period of time than girls. Where girls generally stop growing in middle adolescence, boys' growth continues until late adolescence. Thus, they are continuing to have to assimilate new changes when girls have all but stopped growing. It usually takes longer for male adolescents to form clear images of their bodies and, therefore, images of themselves in relation to others (i.e., the self and object representations which form their late adolescent identities). Boys' feelings of attractiveness, a positive component of their self-image related to their physicality, are most highly correlated with the appearance of facial hair, one of the last of the late adolescent pubertal developments (Tobin-Richards et al. 1983).

The pubertal event for boys that is comparable to menstruation in girls is the experience of ejaculation. Ejaculation signals to boys that real changes are moving them into manhood, and that these changes are sexual in nature. Though the first ejaculations do not, in fact, produce live sperm, adolescent males cannot distinguish between ejaculation that includes live sperm and ejaculation that does not; they thus assume that ejaculation is connected to sexual potency (as girls assume that menarche signals reproductive capacity, even though it usually takes several regular periods for fertility actually to be established). Just as menstruation occurs rather late in the pubertal process, so does ejaculation. It is preceded by a number of other changes.

The first pubertal change for a boy is testicular enlargement. Associated with this change is growth in the scrotum, which becomes larger and darker. Boys then develop pubic hair, which, like girls', is first downy and light, then rough and dark. They start to develop acne, then have a growth in height and penis width and length. This is followed by their voices dropping. First ejaculations tend to occur at this time, often after the first erections that lead to orgasms have already taken place. There is much that pubertal boys do not know; research suggests that they generally have less information at their disposal about their own changes or those of their female compatriots than do girls at this age (Brooks-Gunn and Ruble 1986).

Pubertal young men *do* know, from personal experience and observation, that their penises grow, particularly in circumference; that their testicles descend and change quite dramatically in size, shape and color; and that they have erections for reasons other than direct stimulation (which had been the primary cause for erections in childhood). They often have concerns about these changes: for example, how much growth there will be, whether they will have erections at times they do not wish to have them, or whether their testicles will be more prone to injury because they are larger and more sensitive. They often keep these concerns to themselves. Though there is a good deal of talk among boys about various aspects of their pubertal changes, little serious exchange of accurate information takes place (Brooks-Gunn and Ruble 1986). The privacy of this time contributes to boys' separation and individuation processes, for they are quite focused on what is happening and on mastering the changes that are taking place through figuring out what they look like and how their bodies now work.

Testes change more than any other endocrine organ in the body, for girls or boys, during puberty. They alter in weight, volume, color, sensation, and function. They simultaneously become extraordinarily sensitive to pain (Bell 1964). Though boys are far more ostensibly focused on their penises, in the sense that they talk to and joke with their friends about them, these vast testicular changes are on their minds a great deal and are also the source of a great deal of curiosity and concern. At moments of such concern, they, too, are faced with personal histories that influence to whom they might turn: mothers, fathers, siblings, friends, or others.

When it has been their mothers to whom boys have turned in

the past for answers to questions about their physicality, puberty often brings with it a feeling of great conflict, for relying on past patterns of turning to mother does not feel the same to the changing boys. The same mother who was comforting and a font of information during childhood may feel quite threatening in her knowledge and capacity for offering comfort to the young man. As he stands balanced on the cusp between childhood and adolescence, the experience of being drawn to the mother of childhood can leave him feeling frightened about moving forward into adolescence. Alberto Moravia (1950), in his novella about Agostino, a fatherless 13-year-old boy on vacation with his mother, sums up an aspect of this experience eloquently:

> Why he so much wanted to stop loving his mother, why he even hated himself for loving her, he would have been unable to say. Perhaps because he felt he had been deceived and had thought her to be different from what she really was, or perhaps because, not being able to go on loving her simply and innocently as he had before, he preferred to stop loving her altogether and to look on her merely as an ordinary woman. [p. 50]

Fathers do not pose the same kind of threat to pubertal boys. Though older adolescent boys often struggle with their fathers, in terms of both identifying with them and attempting to define themselves as different from them, early adolescents' conversations with their fathers about manhood can promote a positive male identification at a critical time, and the presence of fathers can ward off fears about and needs for relying on their mothers of childhood.

Pubertal boys also have surges of aggression that are hormonally based and changes in their musculature that make them markedly stronger. The need to test out these new-found strengths and discharge their aggressive surges is great. While both females and males have to contend with a rather constant state of arousal during puberty, males have to learn to manage their aggression as well.

Competitive athletics often offer an important outlet for both sexes, for they provide opportunities for expression of aggression (particularly for the males) and to get to know how their changed bodies function. There is a persistent search for avenues for discharge of tension, however, in both physical and intellectual realms. It is not uncommon, for example, to find adolescents in heated conversations about war, the meaning of life and death, or political battles. These serve to channel and diminish the hormonal surges (through sublimation).

Both female and male pubertal adolescents must contend with their new bodies, feelings, and sensations. Males especially are flooded with aggression, but all adolescents have to find ways of regulating their libidinal and aggressive arousal. Achieving genitality involves the integration and regulation of both sexual excitement and aggression, so that close relationships with others of both sexes are possible.

While these integrations are taking place, adolescents easily become overwhelmed. Helene Deutsch (1944) notes that real life circumstances that would, under most circumstances, be considered difficult but not overwhelming might actually be traumatic because of the biological upheavals of puberty. Adolescents already have so much with which to cope, internally and physically, that otherwise manageable external circumstances can simply be too hard for them to integrate. Not knowing just how to define their ever-changing physical boundaries often leaves adolescents feeling awkward and clumsy. They may lose a clear sense of where they stand in time and space; thus, they may have trouble gauging how much time it takes to accomplish a task (e.g., homework), or how much room they need to get between objects or people (e.g., they may bump into things or people, or feel generally uncoordinated) (Meyer 1995).

There is inevitable disruption in adolescents' sense of well-being and in their family life. Parents must find new ways of relating to their young men and women, as adolescent children must find new ways of seeing and relating to their parents. When the 14-year-old girl quoted at the beginning of this chapter says that she and her father used to be close until her breasts got between them, there are at least three possible explanations: her father felt uncomfortable with her budding sexuality, she felt uncomfortable with her father because of her new sexual feelings, or both. In most instances, the discomfort is shared among family members; in most instances, it is (thankfully) temporary.

MASTURBATION

Masturbation is the activity that permits a meeting of the changed body and mind of adolescents. Early conscious and unconscious fantasies about sexuality are rearoused, new sensations felt, and genitalia explored. Touching themselves gives adolescents an opportunity for forming mental images of their changed parts that are then incorporated into their self-representations. They thereby achieve a sense of bodily ownership (Laufer 1968). Just as early interaction with the physical self permits children to form a body ego (Freud 1923, Hoffer 1950), so does the self-touching of this time permit adolescents to re-form their body egos to take into account their current shapes.

Masturbation is direct and indirect; it involves both specific tactile arousal and arousal that comes from fantasy and association. It also is both intentional and unintentional, though what is most significant at this time is intentional masturbation. Intentional masturbation is conscious activity aimed at physical stimulation. It is intentional masturbation that involves an active effort at mastery and integration of the genitals, genital functioning, and sexual fantasy.

Specific tactile arousal involves the direct stimulation of parts of the body that are sexually exciting, such as the breasts or clitoris for a girl and the penis or scrotum for a boy. Instances of indirect stimulation are experiences such as rubbing up against something that stimulates the genitals, or reading or seeing sexually exciting material. In either case, in healthy development puberty brings with it a *genital* experience of masturbation. The physiological changes of this time produce a markedly different experience of arousal for adolescents. That arousal is located in the genitals, whether it is directly or indirectly produced. (Others, such as William Moore [1975], define masturbation exclusively as direct genital manipulation. A definition of masturbation as direct genital manipulation is focused more on the experience of boys than of girls).

Masturbation provides adolescents with important information about sexual arousal, with particular reference to genital arousal. Genital excitement brings to awareness questions and ideas about adult sexuality that were tucked away at an earlier point in development (the oedipal phase). The adolescent focus on the genitals and adult sexuality anchors them in the present (Reich 1951b) and turns them toward the future, so that temptations to revert back to childhood sources of comfort and definition (through the parents) can be left behind. Blos (1962) sees adolescent masturbation as also performing the role of allowing adolescents to subordinate early forms of sexual pleasure, that is, pregenital sexuality, to genital pleasure. With the changes in sensation emanating from the genitals, and genital growth, the genitalia become the most important focus of sexual pleasure.

At the same time that adolescents are developing a new form of sexual pleasure, they also are concerned about losing the physical and emotional comfort offered by the parents of childhood, and they miss this comfort when it is no longer as possible for them to seek it out. The power that comfort holds for children is memorialized in the "kiss my booboo" requests; it seems to children that a mere kiss from mommy or daddy (usually mommy) can take away their hurt. Growing up means giving up the notion that a mere kiss can do it, and figuring out a way to self-comfort and, ultimately, finding others to offer comfort when it is needed.

The first step away from the "kiss my booboo" approach to comfort is often some form of masturbation, a form of touching oneself that offers pleasure through discharge of tension. It often puts children in a stuporous, autoerotic, primary narcissistic state, one that mimics the post-nursing, satiated state of infants. The memory of the satisfaction of the original feeling of being offered nourishment from someone else is, however, never forgotten. Even when self-comfort is attained, feelings of longing related to that original object-related satisfaction remain. Thus, there is always movement back and forth between self-comfort and object-related comfort. It is one of the pendulums of human development. It also is an example of the progressive/regressive movement of adolescence as a whole, in which adolescents move back into childhood to touch base with early experience in the service of making it a part of their personal history, but also move forward into adolescence and adulthood to experience some of the satisfactions of a life of greater autonomy and self-definition.

Integrating pubertal changes involves attaining a sense of mastery over them. The mastery comes from understanding how the new body parts work and how sexual excitement works, learning how to regulate the excitement and the body parts, and conceiving of ways to bring together the body, feelings of desire, sexual fantasies, wishes for closeness, and needs for sexual satisfaction. Masturbation is a way station along this route of mastery. It permits the adolescent to get to know what is personally sexually exciting and satisfying, and to imagine being aroused while with another person. It endows the genitalia, which first often feel separate from the adolescent, with self-feeling (Spiegel 1961). Ultimately, masturbation becomes a trial action that eases anxiety about actually venturing forth to be engaged physically and emotionally with another person (Blos 1962, Borowitz 1973, Francis and Marcus 1975, Laufer 1968, Moore 1975).

There are differences in masturbatory experience for adolescent males and females (Lampl-de Groot 1950). Males have a much greater tendency to masturbate by direct genital stimulation, for example, and a much greater tendency to talk and joke about it with their contemporaries. They use masturbation as a means to gain a better sense of control over their sexual tension generally, and their erections and ejaculations specifically. They feel a sense of relief at finding a way to deal with what are sometimes unwanted erections, and a way to make themselves ejaculate at will (which inhibits unwanted ejaculations at other times). The later onset of puberty for boys also provides them with more time (than girls) to prepare for the social and emotional implications of the changes, while masturbation provides them with a way to use this longer period of time to integrate their physical functions with what they perceive as their social roles.

Girls usually do not have a great deal of preparation time for the changes of puberty. They are often quite young (8 to 10 years old) when the hormonal changes begin. Masturbation becomes a way to discharge the comparatively sudden increase in bodily tension that accompanies puberty, and then an opportunity to explore their changed breasts and genitalia. It gives them a chance to get to know genital parts that previously were often mislabelled or not labelled at all, such as the labia, clitoris, and urethra (Lerner 1976, Shopper 1979).

Ultimately, as is the case with boys, masturbation also provides adolescent girls with a way to integrate sexual sensations, fantasies, changed body parts, and changed functions. Though they have grown up touching these same body parts, just for the purpose of getting dressed or wiping themselves during toilet activities, the new sensations of this time produced by the same activities must be assimilated.

Some psychoanalytic authors have written about the greater conflict adolescent girls feel about masturbating, as evidenced in fewer reports of masturbation in the analyses and psychotherapies of girls and women (Deutsch 1944, Moore 1975). It may well be that overtly objectless sexual activity is more strongly conflicted for females than males.

A 16-year-old patient was talking about touching herself genitally. She acknowledged that she explored herself, but said that she felt very frightened by it. She thought she might introduce dirt, thus, potential infection. She stopped and asked—what was she talking about? What about if she were with a boy? or using a tampon? There was something about being with herself, intimately, that frightened her—that she felt was wrong. Perhaps this is similar to something an adult woman patient was discussing when she said that she never wanted to use a vibrator to masturbate. She was afraid that she would lose her interest in being with a man if she did. She would, after all, be totally self-sufficient.

Not needing someone or something else frightened these women. This may be the result of the strong emphasis on object relations for women, in comparison to the self-focus emphasized for men (e.g., Gilligan 1982). Girls, female adolescents, and women are certainly socialized to think of their impact on others, and to think of themselves as the caretakers of others.

Pubertal girls also are faced with a daunting developmental task: they must simultaneously take over the comforting function of their mothers of childhood, identify with those mothers as women, and see themselves as young women who are different from their mothers. Perhaps masturbation, an experience that moves them along in this complex process of identification, is avoided or more complicated because of the enormity of this developmental task.

Finally, the greater conflict of pubertal girls about masturbation also may be related to the fact of having orifices that cannot be voluntarily closed and opened, thus suggesting to females that someone or something else must be there, with the first template coming in the form of the early relation to the mother. Another patient, an adult whose mother slept with her up through the time she was post-pubertal, cannot permit herself to be penetrated without pain. She tightens herself, fending off intrusion into her inner space. She seems to feel that she cannot afford to have someone else closing the orifice, for she will be unboundaried in the process.

Whatever the explanation, the reports of adolescent females having greater conflict over masturbation are supported in the research studies published on the subject. Overall, however, it is clear that both female and male adolescents masturbate, and both have some degree of conflict or discomfort about it (Hyde 1990, Kinsey et al. 1948, Kinsey et al. 1953). In one study, boys report masturbating several times a week, girls approximately once a month; both said they felt guilty, ashamed, or embarrassed (Hass 1979). In another, the differences reported by first year college males and females were even greater; 45 percent of the males reported masturbating once or twice a week, while only 15 percent of the females did; only 16 percent of the males reported never masturbating, while 47 percent of the females reported that they had never masturbated (Jones and Barlow 1990).

It may well be that one of the reasons that adolescents are somewhat uncomfortable with masturbation is that they are still residing in their parents' homes. It is difficult, under those circumstances, for them to feel free to explore their sexuality, which requires a revisiting of early fantasies about their parents' sexuality. This is what is entailed in the early adolescent Oedipus complex.

THE EARLY ADOLESCENT OEDIPUS COMPLEX

The Oedipus complex, as it is being used here, refers to the inner representation of a constellation of familial relationships, including all the combinations and permutations that are possible among and between parents and their child. In earliest development, children fundamentally take in one person at a time. The basic paradigm for relationships is dyadic. Once they reach the age of about three, children begin to appreciate more complexity in relationships. They are able to see that their parents have an exclusive relationship with each other, that each parent has a relationship with the child, and that they as a unit have a relationship with their child. These children can now understand that relationships of different kinds are possible and that relationships between people can take the form of a unified dyad relating to a third person, as the parents do to the child.

This realization is not a neutral one for children. It now becomes clear, for instance, that parents may choose each other over the child. This new awareness often leads children to feel a whole range of emotions, including jealousy, anger, resentment, fear, and need. They also may scheme to interfere with the exclusive relationship that they see between their parents in the hope of recreating a prior sense of being the most important person in the parent's life. In any case, children begin to think about what it is that their parents might be offering each other that their child may not be privy to or able to offer as well. What is to them still an elusive notion, "sex," often comes to their minds. They know that this is a grownup activity, that it is related to making babies, and that it involves the private parts of their bodies (that everybody makes such a fuss over), but they do not know what "sex" is in the sense that adults do. They do not know its real significance in adult relations, they do not know what it feels like, and they do not comprehend the act itself.

Children of this age develop theories about why their grown-up parents want to be alone, engaging in the activity known as "sex." They also store fantasies about what sex is, imagining physical positions, motivations, and what the grownups are giving each other. All of these compose the Oedipus complex, so named because the original myth involves a whole set of these theories, fantasies, and relationships. In this instance, the boy child's anger at his father for taking his (prized) mother away from him is reacted to by the son's unconscious wish to kill his father and take his mother as his wife.

The conceptions that children develop do not remain static throughout life. As differentiation becomes greater over time, there is increasing awareness of the more and more complex forms of relationships, ideas, capacities, and sociocultural structures in the world. The theories and explanations that young children have about the nature of their parents' relationship, therefore, become quite outdated. They are markedly different from those of adolescents.

For example, a 3-year-old girl looks up at her mother while being put to bed and says: "I don't understand why you get to sleep with Daddy. You're big and I'm little. I'm the one who gets scared when I'm alone. It's not fair." The mother gathers her wits about her and replies: "Well, Daddy and I don't sleep together because we are afraid to be alone at night. We sleep together because grownups who love each other like to sleep together. Some day, when you're big, you'll be able to sleep with another grownup, too, but for now it's important that you learn that there is nothing to be afraid of at night when you sleep alone."

This little girl had become aware of some form of relationship that her parents had that excluded her. This bothered her, and she was trying to find a way both to understand it and test its solidity. Her mother's response helped her to calm down.

This girl's younger brother, when he was 3 years old, had a different approach to what was probably a very similar awareness: "Mommy, come sleep with me. I won't take up as much of the bed as Daddy does—there's more room for you here."

Both children, at around the age of 3, seemed to become aware of the independent relationship the two most important grownups in their lives had with each other. Both tried, in some fashion, to disrupt this relationship. They had different approaches, different points of view about what it was about, but both seemed to become aware of it, have some difficulty with it, and then accept it.

Every child has to contend with the fact that there are adult relationships that exclude them. The awareness of these adult relationships evokes very strong feelings in the child. These feelings run the gamut from passionate loving to equally passionate hating and are expressed toward one or the other parent, siblings, substitute caretakers, and others in the child's life.

One of the ways in which children seem to move on from this enormous preoccupation is by establishing that there *is* some form of adult relationship. In essence, because it is an adult relationship, a relationship between two big people, they do not have to worry about it because they are still small.

The identifications of this time, the oedipal period, are critical to its resolution. Resolution in this instance refers to children's capacity to become less preoccupied with the relationships of the adults who surround them and more self-focused. But with what are children actually identifying? Are the children identifying with the adults, as men and women, as is usually assumed? Is it developmentally sound to think that children regard themselves as being like adults? And, if so, in what manner?

Another 3-year-old girl said to her father: "I know, Daddy. Let's play a game. You be Jerry [her father] and I'll be Roz [her mother]." This little girl wanted to play at being Daddy's wife—but it was playing at being a grownup. It was not confusing who was big and who was little. Children do not identify with grownups in their bigness, even if they do form identifications with them as male or female, or brown-haired or blond-haired, or liking athletics or reading. Children need to see their parents as big—big and strong enough to keep them safe. It is a comfort for children to regard their parents as big.

When, in puberty, children begin to see and experience themselves as big, the resolutions of childhood no longer suffice. Personal theories about the exclusive relationship of their parents that were based upon the fact that their parents were big and they were small are no longer possible to maintain. The young adolescents are becoming adultlike in body and, at some time that seems to be approaching with more rapidity, they are expected to be adult in spirit and behavior as well. Whatever earlier understandings they had come to about the private parts of bodies, about the private lives of the grownup people around them—that is, about sex—must be revisited. Whatever fantasies had been stored away are now called forth.

Jamaica Kincaid's (1983) novel *Annie John* describes these phenomena in a way that abstract description cannot possibly match.

> The summer of the year I turned twelve, I could see that I had grown taller; most of my clothes no longer fit. When I could get a dress over my head, the waist then came up to just below my chest. My legs had become more spindlelike, the hair on my head even more unruly than usual, small tufts of hair had appeared under my arms, and when I perspired the smell was strange, as if I had turned into a strange animal . . . One day, my mother and I had gone to get some material for new dresses to celebrate her birthday . . . when I came upon a piece of cloth . . . I immediately said how much I loved this piece of cloth and how nice it would look on us both, but my mother replied, "Oh, no. You are getting too old for that. It's time you have your own clothes. You just cannot go around the rest of your life looking like a little me." To say that I felt the earth swept away from under me would not be going too far. [pp. 25–26]

As Annie John so eloquently describes it in this passage, becoming bigger, more adultlike, is a transition replete with the pain of loss and fear of change. There is much conflict involved for both parents and children. The conflict is particularly about leaving childhood behind. During this transition, adolescents must find other ways of seeking and obtaining comfort. Parents must find other ways of expressing their tender feelings and wishes to comfort.

Symbolically, the transition is often experienced as a death of childhood, and certainly, it is a death of earlier notions about life. Seeing childhood as timeless is no longer possible, nor is seeing parents in their prior over-idealized and omniprotective roles.

When pubertal adolescents cannot accept the death of childhood, the loss of the caregiving parents of childhood (object removal), and the development of an adult sexual body (Laufer and Laufer 1984), there is often a breakdown. One all-too-common form of breakdown is that of anorexia, where there is a wholesale denial of the death of childhood. Both the awareness and the acceptance of the changed body of childhood and the advent of adult sexuality are fended off among anorectics. As a 5′ 4″, 90 lb., 18-year-old anorectic adolescent young woman (who had already been in treatment that had been of some help to her) said, "I cannot see how I look in the mirror, using *my* eyes, but when I look at a photograph of myself—which captures how someone else sees me—I can see how thin I am." Having her own eyes see what her body was like involved more ownership of that body than she was yet able to exercise.

Seeing themselves as sexual is one aspect of what early adolescents must integrate; seeing parents as sexual and, as such, having an intense relationship with each other that excludes their children is another. Seeing parents as sexual is an experience that has its precursor in the earlier oedipal period, but it takes on a very different significance during adolescence. Adolescents have a greater awareness of the meaning of sexuality and adulthood and the place these experiences have in life and in the world. This awareness expands over time, especially during middle and late adolescence. Each adolescent subphase supplies more understanding, both personally and socioculturally.

In early adolescence, the awareness of the independent life of parents is an important factor in adolescents' feeling freer to explore their own independence. This is the period of the most significant deidealization of the parents and disengagement from them. Hans Loewald (1979) notes the importance of the fantasy of parricide in the resolution of the Oedipus complex. These fantasies also are important in the deidealization and disengagement processes of adolescence. In order to leave the parents of childhood behind, adolescents must commit a comparable metaphorical murder.

In the context of the adolescent's added size and strength, this metaphorical murder potentially takes on a different (and more real) meaning. Some of the intensity, the ebb and flow, in early adolescents' relationships with their parents derives from their (largely unconscious) parricidal fantasies and the fears and conflicts that result. These fears and conflicts are heightened by the adolescents' potential to do actual harm to their parents. In becoming big, adolescents see adults eye to eye, both figuratively and literally. The words of a 14-year-old male patient are illustrative of this experience:

> I played tennis with my father for years. He never let me win or anything. It was pure tennis every time. I felt so small. I used to dream about killing him—wiping him out—6-0, 6-0. Well— guess what. I beat him. I *really* beat him. But it was weird— instead of feeling on top of the world, I felt bad for him. What kind of sweet victory is that?

Thus we hear represented the elements of competition, bigness and smallness, the oedipal "death" wish, and the sense of loss that must be part of our understanding of the oedipal constellation and the adolescent deidealization and disengagement processes.

Early adolescents are exploring their own bodies and trying to come to terms with the fact of their incipient "big-ness" and what that means. Their parents are going through a similar process. The adolescents see themselves as having parents of childhood and parents of the present; parents see themselves as having had small children who are now on their way to becoming young adults. Parents' cognitive and psychological maturity permits them to see both further back in time and further into the future. Parents and early adolescents thus find themselves with worldviews that often are not consonant with one another.

An important implication of the earlier onset of puberty is that adolescents must contend with these issues at an earlier and earlier point in their lives. This is particularly the case for girls, who, as previously noted, generally reach puberty two years before their male counterparts. For a 10-year-old girl to contend with the avalanche of fantasies about "big-ness" and sexuality that follow the advent of puberty is very different from a 12-, 14-, or 16-year-old having to do so. As one 11½-year-old said, with tears in her eyes, to her mother upon menstruating for the first time: "This doesn't mean I'm a woman now, does it, mommy?" For such a young girl to begin to see herself as becoming big, as becoming a woman and a potential mother (with the host of attendant adult female identifications), is an extraordinary task.

More and more early adolescents are having difficulty with this task. Males and females alike must contend with "growing up" when they are younger than was the case for previous generations. The increase in early adolescent onset of eating disorders is one reaction to this. The increase in adolescent suicide is another. These young adolescents cannot comfortably take over caring adequately for their bodily needs, which is the role of the parent of childhood. They are not yet developed enough as individuals; they simply are not yet old enough.

There is a shift in focus during middle adolescence. Adolescents of this age are not as concerned with whether their parents will still take care of them, what their parents are doing, or whether they have longings to return to childhood. The change of this time is similar to that of the postoedipal shift into the world of peers and skills. Middle adolescents are preoccupied with those like themselves, and are far less concerned with being bigger, the implications of being adult, or having a past. They are very much involved in the present: how they look, with whom they are associated, and what they wish to be doing. Rather than being concerned with revisiting earlier fantasies, they are deeply involved in both enacting the fantasies and engaging in new life experiences. They are tuned into the intellectual and sociocultural worlds and often very excited by both.

Middle adolescents' fantasies about sexuality are far less concerned with their parents than they are with their own behavior and that of their friends. They need and want to test out their physical capacities, including those in the sexual realm. They know about sex (or at least see themselves as knowing about sex) and want to connect what they know with what they do (or have done). There is much discussion and comparison among same-sex friends, and there is often the beginning of similar discussions between the sexes. The exploration of intimacy between females and males often lags behind the exploration of intimacy between those of the same sex.

Late adolescence brings a different need for forming adult identifications with parents and others. Late adolescents are very much aware of the need to see themselves as adults; they are far more focused on the adult world and where to place themselves within that world. For the most part, they feel a greater sense of ownership of their bodies, including their sexuality. They have clearer ideas about who they are attracted to, what is sexually pleasing to them, and how their bodies work. They think and talk to each other about intimacy, long-term relationships, and integrating love and work in their lives. In general, they are comfortable with both sexes.

It is fortunate that the capacity for abstraction emerges during adolescence, for clearly there is an extraordinary amount to assimilate and integrate during this time of life. Adolescents must come to terms with their increased physical size (i.e., their "bigness"), their sexuality, and the sociocultural aspects of gender (see Chapter Three). They must come to see their parents simply as adults in an adult world that the adolescents are about to join, rather than as the grownups who loomed so large in childhood.

The changing relationships between children and parents through the subphases of adolescence can be clarified by viewing them in terms of the Oedipus complex, but only if the Oedipus complex is reconsidered to take into account its differing meanings and significance at each developmental point. Too often, the Oedipus complex is referred to as if it were a static set of feelings and fantasies that remain unchanged from the time they first emerge. In light of the vast changes in the meaning of the Oedipus complex during adolescence described above, this static conception is clearly inadequate for understanding what is occurring between adolescents and their parents, both developmentally and clinically.

Indeed, the literal terms of the Oedipus complex may also obscure an age-appropriate understanding of a child's experience at earlier developmental points. For instance, did the first little 3-year-old girl described in this chapter want to kill her mother so that she could sleep with her father? Did she want to kill her mother's husband (her father) so that she could sleep with her mother? Or was she inquiring about why small children had to be alone when big people did not (or asking for some other clarification about the different worlds of children and adults)? *How* do we know— and *what* do we know about the meaning of these questions? It is easy to make assumptions about these kinds of meanings too quickly, both in the moments in which they occur and reconstructively in adolescent and adult treatments.

It goes hand in hand with the ever-expanding world of children that they gradually become aware of more and more complex relations in the world and that they therefore find it necessary to make sense of (and come to terms with) the fact that their parents have an exclusive relationship with one another. They also observe that their parents have a relationship as a unit with them. These observations are a natural next step from the prior awareness of one-to-one relationships and are followed by the awareness of other kinds of increasingly complex relationships in the world, such as groups, institutions, and political parties.

It is developmentally asynchronous to assume that young children of 3, 4, 5, and 6 years of age truly form identifications with big people as big people, even though they do form identifications in other ways. They come up with answers to the questions of this time or are supplied with answers, somehow calm themselves or are calmed, and move on to the next set of questions.

The mysteries of exclusivity in relationships, sexuality and the role of private body parts therein, and "big-ness" are submerged into the less conscious minds of children until they are somewhat more equipped to contend with them. They re-emerge during early adolescence, when the now pubertal children have no real choice but to revisit the fantasies and explanations of their early years. Now they are thrust into the throes of new and different sexual feelings, the growth of the private body parts, and a capacity to observe and understand their parents and other adults in the world that is dramatically different. They have joined the world of the Big Ones.

In early adolescence, when a girl must come to terms with her changing body and her womanliness, for example, she is forced to see herself as like her mother in a way that is qualitatively and quantitatively different from what occurred during the oedipal period. She must leave the mother of childhood behind, see herself as both like her, in her femaleness, *and* different from her, in that they are separate people. There is a strong and conflicted wish to be close to her, that is, a negative oedipal reaction.

Early adolescent girls are very drawn to their mothers. This attraction is extremely conflicted. They are drawn to their mothers as representatives of being cared for and taken care of—as, therefore, the mothers of childhood. They are also drawn to their mothers as female objects of identification in the world. These are most often the women that adolescent girls know best. In both instances, these mothers are very powerful to these girls. Indeed, too powerful, at times, especially in the context of the early adolescent's need to become her own young woman in a future that now feels as if it is upon her. This often results in a turning out into the social world for a best friend and/or a non-parent female mentor.

In the context of what is called the negative oedipal situation, this brief description of the early adolescent girl's relationship with her mother immediately conjures up images and questions about her relationship with her father. At this time particularly, however, the relationship with mother and the relationship with father are on two separate tracks. The girl's need to deal with her mother is a rather distinct phenomenon, and very much dominates her psychic picture. It is not that her father is absent, it is just that her mother is omnipresent. The reflexive ways loving mother and hating father are associated when thinking in oedipal terms (to oversimplify it) simply do not apply at this time. (Perhaps they never do, but, at the very least, they do not during early adolescence).

In *Annie John* Jamaica Kincaid describes an early adolescent Annie at the lunch table with her parents:

"When my eyes rested on my father, I didn't think very much of the way he looked. But when my eyes rested on my mother, I found her beautiful. Her head looked as if it should be on a sixpence." (p. 18)

She goes on with her impassioned description of her mother, then closes with: "We ate our food, I cleared the table, we said goodbye to my father as he went back to work, I helped my mother with the dishes, and then we settled into the afternoon" (pp. 18–19). This aptly captures the early adolescent girl's rich relationship with her mother and the comparative lackluster relationship with her father. It demonstrates both her longing for mother, with its more adult sexual tinge, and her wish to be like her mother, doing as she does.

In "Psychoanalysis as an Art and the Fantasy Character of the Psychoanalytic Situation," Loewald (1980) writes about the reciprocal relationship of the past and present as it is represented in the analytic relationship. The past regains meaning in the present because of the very real quality of the transference relationship with the analyst, in which a past experience is brought into the present; conversely, the present relationship with the analyst is intensified because it is understood in the context of the past. Normal adolescent development reengages the fantasies of childhood in a similar fashion.

By virtue of the visceral experience of sexual feeling and the body becoming big (that is, more adultlike in form), pubertal children find themselves in the throes of integrating past experiences of sexual feeling and ideas about big-ness with present experiences. This is an example of the process of differentiation: the revisiting and revising of experience that occurs throughout life, a process that results in the integration of more and more complex experience. The young adolescent who, on the one hand, longs to rush into the arms of a parent for comfort during this time of enormous change and, on the other hand, is all too aware of a changed feeling within and on the part of the parent that makes such sources of comfort distressing (and often impossible), exemplifies this differentiation process.

Where the awareness of the other person in the early dyad (as has been aptly pointed out by many, particularly in the last decade), including the father, is present from infancy (e.g., Benjamin 1988, Blos 1991, Stern 1985, Stern et al. 1977), this awareness markedly grows during early adolescence. The effect of becoming big is profound. In an earlier paper of Loewald's (1980), "Internalization, Separation, Mourning, and the Superego," he says, "As we explore the various modes of separation and union, it becomes more and more apparent that the ambivalence of love–hate and aggression–submission . . . enters into all of them and that neither separation nor union can ever be entirely unambivalent" (p. 264).

What changes during this developmental period is, in part, the capacity of adolescents to be more aware of the complexity of their feelings. The relative simplicity of the child's experience is lost.

As a 14-year-old, the first 3-year-old quoted in this chapter made an important move into a new school. At that point, she went to her mother and said she was having a severe case of the "what ifs." When asked what she meant, she replied: "Well, I began to think—what if something *really* happened to you? or Dad? I mean, I guess I'd just have to go on with my life, but it would never be the same. It would all be different. The way I looked at everything would be different." Now, perhaps, we can hearken back to her wish not to be alone as a 3-year-old and what that may have meant. Is this the later manifestation of her wish to be rid of her mother? Perhaps. But this hardly does justice to the complexity of her experience, as a 3-year-old or an adolescent.

The infantile sexuality of the oedipal period is mediated by a bigness/smallness factor. When there is a pubertal resurgence of this constellation, the mediating factor dissolves. Infantile sexuality must be understood as a child's form of sexuality, specifically. The resources a child brings to bear on understanding the exclusive relationship of the parents are those of a small child. To make this understanding equivalent even to that of the now big adolescent is to "adultomorphize" the child.

What is seen and felt, what is perceived, continues to change, evolve, and become more complex over time. In the early part of their development, adolescents identify with their parents as people who had once cared for them when they were unable to care for themselves. As development proceeds, they identify with their parents and other adults as grownup, gendered, and sexual people. All of these identifications contribute to their middle and late adolescent capacity to achieve genitality.

Exploring the Social World

3

Middle Adolescent Genitality: Gender and Sexuality in the World of Peers

It is important to understand clearly that the concepts of "masculine" and "feminine," whose meaning seems so unambiguous to ordinary people, are amongst the most confused that occur in science.

Sigmund Freud, *Three Essays on Sexuality* 1905

Deciphering the concepts of gender and sexuality presents a knotty problem to those who try to comprehend human nature. Often, important elements of each are seen as if they were opposites: male/female (biological gender), masculine/feminine (social gender), and heterosexual/homosexual (sexuality). Such absolute terms are typical of childhood, where good and bad or right and wrong are conceived of in simple, binary terms. Binary thinking, however, is left behind when adolescents bring their new cognitive and integrative resources to bear on their perceptions of the world. With these new perceptual capacities, they can see the ambiguities and the continua that actually constitute gender and sexuality, as well as the confusions caused by trying to impose binary categories on more complex phenomena.

From biological, social, or psychological perspectives, gender and sexuality cannot be reduced to binary terms. Each person is a mélange of female and male hormones, feminine and masculine traits, and homosexual and heterosexual attractions. Behavior is often belied by fantasy, appearance by underlying motivation. A woman can be having sex with a man, for example, and imagining that she is with another woman. A man can appear to be masculine in dress and overall appearance, but feel himself to be a woman (Money 1975, Walters and Ross 1986), or a man can express his love of women by wishing to look like them through crossdressing (Allen 1989).

Adolescents, whose self-representations are in a state of great fluidity, are often quite conscious of their particular admixtures. Indeed, these are frequently the source of personal conflict. This conflict often derives from a belief that gender and sexuality are supposed to be experienced in binary terms, when the adolescent's actual experience is far more complicated.

Postpubertal adolescents emerge from childhood into the social world more physically developed (in ways that bring gender into relief) and ostensibly more ready to explore their sexuality. Middle adolescence is dominated by the emergence of the adolescent's gendered and sexual self from the family into the social world. Middle adolescents move out from their families into the world of their peers to explore how their more definitively shaped bodies work, how they are seen, and how they wish to be seen. This exploration takes place on the playing field as much as it does in affectionate and intimate relationships. Adolescents of this subphase primarily focus on how friendship and more intimate relationships are formed and sustained. In terms of this exploration, the importance of family life pales in comparison to their lives outside the home.

Adolescents become aware of the sociocultural world at this time in a way that is very different from any ways they have seen it before. They become aware of political ideologies, the influence of media, religious and historical ideas, philosophical and literary concepts. What it means to be an adult, particularly what it means to be a female or male adult, becomes extremely important. Once adolescents' bodies change in directions that make them more aware of themselves as definitively female or male, the social significance of that designation shifts into the forefront of consciousness.

The development of self-representations of gender are a critical aspect of middle adolescence. Their formation requires looking both inside and out, and creating images of ways of being in the world that feel female to females and male to males. To create such images, adolescents must look within and become aware of the personal meaning of being female or male. They must also take actions in the world that present them as female or male. Both how feminine or masculine they wish to be and how clearly gendered they want their presentation to the world to be are significant in the development of their self-representations of gender.

The world of sexuality also dominates the middle adolescent picture. Adolescents must permit themselves to become aware of those to whom they are attracted, what they wish to do with them, and how it feels to be involved physically and emotionally with the same person. Often there is an initial separation of physical closeness and emotional closeness: there is sexual activity simply for the purpose of gaining experience; there are crushes on people the adolescent does not even know. The complexity of sexual life becomes more apparent, while childlike notions about the nature of sexual activity are revised. Sexual feelings, fantasies, and urges become the focus of attention as adolescents form representations of themselves as sexual people.

These are the issues in middle adolescence that form the foundation of genitality, the concept I use to describe both the integration of the mature genitals into the sense of self and the development of the capacity for intimacy in object relations. Middle adolescent genitality is preceded by the early adolescent issues of integrating the physical changes of puberty and achieving some greater degree of bodily ownership through masturbation and the revisiting of the Oedipus complex. Late adolescence brings with it a focus on individual aspirations and values, as well as a synthesis and integration of identifications that prepare the adolescent for entry into the adult world.

Individual development, however, must not be regarded as linear. Development is not a simple layering of experiences that each individual records, where each subsequent layer replaces the previous one. We are not formed as trees are formed, where there is a layer of bark visible to the outside observer and many layers underneath, each one having formed over the one that preceded it.

Each developmental phase leaves its mark, which is in the form of a reintegration of prior experiences. The prior experience is *re-formed*, not simply recorded. With each developmental advance, children, then adolescents, then adults, are able to look forward and backward, and conceptualize experience in the terms (and with the capacities) now available to them. When adults recall experiences of adolescence, for example, they fill in and rework the recollection with the means of organizing and understanding experience that are available to them in the present but were not available to them as adolescents.

Adolescents also are able to look forward, backward, inward, and outward with more complexity than children. Their view, for instance, is one that extends further back and further ahead, especially over time. As adolescence proceeds, adolescents are able to look further back into their personal histories and further ahead into their anticipated futures. Indeed, one of the important differences between late adolescence and middle adolescence is the greater ability and proclivity of the late adolescent to look into the future. This is an aspect of the ever more complex sense of time that evolves generally during development.

Recognizing that there is constant revision of experience in light of new knowledge and new capacities for perception and integration is critical to understanding the development of gender and sexuality. Children's earliest conceptions of both are revised repeatedly, indeed, continuously as they grow. Irene Fast's (1984) model of progressive gender differentiation aptly describes the manner in which these conceptions evolve. Her position differs from Freud's view of girls as castrated boys or the position (that sex difference is primarily a cultural notion) of the psychological researchers who are social constructionists. She emphasizes that boys are biologically male, girls are female, and that physiological factors contribute to sex differences. She sees social factors as predominating in their influence on gender development and notes that there also are differences from the very beginning in how caretakers treat girls and boys. She proposes that early gender awareness

> is undifferentiated and overinclusive. That is, in the early processes of identification or establishment of self representations, the child has little sense that the characteristics of either femaleness or maleness, feminity or masculinity , are excluded for her or him respectively. Self representations or identifications are in this respect indiscriminate and overinclusive. . . .[pp. 11–12]

She further elaborates her view:

> . . . initially boys and girls may internalize a wide range of characteristics of people in their environment. No attribute is excluded because it is inappropriate to the child's actual sex and gender. Only retrospectively, when sex differences become salient, will the girl and boy become aware that attributes not included in their developing self structures cannot or must not in fact be theirs. [p. 13]

Wendy Olesker's (1984, 1990) longitudinal observational data records early and consistent differences between boys and girls on a number of behavioral and psychological factors, and consistent differences in the way that girls and boys are handled by their caregivers. She sees strong gender-linked differences from very early on in development, which are further elaborated as social influences are integrated.

The point of view that I find most effectively describes the developments in gender that characterize adolescence incorporates Olesker's findings and Fast's observations. There are gender-linked differences from birth, but children internalize characteristics of both significant females and significant males. They also are treated differently by those who take care of them, depending upon whether they are female or male. Characteristics keep getting internalized and shed, based upon the child's sense of what is acceptable, given their femaleness or maleness.

Children enter adolescence knowing that they are biologically female or male, but must come to terms with what this means to them. Gender differences thus become especially salient: adolescents focus intensely on the sociocultural environment for cues about gender and are exquisitely sensitive to what they perceive as appropriate for them on the basis of gender.

Fast's thinking is in the tradition of Robert Stoller (1964, 1968, 1975, 1985), whose groundbreaking work on gender firmly establishes the centrality of the concept of core gender identity (conviction that one's biological sex assignment is correct) and the critical significance of the nonbiological social and cultural influences on gender. He sees the first stage of gender as protofeminine because of infants' earliest attachments to their mothers, and describes how social influences are incorporated into gender identity over time. A woman is not simply an incomplete man, as Freud (1905a, 1925, 1933) described, and masculinity is a state that must be achieved by males, rather than a natural stage (Stoller 1985).

Fast's model does not designate a protofeminine stage for both females and males in early development. She emphasizes that we begin with an overinclusive and indiscriminate (with regard to biological differences) sense of gender that develops in the direction of more gender-specific identifications. Her model incorporates the cognitive/developmental work of Heinz Werner (1957) and Inhelder and Piaget (1958), for she emphasizes the changing nature of thought processes over time. She does not delineate, acknowledge, or explain the range of differences between girls and boys, however, that is aptly explicated by Olesker (1984, 1990).

The differentiation processes that Fast describes *are* important elements of separation and individuation. Separation is the process by which we become more and more aware of ourselves as distinct from the significant people in our lives; it is generally a process that involves what happens between people. Individuation is the growing capacity to see ourselves in complex ways and relate to others in a manner that encompasses our complexity; it is generally a process that involves what happens within people. Fast does not segregate these processes, however, by looking at how they function within separation as compared to individuation, or how they differ between females and males. Instead, she has developed a refined model for looking at the overall evolution of female and male gender identity through the use of cognitive/emotional (perceptive and organizational) processes. The model she develops is tremendously useful for understanding how concepts of gender and sexuality evolve during adolescence.

In separating from their families, adolescents must form independent conceptualizations of gender and sexuality. The conceptualizations they formed in their families are the foundation for those they form during adolescence, a time when the world of peers and the sociocultural world at large takes precedence in their minds' eyes. To individuate, adolescents must develop self-derived formulations of their own gender and sexuality. These formulations come from more complex and reality-based perceptions. These personal integrations, which take the form of mental representations, are crucial to adolescent development. They begin with early conceptions of gender.

GENDER IN THE WORLD OF PEERS

The earliest sense of gender, "I am a girl" or "I am a boy," is based upon the recognition of children's external genital differences, both by the children themselves and the adults around them (Olesker 1984, 1990, Roiphe and Galenson 1981). As children mature, they become aware of feeling that they are girls, boys, or some more fluid, undefined (perhaps, genderless) person. Boys whom adults or older children see as "sissies," girls who are seen as "tomboys," are obvious examples of children whose gender identities are in a fluid state, but it is probable that most children have feelings that span the continuum of girl to boy, or feminine to masculine. Their language and levels of cognitive organization lead them to describe themselves, however, in binary terms. It is rare that children say, "sometimes I feel like a girl, sometimes I feel like a boy"; they are far more apt to describe themselves simply as girls or boys. In using these designations, they are referring to their biological assignments as female or male. Their sense of gender is more complex than they have language to describe.

The advent of puberty induces children to confront their sense of gender. Their comparatively androgynous bodies (apart from the gentialia) become more definitively gendered. Before this time, children are far more overt in demonstrating the fluidity in their sense of gender. They may well know that they are (biological) girls or boys, but the meaning of that designation is far from cast in stone.

A number of writers note this prepubertal fluidity in gender identifications, though the language used to describe this experience varies from theorist to theorist. Marjorie Harley (1970, 1971) and Blos (1962), for example, describe the "bisexual identifications" of prepubertal children. They are writing about the relative ease with which both girls and boys see themselves as like their opposite biological gender.

One little 11-year-old that Harley (1971) describes puts it well: "she thought she must be queer" because she has "so much boy" in her and yet still was a girl who wanted so much to be a girl; "it was as though she were some 'half-and-half creature'" (p. 390). In describing the 12-year-old female protagonist in Carson McCullers' *Member of the Wedding*, Dalsimer (1986) also writes about this experience: "the fluidity with which she thinks of herself, either as female or male, is suggested by her getting dressed up to go into town either in a Spanish shawl or in a football suit—while her friend just as easily took the other costume" (1986, pp. 15–16).

Political activist and novelist Leslie Feinberg (1993) presents still another vantage point on this developmental period when she writes of a woman who grew up transgendered (biologically female, but feeling like a male) in the fifties. This protagonist knew she was a biological female, but simply did not *feel* like a girl. Puberty, therefore, was a painful transition for her, for it made her femaleness clear to others:

Just when it seemed like it couldn't get worse I noticed my breasts were growing. Menstruation didn't bother me. Unless I bled all over myself it was a private thing between me and my body. But breasts! Boys hung out of car windows and yelled vulgar things at me. Mr. Singer at the pharmacy stared at my breasts as he rang up my candy purchases. I quit the volleyball and track teams because I hated how my breasts hurt when I jumped or ran. I liked how my body was before puberty. Somehow I thought it would never change, not like this! [p. 23]

When children reach puberty, they begin to look at themselves and their friends quite differently. The choice for girls to dress as boys, or boys as girls, for example, is one which comes to have larger implications. Where children may play at being one gender or another, adolescents are seen as exhibiting an aspect of their identities when they do so. Suddenly, they may be categorized as "crossdressers," rather than kids who like to play at being the opposite sex.

This is an example of how the sociocultural meanings of gender enter the picture: adolescents begin to see that the way they present themselves in relation to gender has significance in a social context. Their presentation potentially places them in one sociocultural group or another, and is seen as defining an aspect of their identity. There is constant attention paid to how they fit into their peer group, and gender identity is an important component of that categorization process. The identity formation process is both an individual and a collective one: adolescents form personal identities simultaneously with placing their friends in identity categories.

The adolescent turning point with regard to gender is puberty, for it is with the pubertal changes that their bodies become unmistakably female and male (Savin-Williams and Weisfeld 1989). How individual adolescents experience these pubertal changes, reinforce them, or attempt to hide or disguise them is based upon their individual histories and relevant sociocultural influences.

Each pubertal girl and boy has had a personal history in which bodily processes were invested with particular meaning because of the ways the significant people in their lives reacted to bodily changes and events. Whether toilet accidents led to angry parental reactions, sympathetic ones, or humiliating ones, for example, might lead a child—now adolescent—to feel guilty, matter-of-fact, or ashamed about the transformations of puberty. This is the individual-historical context. It can lead pubertal adolescents to have a whole gamut of feelings about their bodily changes.

The pubertal changes also thrust adolescents into a situation in which they must contend with the fact that their physical possibilities are not limitless. This is an aspect of the differentiation process to which Fast (1984) refers when she describes a gradual change from narcissism to object relations: omnipotent, all-inclusive fantasies give way to more accurate perceptions of personal attributes and potentials.

> Both boys and girls must come to terms with their limits. In the course of doing so both may envy the sex and gender attributes of the other sex. Both may perceive the fact of not having those attributes as a loss or an incompleteness, and demand restitution. Both may, after they have recognized their own limits, attribute bisexual "completeness" to others. For both, success in coming to terms with limits requires giving up a focus on not having the sexual attributes of the other sex and committing oneself to one's own actual sexual identity. [pp. 22–23]

Fast is describing the changes and awarenesses of early childhood. The words of a 2½-year-old girl upon seeing her newborn brother on his changing table for the first time exemplify her observations:

"Mommy . . . I have a penis."

"Oh," Mom replies. "You have a make-believe penis?"

"No," responds the little girl. "I have a penis."

"Well, where is it?" queries Mom.

"In my 'gina," she says as she quickly exits the room.

This little girl wants everything. In fact, she believes she has "everything." There comes a point in time when such belief is untenable. It becomes untenable because reality intrudes. One person cannot have the genitalia of both females and males (except in very exceptional physical circumstances). The realities of gender difference become clearer over time, as Fast (1984) and others have noted. Puberty is a nodal point in this growing awareness.

In becoming aware of their pubertal changes, adolescents, like oedipal children, must face the fact that their bodies are not all-inclusive. They, too, must contend with their limitations: they must see and organize a sense of personal gender and a sense of personal sexuality.

In normal development, children arrive at this time with a core sense of gender, a primary identification as a biological female or male (Stoller 1964, 1968, 1975, 1985). (Stoller refers to the biological as "sex," a term I wish to reserve for matters relating to object choice in intimate relations.) The development of gender, gender role, and gender role identity are subjects that have been explored in depth not only by Stoller, but by a number of other prominent contemporary theorists and researchers.[1] Some take the position that gender is fundamentally a social construct.[2] This relatively recent work has significant psychoanalytic predecessors.[3]

Puberty, however, brings with it a particular evolution in gender role identity. Gender role identity is being used here to refer to the psychological sense of gender: what it means to be a female or male in our society, and what it means to be feminine or masculine. Adolescents are driven to define themselves in these terms. Much of their energy is directed toward recognizing and integrating the social and cultural meanings of gender. This may be described as a

---

1. Examples of those who have made significant contributions to this literature include Bem 1993, Benjamin 1988, Bernstein 1979, 1990, Chodorow 1978, 1989, Dinnerstein 1976, Fast 1984, Miller 1973, 1976, Money and Ehrhardt 1972, Olesker 1984, 1990, Person and Ovesey 1983, Roiphe and Galenson 1981, Silverman 1987, Tyson and Tyson 1990, and Wisdom 1982.

2. These social constructionists are primarily psychological researchers: Douvan and Adelson 1966, Hare-Mustin and Maracek 1990, Hill and Lynch 1983, Huston and Alvarez 1990, Kessler and McKenna 1978, and Unger 1990.

3. There are many who could be cited in this context. Those listed span a wide range, both theoretically and historically: Blum 1976, Chasseguet-Smirgel 1970, Deutsch 1944, Freud 1905a, 1925, 1931, 1933, Greenacre 1958, Jones 1927, Kestenberg 1968, Kleeman 1971a,b, 1976, and Zilboorg 1944.

focus on what it means to each individual adolescent to be a woman or man. The particular evolution of this time is in the psychological incorporation of the sociohistorical context.

Focusing on the importance of the sociohistorical context involves the recognition that the meaning of femaleness and maleness, feminity and masculinity, changes over time. Each historical period emphasizes different definitions of gender roles; different developmental periods in a person's life involve changed aspects of gender; and different generations in a family may have varying conceptions of gender role. One need only look at the changing models of beauty represented by such icons as Kate Moss, Jared Leto, and Johnny Depp in comparison to Sophia Loren, Cary Grant, and Rock Hudson to grasp the meaning of the first part of this statement. The current icons represent far more androgynous models of beauty than those represented by the icons of the 1950s. Where teen magazines in the fifties emphasized chest-building for girls, those of the nineties stress quick weight reduction techniques. The professionally powerful, sexy woman and the fit, ornamented man, commonplace images of today, were virtually nonexistent a generation ago.

In terms of the changed perceptions about gender that individuals experience, it is during the middle adolescent shift of focus from home to sociocultural world (i.e., from the family to the world of peers) that a particular awareness develops of the social definitions of gender roles. The girl who prefers looking boyish, for example, may now be categorized as "butch," a designation that is likely to define her social group.

Adolescents' parents may well confront them with historical differences in definitions of gender role as well. For instance, comparing models of beauty that were dominant when the parents of today's adolescents were teenagers with models to which their adolescent children are exposed today may lead to confusion or tension in adolescents' families. A girl considered beautiful by her parents and their friends may feel she is overweight or unattractive in terms of the images valued by her peers.

The current sociocultural context has profound implications for the adolescent's development of a sense of gender in a number of ways. Articulating some of these will provide a way to understand the particular pressures that contemporary adolescents face as they attempt to come to terms with both their personal sense of gender and their collective identifications.

As Americans in the nineties, for instance, we live in a time and place where there is great sanitization of girls' bodily processes, an exaggerated emphasis on their cleanliness and orderliness. Girls use "ladies" rooms and rarely refer to what they are going to do in them; boys are much more specific about what they are going to do, often using graphic terms, and more often than not, are going to "men's" rooms (rather than gentlemen's rooms). Sometimes, males simply refer to the toilet activity they are about to undertake, a practice virtually unheard of among females!

Shopper (1979) wrote a wonderful article about the (re)discovery of the vagina through the use of menstrual tampons. In it, he noted that tampons without applicators are popular in Europe, but there is almost no market for them in the United States. There is, however, a market for all kinds of feminine hygiene products like deodorized tampons and douches. All this introduces pubertal girls to a world in which their genitalia may be regarded as dirty. Indeed, there is a pervasive suggestion that girls should not exhibit their bodily needs or processes in any way. One rarely sees girls or women portrayed as having healthy appetites in any sphere. This may well have contributed to the extraordinary rise in eating disorders in the last few decades. Charles Hogan (1992) suggests that changes in sexual mores, another sociocultural factor, also has played a significant role in this rise.

The comparative ease with which men are expected to talk about and even show their genitalia and bodily processes imposes pressure on adolescent males. What adolescent females are "supposed to" hide, adolescent males are "supposed to" display. If boys are shy or slow to develop, they easily can become the objects of ridicule among their peers. If their appetites in the bodily or sexual spheres are not great, they can be categorized as lesser males: the "wimps" or "dweebs" of their peer groups.

Gender-role (also called sex-role) stereotypes, the often exaggerated sociocultural notions about what females and males are "supposed to" be like, exert a very powerful influence on adolescents' behavior. These stereotypes support the childlike, binary notions about gender with which adolescents struggle. Adolescents tend to be overly influenced in their behavior (though not necessarily in their thoughts or feelings) by these sex-role stereotypes. They often act in ways that reflect this influence. Middle adolescents are especially subject to such influence, because of the deidealization process. This process leaves them less invested in their parents' points of view, more invested in their friends' points of view, and more generally focused on what they see as sociocultural facts.

The emphasis on being "macho" is commonplace in discussions about adolescent males, but there is also a recurrent theme among adolescent (and adult) females of whether they are "woman enough." Among female patients, this issue often arises in the context of comparing themselves to unrevised images of their early mothers. In these images, women loom large and seem inordinately powerful. The adolescents cannot imagine themselves to be like these larger-than-life women. It is only in coming to terms with adolescent issues such as fertility, sensuality, and sexuality that an identification as a woman can take place—a woman as her mother was a woman.

Caroline

Fifteen-year-old Caroline had asked her parents if she could see a therapist. When they asked her what was wrong, she simply replied, "Girl stuff."

The slim, lithe girl with sandy-colored hair looked a bit younger than her years. In response to my inquiring about what had brought her to ask to see a therapist, she quietly responded:

"I just don't feel normal. I really think there's something wrong with me."

"In what way?" I asked softly.

Caroline's eyes filled with tears. "I don't feel like I'm really a girl. I don't feel like a boy, either. But I don't feel like a girl, you know, on my way to being a woman. I know I'm supposed to, but I just don't. Maybe I can't."

"Well, what do you think of as a real girl—or a woman, for that matter?"

"Well, I like little kids, but I'm terrified about the idea of being a mother. It's just, like, too much to imagine. And I know I'm a girl, but I don't feel particularly feminine. I'm not the girlie type."

"Sounds like you're comparing yourself to some specific images of what girls and women are like."

"I guess so. But, you know, I'm not the only one. All the girls do this. There are a million pictures in all the magazines, there are all those girls on TV. They're so similar to each other. And it's just not me."

Adolescents like Caroline are keenly aware of what they are "supposed to" look and be like, and just as keenly aware of what they *do* look and feel like. The comparison between the two is often what leaves them feeling less than female, not "woman enough." The concern with this issue is one that is shared among Caroline's friends. They constantly compare themselves, as does Caroline, to how they see women portrayed in the sociocultural world.

Brian

Sixteen-year-old Brian had reached puberty at the age of 15. Until shortly before that time, he was just over five feet tall and slight of build. He had looked significantly younger than most of his male peers, and was often the butt of jokes. His nicknames were "Shorty" and "Mouse" (short for Mickey Mouse). The young man who presented himself to me, however, looked nothing like a "Shorty." He was at least 5' 9", muscular, and quite good-looking.

"I can't believe I'm seeing a shrink. I mean, I know I asked for it. But this seems really lame."

"Well, let's see if we can make the best of it. What was on your mind when you asked about seeing someone?"

"Girls. Guys. The whole thing. I can't see how I'm supposed to get myself to ask some girl out. All these years they all made fun of me. Treated me like I was some kind of a younger brother or something. Y'know, I was teased all the time for being puny. It's not like I could have done anything about it or anything. I sure as hell didn't—oh, sorry . . ."

"Don't let that stop you. Go on, please."

"Well, anyway. Now everything's supposed to be different. I'm supposed to be the big guy. Pick up the phone and ask some girl out. Can't do it. Just can't do it. I try, but I just freak out. I get a big lump in my throat—feel like I'm about to cry or something. . . . I'm such a pansy."

As a general rule, adolescent males develop later than their female counterparts. It is not until middle adolescence that most females *and* males have reached puberty. Females of this age tend to be nearly finished growing; males have grown significantly, but tend to continue growing for a few more years. It is the first time, however, that most males are bigger and stronger than females; thus, they often are cast into traditional male gender roles at this time. The transition, as Brian describes, is not always a smooth one.

In middle adolescence, there is, then, a definite focus on what it means to be a woman or man, but also a sense that one is rarely whatever it is that is designated as such. Often, this is because there is such strong emphasis on absolute notions of female and male. These absolute notions derive from early conceptions about mothers and fathers; these notions evolved before deidealization took place and have yet to be revised in light of adolescent knowledge and experience.

The reactions to these absolute notions are manifold. One reaction is described in the clinical illustrations above, a reaction which involves strong personal conflict leading to distress. Another is exemplified by thinking about the adolescents of this subphase who look androgynous. They may well be externalizing inner conflicts and confusions by making overt a wide range of feelings, thoughts, and images they have about gender roles. The males of this type may be long-haired and wear earrings but lift weights and talk sports with their friends. The females may have their heads shaved and wear jeans and tee-shirts but be highly flirtatious with their male counterparts. Adults around them are often overheard saying, "Is that a boy or a girl?" The relative comfort with crossing over traditional gender-role lines that adolescents in the nineties sometimes demonstrate may create strong feelings of discomfort among the adults around them who grew up in times when strict adherence to gender roles was more common.

Ultimately, however, it is not the adults around them who are most significant to middle adolescents. It is their contemporaries. How they see their friends and how they are seen is of paramount importance (Mussen et al. 1974). Adolescents must refine a sense of gender that integrates their personal visions, a sense of how they are seen, how they wish to present themselves, and how their social presentations will be categorized by others. Their fundamental sense of themselves as female or male cannot waver in the face of sociocultural assumptions about gender. How they react to these assumptions will aid them in placing themselves along a feminine-masculine continuum. In the end, however, self-representations of gender must gel as they proceed into late adolescence with greater clarity about their femaleness and maleness and their feminity and masculinity.

These self-representations of gender constitute a critical aspect of genitality during middle adolescence. The other major aspect to be integrated is in the broadly defined domain of sexuality. This broad definition includes adolescents' attachments, attractions, desires, fantasies, and intimacies.

SEXUALITY IN THE WORLD OF PEERS

One of the most important elements of differentiation during middle adolescence is the elaboration of what constitutes a satisfying sexual life. Contemporary thinkers about adolescence such as Moses and Eglé Laufer (1984) "see the main developmental function of adolescence as the establishment of the final sexual organization" (p. 5), and view breakdowns among adolescents as most often stemming from difficulties in accepting the bodies and urges that accompany their sexual development at this time.

Middle adolescents of this age must permit themselves to explore their feelings, sensations, and desires toward other people. At first, this may happen through developments in the masturbatory process; subsequently, fantasies and feelings are explored in the context of relationships with others.

I want to emphasize that the way adolescents masturbate is not fixed. At first, they arouse themselves with direct and indirect physical stimulation accompanied by fantasies that are largely unconscious and preconscious. What they are aware of is images of their bodies and body parts. These images and the knowledge they develop about how their bodies work form the foundation for self-representations of early genitality.

As adolescents move into their middle period of development, conscious masturbatory fantasies often involve general sexual images of others' bodies or some desired person initiating sexual contact. Later in middle adolescence, the fantasies involve more reciprocal relations with others.

Late adolescence ushers in a focus on particular people. The shift from largely unconscious and preconscious to more and more conscious fantasies signals a growing acceptance of sexuality for the adolescent. The shift also signals a greater capacity for object relationships. I want to make clear here that unconscious fantasies remain present in adolescents, and the derivation of even the conscious fantasies remains unconscious, but there is an important change that takes place during adolescence that involves both the quantity and nature of conscious sexual fantasies.

When Fred Pine (1985) describes the "metabolization" of new experiences into the self, he uses the adolescent's integration of sexuality as an example of this process. He notes that sexuality is first "almost 'watched' by the adolescent as it 'happens,' but later on it is taken for granted, owned, as part of one's own being" (p. 120). Spiegel (1961) notes that sexuality first acts on the individual adolescent, rather than expressing something about that individual.

The integration of sexuality is a complex and multifaceted process that takes all of adolescence to achieve.

The definition of sexuality that I use is a broad one. Sexuality encompasses: adolescents' awareness of the objects of their desires, that is, to whom adolescents are attracted and what they wish to do with those to whom they are attracted; desires, including those that are acted upon and those that remain in an adolescent's fantasy life; and attachments ranging from friendship to emotional and physical intimacy.

Each of these elements of sexuality takes years to define, and there are stages of development for each. Each of the subphases makes a contribution to the development of sexuality, but it is in middle adolescence that some of the most important elements are explored and integrated. The exploration takes place within the world of the adolescent's peers. It is preceded by the early adolescent awakening to new and intense sexual urges, and followed by the late adolescent's refinements of sexual self-representations through involvements with individual partners.

This sexual development requires the articulation of a set of personal beliefs about sexual activity. These personal beliefs are developed when adolescents accept their changed bodies and accompanying sensations and desires. In order to establish a current system of beliefs, middle adolescents must continue to revisit their early theories about sexuality and reexamine ideas that developed during the oedipal phase in the context of their present knowledge and experience.

These early theories, if left unexamined, may create intense conflicts for adolescents about initiating or participating in sexual activity. If young children imagine that physical contact between their parents involves, for example, dominance and submission, as adolescents they may be terrified of sexual involvement for fear of being hurt by or hurting their partners. If as young children they imagined that their parents' physical relationship involved some form of soiling, as adolescents they may have a dread fear that having sexual contact will contaminate them.

Personal beliefs about sexuality are strongly influenced by social and historical contexts. Helene Deutsch (1944), who wrote her major treatise on female development during World War II, notes that the social milieu of development has a significant influence on its shape. Samuel Ritvo (1971) states that "the duration and style of adolescence are influenced more by cultural and social factors than any other developmental period" (p. 243). Aaron Esman (1990) writes that the experience of adolescence is shaped by the culture, socioeconomic class, historical time, and ethnic group in which it takes place. In a general essay on "Sex and Society," historian Ellen Ross and anthropologist Rayna Rapp (1983) state that "Sexuality cannot be abstracted from its surrounding social layers . . . [it] is shaped by complex, changing social relations and thus has a history" (p. 54). They write about how social influences structure the availability of sexual partners, the transmission of sexual knowledge (including what is taboo), and how the erotic is related to what is taboo. They observe that there is extraordinary variability across cultures and throughout history in each of these areas.

This is an era, like that to which Deutsch makes reference, in which adolescents are faced with life-threatening circumstances. In this instance, however, it is sexual exploration itself that may lead to death. Sexually transmitted diseases such as AIDS, herpes, and hepatitis B are part of the current social mileiu. Adolescents' early fantasies, in combination with these social circumstances, can create significant interferences in the development of sexuality for middle adolescents.

Brian

Brian was now just shy of his seventeenth birthday. He was 5'11" tall and much more self-assured. He had a number of male and female friends, academic success, and had shown leadership in his community. He was still struggling with issues about sexual contact and having a steady girlfriend.

"I can't believe I'm going to tell you this. You know, I don't usually like to talk about this stuff here. But I'm feeling weirded out about it, so maybe you can give me something to think about with it. . . . Jesus. That was really lousy English. Okay. Here it is. I think I am overly worried about getting AIDS or something. I know you don't get it from kissing. But I thought it was transmitted through the blood . . . and saliva is biologically connected to blood. So. . . ." Brian fell silent, looked uncomfortable, and stared out the window as if he were eyeing something outside very intently.

"What's this? Looking outside instead of inside or something? You seem so uncomfortable. I guess this makes you nervous . . . you and a lot of other people, you know."

"Is that true? You know, no one talks about this."

"I've talked to many a kid and many an adult with these kinds of concerns. What made you assume yours were exaggerated?"

Brian was visibly more relaxed.

"I know guys are supposed to be knowledgeable about these things. And certainly experienced and comfortable and all that. But it worries me that there are all these diseases around and everything. And it's not like it used to be. Like, the girl getting pregnant. I mean, people can die from these things."

"True. But do you think there's more to it for you?"

"Yeah."

"I had that feeling. Almost seems like you are worried that sexual involvement could be dangerous."

Brian had been in therapy for most of a year. This was the first time he had broached the subject of sex. He had reached a point in his physical, social, and emotional development that brought the issue of sexual contact to the forefront of his mind. Old theories about sexuality were keeping him from feeling comfortable pursuing sexual involvement with any of his female friends, toward whom he felt attracted. His fears of contamination were rooted in early soiling experiences and fantasies; early notions about sex being potentially dangerous, which permitted a childhood resolution of his oedipal concerns, were a serious obstacle for him as a middle adolescent. The opening up of the discussion with me was an active effort to deal with the conflicts he knew were within him. He had been feeling the pressure of these conflicts, without knowing exactly what they were.

While revisiting the oedipal situation in early adolescence allows adolescents to feel bigger, thus leaving the smallness of childhood behind, in middle adolescence this revisiting process permits adolescents to pursue new sexual theories and experiences. Louise Kaplan (1984) notes that adolescents also must link these early theories with activities in the present in order to establish a satisfying sexual life.

Masturbation is the primary sexual experience of early adolescence. Knowledge they gain through self-stimulation and observation aids these adolescents in feeling comfortable pursuing sexual contact with others. Sexual experimentation with peers is the primary experience of middle adolescence. It is through this experimentation that adolescents of this age come to see how their bodies work in concert with others.

There are stages of development not only in the ways that adolescents interact physically with others, but also in the ways that they form relationships with others. Initially, adolescents focus most intensely on relations with same-sex peers. Harry Stack Sullivan (1953) notes that these relations, which he calls "chums," permit young adolescents to have a basis for comparison about their bodily changes and, generally, to develop a broader range of standards. Certainly, in the context of coming to know their newly changed bodies, early adolescents constantly compare themselves to their same-sex friends: who has developed what, how are they the same and different from those around them. Girls and boys look to see who has developed breasts, how tall their friends are, and how much their bodies have changed.

As middle adolescence is reached, relations become a mix of same- and opposite-sex connections. Within these relations, adolescents often look for how they are the same as those to whom they are drawn. In discussing *The Diary of Anne Frank*, Dalsimer (1986) writes that the sense of separateness with which adolescents of this age contend, in response to their growing independence from their families, leads them to wish to feel the same as their friends: "There is relief and exhilaration in the breaking down of boundaries; the sense of separateness is alleviated as each finds in the other a reflection of the self" (p. 64). She goes on to quote from middle adolescent Anne's diary: "Peter and I are really not so different as we would appear to be . . . we both lack a mother . . . both wrestle with our inner feelings. . . ."

Early adolescent sexual relations with the opposite sex are often more rooted in relationships with same-sex friends than they are in the actual opposite-sex relationships. At this time, adolescents are fundamentally more focused on being observed in opposite-sex relationships by their same-sex peers than they are involved in the opposite-sex relationships. Here is a common case in point:

> A 14-year-old female adolescent excitedly calls up her girlfriend upon returning home from a date with a boy they both know from school:
> "So, did you do it?" inquires the friend on hearing who it is on the telephone.
> "Ugh, yes . . . I'm washing out my mouth right now. I can't believe anyone ever thought this was fun."

These girlfriends had made a pact. Whoever tongue-kissed a boy first would immediately call the other to report on what it had been like. The more intimate of the two relationships was between the girl and her girlfriend. It was partially for the benefit of her girlfriend that the girl on the date kissed the boy. It also may be that she was strengthened in her capacity to take this step in her sexual development because of her girlfriend's interest and support. The trading of information about early sexual experiences is typical of both female and male early adolescent friendship.

> This is taken from a conversation quoted by a 15-year-old male that took place between him and his friend:
> "So, where did you get?"
> "Under her shirt."
> "Awright . . . good shootin'."

The young man who was quoting the conversation brought it up because of the sports allusion. He noted that among his friends, sex was discussed as if it were an athletic endeavor.

Just as is true with early adolescent girls, at first male adolescent sex is separated from emotional attachments. Sexual activity is more of a rite of passage than it is an aspect of a close emotional relationship. The integration of emotional attachment and sexual activity most often begins in middle adolescence. Who is dating whom and what they do with each other (sexually) is important in the middle adolescent gossip mill.

Caroline

"I hate this. Everybody knows everybody else's business. I don't want every kid at school to know what's going on with Billy and me. It's, like, you can't just have a relationship with someone. It has to be a public thing."

"How does anyone know what anyone else is doing?"

"Well, you know. I told my friend Sandy. She probably said something to her boyfriend. Then he tells someone. And on and on."

"What happens if you tell Sandy in confidence?"

"That's tacky. She'd probably think I was ashamed or something. It's no big deal for people to know what I've done. I'm no slut or anything."

"Is it my imagination or are you saying two contradictory things here? It bothers you for people to know, but you really don't mind if they know?"

Middle adolescents frequently begin sexually intimate relationships to mark their entry into another realm of social experience. This, more often than not, is carried out in the social domain. It is important to them that others know that they are sexually experienced. In going through this rite of passage, however, close relationships between the two sexual partners often form. Middle adolescents in relationships get to know each other in ways that are new to each of them, both physically and emotionally.

> Caroline was discussing a recent conversation with her boyfriend.
>
> "Billy kept looking in the mirror, so I asked him if he was worried about something. He said he hated his hair. It never went the way he wanted it to. I couldn't believe it. I would never have known that he cared one way or the other."
>
> "Is it because you've always thought that only girls care about how they look? Or is it particular to your sense of Billy?"
>
> "Well, I definitely didn't think that Billy cared about his looks. But, in general, I didn't think that boys did . . . except an occasional narcissistic type or something. This really surprised me about Billy, though, because he always acts so confident."
>
> "Sounds like you're getting to know him better."
>
> "Yeah, definitely. It's interesting. Not having any brothers or anything, I really never have known a guy this well."

Ultimately, there is an important shift in the level of object relations that middle adolescents demonstrate in their dating/ sexual relationships. What at first may be a rite of passage among their contemporaries comes to be a personal journey shared by two people who get to know each other well, both emotionally and physically. On the one hand, they come to know more about the general attitudes, feelings, and actions of their partners; on the other, they come to know what is sexually pleasing to their partners and how their excitement is expressed. G. Stokes' (1985) study on adolescent sexuality notes that 40 percent of adolescents who engage in intercourse say their primary sources of information about sexual techniques are their partners. These early relationships are significant forces in the integration of the emotional and the physical that takes place within each adolescent, and between the two who share a relationship.

It is usually in these evolving relationships that adolescents are faced with decisions about how far they wish to advance, in sexual terms. In America, the rise in adolescent intercourse and decline in the age of initiation is well documented (Coles and Stokes 1985, Dyk et al. 1991). When to have sexual intercourse is a major topic of concern.

Esman (1990) describes the most common relationship pattern among adolescents in contemporary American society as that of serial monogamy, and notes that differences between females and males with regard to sexual activity have dramatically decreased. I have observed a similar pattern of relationships and a similar lessening in differences between female and male adolescents' concerns.

Brian

Brian seemed agitated.

"Okay, I have two questions for you. How do you know when you're in love, and how do you know when to have sex?"

"Since these are both deeply personal subjects, I think we should start with some statements from you rather than simple answers from me, don't you? Otherwise, rather than your getting answers that are totally for and about you, you're getting general answers that may or may not be relevant."

"All right, all right. Nothing's simple with you, is it?"

"Maybe nothing is simple, period, when it comes to human nature."

"I'll grant you that. . . . Okay, on the love front . . . I think I may be in love with Christine."

"So, what does it feel like?"

"I dream about her, I even daydream about her. I stare at her, think she's the most gorgeous girl in our class. . . . well, maybe that's pushing it. . . . but she's gorgeous to me. She's the sweetest, she's the smartest. She's fun. I feel lucky to be going out with her."

"You wonder what to call all this?"

"Well, I think I'm totally in love with her."

"So, what's the question, exactly?"

"I don't know if this is what people call 'love,' that's all."

"Which people? Certainly sounds like it's what feels like love to you. Is someone else supposed to be deciding this?"

"Not really. But it's related to the second question. Christine says she's in love with me, but she only wants to have sex if I'm in love with her, too."

"And?"

"The truth is . . . I think I'm just nervous about having sex. Like, what if I don't know what I'm doing—and it doesn't work out the way it's supposed to."

"How is that?"

"Um . . . you have a real talent for making me question my preconceptions, don't you?"

"I try."

Brian's fears and concerns about love and sex are frequent topics of discussion among middle adolescents (in and outside of treatment). Fantasies about what each of these means often reveal the presence of early sexual theories and societal assumptions about "appropriate" gender roles. Both female and male middle adolescents struggle with what they feel and what the implications are of what they feel.

The first experiences of adolescent love are intense and, like Brian's, often filled with hyperbolic description. Dalsimer's (1986) essay on Shakespeare's adolescent lovers, Romeo and Juliet, eloquently captures this experience. She describes the function of this love in the separation process: childhood ties to the family are relinquished when powerful relations outside the family are formed. She also notes the intensity of these relationships, and the anxiety they often engender in adults who observe them. The friar who counsels the young couple to "love moderately" speaks for the adult generation; adults are startled by and concerned about the urgency of adolescents' feelings. These love relationships are critical in adolescent development not only for their role in the separation process, as Dalsimer notes, but also in the individuation process, for they afford adolescents opportunities for refining their sexual and emotional feelings, sensations, and attachments.

In the context of defining bodily functioning in the sexual realm and the nature of desire, middle adolescents must come to terms with who it is that attracts them, and what they wish to do sexually with their partners. In an essay that mentions her prior (middle adolescent) "coming out" as a lesbian, performance artist and author Rachel Kaplan (1992) aptly describes her current experience of herself as bisexual: "i [sic] know that my sexuality changes a lot, along with other pictures of myself, so coming out has become the process of trying to articulate my reality" (p. 71). She notes the insufficiency of categorization: ". . . language makes boxes and boxes are bad if you're forced into them, but if you're choosing a box where you want to live, it's important to find one that's comfortable" (p. 72). She sees bisexuality as being the "box" that permits her the highest degree of freedom, and the one that most thoroughly describes her actual experience of desire. She is struggling with self-representations of sexuality.

Kaplan captures the difficulty of accurately describing sexuality both to oneself and to others. In describing the concepts of self and identity, and the experience of separation and individuation during adolescence, Roy Schafer (1973) notes that there are two significant realms of description: that of the behavioral, interpersonal (object-related) and that of the inner representational (self and object representations). This distinction is enormously helpful in attempting to define the adolescent's evolving sense of sexuality, for the evolution incorporates both realms of experience.

Middle adolescents are observed in their social and sexual activity. The observations lead them to be defined as heterosexual, homosexual, or bisexual. The defining is carried out by their peers, the surrounding social world, and themselves. Their peers and others define adolescents by their appearance and interactions in the world; privately, however, the adolescent often finds it difficult to achieve clarity in self-definition.

Caroline

Caroline seemed anxious.

"Sometimes when I'm with Billy, I think about what it

would be like if it was Sandy kissing me instead. It really freaks me out—does this mean I'm gay or something?"

"Well, I think we really have to start by distinguishing between thoughts and actions, don't you?" I responded.

"Yeah, I guess so. I mean, there's a lot of stuff like this that I think about. Sometimes I think I'm completely obsessed about it. I talked to Sandy a little about it. She says she thinks about it all the time, too. Like, how do you know if you're really gay or straight? Maybe I'm bi? How do I know? I've never kissed a girl the way I've kissed a boy. Maybe I'd like it."

Caroline (and Sandy) are preoccupied with sorting out their sexual feelings, fantasies, and actions. In so doing, self-representations of sexuality form. Reactions from others, personal reactions to others, and physical sensations figure prominently in the sorting-out process.

Female high school student Jess Goldberg, in Feinberg's (1993) autobiographical novel about a "butch" lesbian who came of age in the 1950s, describes a part of this sorting out process:

> I had a new secret, something so terrible I knew I could never tell anyone. I discovered it about myself during the Saturday matinee at the Colvin Theater. One afternoon I stayed in the bathroom at the theater for a long time. I wasn't ready to go home yet. When I came out, the adult movie was showing. I snuck in and watched. I melted as Sophia Loren moved her body against her leading man. Her hand cupped the back of his neck as they kissed, her long red nails against his skin. I shivered with pleasure. [p. 24]

At the same time, when Jess walked by in school, girls would squeal, "Is it animal, mineral, or vegetable?" The personal definitions and the social definitions run in tandem; middle adolescents struggle to find a way to form a cohesive set of sexual self-representations. All such self-representations are a combination of idiosyncratic leanings, fantasies, sensations, and experiences, looked at in the context of an individual's social world—including its relevant linguistic categories for sexual behavior and feeling.

British novelist Radclyffe Hall's (1928) autobiographical novel of growing up as an upper-class woman who felt like a man (and was sexually attracted to other women) articulately describes the added pain and confusion that the lack of social category creates for those who do not fit neatly into the categories of their time and place. The protagonist is agonized over feeling unnatural because of her gender and sexual leanings. The only social group in which she feels any sense of belonging, that of other homosexuals, is in a different country from the one in which she grew up and is, in general, less educated and more wild (socially). She is without an adequate social category.

The added conflict produced by limited and prejudiced social definitions of gender and sexuality leads social-activist lawyer Martine Rothblatt (1995) to call for the abolition of sexual categories: ". . . there is no socially meaningful characteristic that defines humanity into two absolute groups, men and women. There are five billion people in the world and five billion unique sexual identities. Genitals are as irrelevant to one's role in society as skin tone" (p. xiii). Others simply aver that gender and sexual choice must be thought of as independent of biological sex.[4]

In any case, contemporary American society does offer a wider range of sexual categories and a wider degree of acceptance for sexual variation than was the case in Radclyffe Hall's time, even though adolescents may not immediately feel the effects of this opening up in society. Adolescents themselves still may feel quite frightened by what they perceive as their differences from their peers in the sexual realm.

---

4. Researchers such as Green 1974, Kessler and McKenna 1978, Money 1975, Money and Ehrhardt 1972, and Sherif 1982 are examples of those who take this position.

Brian

Brian looked distressed.

"I think I'm screwed up. I tried to ask Tommy about this, but . . . no way. He looked at me like I was crazy or something."

"What's going on?"

"Well, to be honest, I really don't like oral sex. Well, to be even more blunt . . . I really don't like going down on a girl. I don't mind when she does it to me—actually, I like it. But, it's the other way that bothers me."

"What is it about it that bothers you, do you know?"

"Well, you know I've been thinking about it."

"I figured as much."

"I think it's two things. One, it's kind of gross—just physically. Sorry, but it doesn't smell so great. And, two . . . and this really gets me . . . it makes me wonder whether I'm gay or something."

These are far from unusual concerns. The fact that Brian feels he has to be either gay or straight contributes to his discomfort, and the fact that being gay is troublesome to him escalates the amount of discomfort he feels. Though this is an era in which homosexuality has far greater acceptance than it had in previous times, adolescents are often the last to feel that this is the case. Their exploration of sexuality and the confusions they feel in response to this exploration often makes them less open-minded than they might eventually become.

Adolescents are extremely concerned with their "normality." This concern stretches from their feelings about their relationships with their parents to their feelings about their relationships with their peers, from concerns about their bodies and appearance to concerns about their sanity. Whether they are sexually "normal" is definitely high on their list of concerns.

In talking to adolescents about sexual normality, I describe normal sexuality as that which is based on love and attraction rather than hatred or fear. I emphasize the importance of reciprocity, passion, and emotional closeness. I attempt to portray sexuality in the very broad terms with which I introduced the topic earlier in this chapter. This is the sexuality with which middle adolescents become familiar. It is not until late adolescence, however, that it becomes possible for adolescents to pursue the depth of relationship implied by this description.

Individual Integration

4

Late Adolescent Genitality:
Adult Identifications and
A Mature Ego Ideal

"When I grow up to be a man . . . will I dig the same things that turned me on as a kid? Will I look back and say that I wish I hadn't done what I did? . . . Will my kids be proud, or think their old man's really a square? When they're out having fun, will I still have my share? Will I love my wife, the rest of my life? When I grow up to be a man, what will I be?"

Lyrics excerpted from "When I Grow Up To Be a Man"
by Brian Wilson, The Beach Boys

Pursuing love relationships based upon reciprocity, passion, and emotional closeness seems to become possible when adolescents are able to perceive themselves as *adults-to-be.* Early adolescent oedipal identifications as "big people" are supplanted by these late adolescent identifications as near adults. Especially in the context of what they seek in intimate relationships, late adolescents become aware of the large and small differences between themselves and others. They are able to fine-tune their values and beliefs, and to sharpen a sense of who they are and what they wish to be. Entering the world of adult sexuality and forming a more self-derived system of values, beliefs, and aspirations are the two most important aspects of late adolescent genitality.

The two previous chapters of this section on identity formation discuss the integration of a more complex sense of the genitalia, a process that is part of the sexual differentiation of puberty. This is crucial to adolescent individuation. In the sexual differentiation process, the genitalia come to be seen in a manner that is more defined, both intellectually and proprioceptively. This more differentiated apprehension of the genitalia must be incorporated into each young adolescent's sense of self.

The genitalia are integrated not simply as larger body parts, like so many other parts of the body, but as body parts with important functions in the sexual realm and beyond. Adolescents come to see themselves as sexual beings, which incorporates more than functioning genitalia—it incorporates seeing themselves as being able to use those genitalia in the context of intimate relations with others. It thus connotes that mind, body, and spirit can be interconnected. It is not sufficient to be sexually active; full genitality is achieved when adolescents are able to be both physically and emotionally close to the same person. This is the first of the two critical aspects of late adolescent genitality to be discussed in this chapter.

The genital stage involves the integration of mental representations of the changed body, self, and self in relation to others. It incorporates the identifications of the adolescent Oedipus complex, which include a vision of oneself as being like one's parents, particularly with reference to the possibility of being an adult in a couple that is sexually involved with one another. This is a pivotal resolution of the late adolescent Oedipus complex.

The achievement of late adolescent genitality is a point at which the processes of separation and individuation coalesce, for there are aspects of self developing simultaneously with the formation of important aspects of identity. There is a growing awareness of not needing primary caregivers as one once did and not being a child any longer—elements of the separation process. There is also the awareness that one's physical dimensions and inner feelings have changed—elements of individuation. At the same time, object relationships reach a new level, for changed physical capacities and matured capacities for closeness come together to permit a different form of connection with other people.

From the vantage point of late adolescent development, connecting to other people involves the integration of self and object representations and a set of self-derived values. How one wishes to be, who one wishes to be, to what one aspires, what one believes in—all of these constitute the mature ego ideal. The mature ego ideal represents the culmination of adolescent development, and requires the integration of all that has preceded it in early and middle adolescent development. Late adolescent identifications are significant in the ego ideal maturation process, for it is through the integration of these identifications that the ego ideal becomes more realistic. Before this, the ego ideal is rooted in children's fantasies of what is loved and approved of by their parents. The maturation of the ego ideal is the second of the two critical aspects of late adolescent genitality that I will discuss.

The late adolescent identity formation process utilizes the more mature perceptual, cognitive, and emotional capacities that are available. Adolescents are now able to integrate the valued traits that have been observed in others into a sense of self. Identifications with parents as significant adults in their lives are especially important in this integration process. Once these are integrated, the adolescent is able to move into adulthood feeling comparatively whole and self-defined.

SYNTHESIZING ADULT IDENTIFICATIONS

The awareness of becoming an adult has an air of unreality to it throughout adolescence, until the last stage of adolescent development is reached. Early adolescents are aware of being bigger, but rarely think of themselves as moving toward adulthood. Middle adolescents are primarily focused on each other, often in contrast to the adult world. Late adolescents begin to look at themselves as individuals. In so doing, they become increasingly concerned with how they want to be, who they want to be, and whom they admire among the adults they observe.

Whether in school or in the work place, late adolescents often seek out adults who are objects of their admiration. These may be coaches, bosses, teachers, therapists, relatives, parents of friends, or friends of parents. In any case, adolescents wish to get to know these adults better and differently. It is part of the process by which they come to see themselves more and more as young adults, and less and less as their younger adolescent selves. They often model themselves after traits they see in these adults. These adults also may serve as bridges between the adolescents' childlike ways of relating to their parents and the ways they will relate to their parents in the future.

Alison

Especially in high school, Alison had a difficult home life. Her mother drank heavily and abused prescription drugs such as diet pills, tranquilizers, and sleeping pills. Her father was absent in two senses of the word: he left home early in the morning and returned home late at night, and when he was at home he was mostly uncommunicative. Her parents also fought regularly, usually over her mother's inebriated state, her father's absence, or money.

Alison was the oldest of four children. Her other siblings were boys. Whenever her mother was incapacitated, Alison was expected to feed the boys, help them with their schoolwork, and get them to bed. She hated the fact that this was what her parents expected of her, though she enjoyed some of the aspects of caring for her brothers.

In school, Alison was very successful. Her grades were excellent and she was a leader in a number of school activities. She had friends, though she said she only felt really close to one of them. Most of her afternoons were spent at this girlfriend's house. She dawdled on her way home as much as possible, always dreading the moment of opening the front door of the house. She never knew the state in which she would find her mother.

Alison was not someone I saw in treatment, but she is someone I came to know well. She spoke to me at great length about these years, in the context of a relationship with me as her professor (I met her when she was a college student). Her attachment to me was strong. She said it mirrored the relationship she had with her best friend's mother when she was in high school.

"My relationship with Laura's mother saved my womanhood. It was so hard for me to want to be a woman. I was a complete tomboy as a kid; for years, most of my friends were boys. I just didn't see anything good about being female. My mother bitterly complained about my father and about having to take care of us. She said I should never get married. And looking at her sure didn't make being a woman seem like a positive thing."

She described her utter fascination with Laura's mother. "She was so pretty, and so smart. I thought Laura was incredibly lucky to have her as a mother. I used to ask Laura and her mother endless questions about the details of their lives. Like I was trying to find out, how did a normal household function, anyway? I started dressing more like Laura's mother, using eyeliner the way she did. Maybe it was weird, I don't know. But I think it saved me, in some way."

Alison's involvement with me revolved more around how to integrate a career and a family life. Neither her father nor her mother had successfully created such an integration. She very much wanted to believe that it was possible. She pursued a relationship with me as a professor she admired in her chosen department as a way of bolstering her commitment to her own hopes and dreams. If I could do it, perhaps she could as well. Our relationship became a vehicle for her to further define her own aims.

Involvements (such as the one between Alison and me) with other adults make alternatives to the adolescent's own family life seem more possible. Fantasy is supplanted by reality; the reality principle increasingly takes precedence over the pleasure principle. This is an important piece of cognitive development during late adolescence. The capacity to perceive reality accurately expands, for it is less impeded by psychological demands. The developing ego is capable of greater and greater complexity in perception. It can synthesize more and more diverse stimuli.

"Synthesis" is key to late adolescent development. Erik Erikson (1956), for instance, sees "ego synthesis" as a critical accomplishment of this time. In late adolescence, the achievements of middle adolescence in the realms of gender and sexuality must be integrated into the "self." This means that there must be representations of experiences in these realms that feel integral to the adolescent. These are internally bonded in a way that feels coherent with the rest of what is experienced as self. This is the beginning of the "integration" processes that constitute an "identity."

I put these terms in quotes because there is so much confusion in the literature in the way they are discussed and represented. Schafer (e.g., 1960, 1967, 1968, 1973) has repeatedly (and accurately) pointed this out. These are complicated terms that are used in ways that are too diverse and, as Schafer (1973) emphasizes, too reified. They refer to ways of conceiving of who we are and how we are, not to actual entities. I feel it is incumbent upon me to explain how I am using them here.

"Self" is an immediate sense of who we are, made up of images of oneself alone and in relation to others (i.e., self and object representations). Each person has many such representations, for example, social, private, work/school place, intimate/family. Adults are not usually conscious of these representations, but can be made conscious of them; there is a preconscious awareness, available at will to consciousness.

Adolescence is a developmental period, however, in which there is a great deal of self-consciousness. Early adolescents become more self-conscious in large part because of their bodily changes. They need to find ways of seeing themselves that take these changes into account. Middle adolescents interact in the world of peers to glean a sense of how they compare to others who are in a similar state of flux. Late adolescents focus on refining a sense of self that feels real and coherent to them. Their self-consciousness leads them to notice and bristle at seeing themselves acting differently in different situations. They want to feel that their sense of self is stable and continuous.

Adolescents are generally more aware of themselves than they will be once the adolescent process is left behind. This awareness is in the service of defining a more distinct sense of self, especially one that feels authentic. Along the way, there are contradictory versions of self that are sorted out; some are discarded, some are maintained.

There is a conscious awareness of these different aspects of self, but the discarding process itself is an unconscious one. Identifying with others plays a role in aiding adolescents to define different ways of being that either appeal to them or that they dislike.

Deutsch (1944) notes that the weaker the ego, the more a child turns toward identification with adults. The adolescent ego is under a great deal of pressure to integrate the influx of energy stemming from instinctual forces (id) and the new expectations that come from the external world, simultaneous with the adolescent's disengaging from the parents of childhood (who offer ego support). The adolescent ego is, thus, also in a weakened state. Adolescents, like children, turn to identifications with others to refine a sense of self.

Edna Furman (1973) discusses how identifications with parents aid adolescents in decathecting from them as incestuous objects. This decathexis from the parents permits adolescents to pursue sexual relationships outside the family. The necessity to derive the new identifications from the old, to build organically upon the foundation of the past, is noted by Edith Jacobson (1961). Each of these thinkers is aware of the importance of identifications with adults during adolescence. I would like to stress that the identifications are with a wide spectrum of people: adults, both parents and non-parents; older peers; and same-age peers. The integration of these identifications, particularly those of late adolescence, ultimately leads the adolescent to feel more authentically adult.

"Identity" differs from "identifications" or "self." It is a pulling together of representations that include social, physical, and private images of who we are and with whom we belong. When asked what we are, we answer with different elements of our "identity." These may include a sense of our nationality, religion, vocation, or ethnocultural background. In any case, identity connects us to other people or organized social institutions. It is the outgrowth of a feeling of belonging or a way that we believe we tend to be seen. For example, one's identity might consist of being an Italian Catholic female dancer, a Jewish American male artist, or a Latin American socialist female writer. Where "identity" connects us to abstractions that define us, "self" connects us to images of how and who we actually are in our everyday lives.

To "synthesize" the images (representations) that constitute self and identity is to use the new cognitive and emotional resources available to late adolescents to combine the representations into an entity that feels authentic and cohesive. Jacobson (1961) describes adolescent identity formation in a similar fashion. She sees it as an increasing ability to preserve the whole of the psychic organization as a highly individualized, coherent entity. This is what I see as constituting "I." The experience of "I" involves the integration and synthesis of disparate elements.

Late adolescents have more energy available for this complex identificatory and integration process. The availability derives from the freeing up of energy that had been engaged in the relationship with their parents during childhood. This added energy also fuels the individuation process. Getting to know themselves, a primary task of this subphase, means getting to know which self-images feel real. This is what occurs in late adolescent identity formation. As Schafer (1973) notes, this takes a good deal of time:

> Genuine emancipation seems to be built on revision, modula-tion, and selective acceptance as well as rejection, flexible mastery, and complex substitutions and other changes of aims, representations, and patterns of behavior. These changes are necessarily slow, subtle, ambivalent, limited, and fluctuating. [p. 45]

Once such an emancipation and subsequent integration of changes have taken place, there is far less consciousness of self or identity. As a matter of course, most adults simply are who they are; they give far less (and qualitatively different) thought to the experience of "I." They are, for example, much less concerned with how others perceive them than are adolescents. Developmental crises of adult-hood, however, sometimes bring the kind of consciousness to "I" that is typical of adolescence.

The necessity to undergo major surgery, the death of a spouse, or the death of a parent are examples of adult crises that may precipitate this kind of consciousness. Surgery brings one's physical shape and capacities into focus, much like the bodily changes of adolescence. The loss of a spouse brings to mind the kind of intimate relationship one has had and raises questions about what kind of relationship might be sought in the future. These, too, are an important aspect of adolescent development. The death of a parent leads an adult to consider the limits of life, the inevitability of death, and the final abandonment of the role of child. All of these are considerations of adolescence as well.

The focus on an evolving sense of self is an outgrowth of the shifts in narcissism during this developmental phase. The narcissistic preoccupations of the early and middle subphases, which aid the adolescent in separating from the family of childhood and in individuating, give way to interests in the actual external world during late adolescence. Ritvo (1971) emphasizes the vital importance of the intimate sexual and emotional relationships that adolescents seek in the external world in their emergence from what he terms "the narcissistic retreat" (p. 252). These partners in the external world help adolescents to stabilize (adult) identifications with oedipal objects; the early, charged relationship with oedipal objects is neutralized through contact with real, permissible love objects in the present. Energy is thus freed that had been bound up in the earlier relationships. Ritvo emphasizes the blending of the old object representations with the new.

Carl Adatto (1991) describes the difference between the intimate relationships of late adolescence and those of the earlier subphases. He aptly notes that the focus shifts from detaching from the old important relationships to the forming of new and more permanent ones. What the adolescent wants in and from relationships is more defined; in late adolescence, the relationships themselves serve to demonstrate to the adolescent how possible it is for these wishes to be met.

Nathaniel

Nathaniel had just graduated from college. He felt unsure about what to do in almost every context. He had no job, though he was very bright and multiply talented. He had a girlfriend for whom he cared a great deal, but could not decide whether to live with her or not. He was temporarily living with his parents, but was quite dissatisfied with what he felt was a regressive situation.

"I'm stuck. I'm just stuck. I feel like I really don't know myself, and I should by now. I just dealt with college like it was high school—sort of breezed through, barely paying attention. And now what? I've got nothing. I can act, sing, write, think philosophically or biochemically. And where does it get me? Christie [his girlfriend] thinks my problem is that there's *too* much I can do well. She also thinks my godlessness is a problem. I would be better off if I believed in someone or something. I can't help the fact that my parents were anti-religious atheists."

"And what do *you* think?"

"I don't know what I think."

"Certainly makes it hard to make decisions for yourself."

"Look. I don't even know what I really feel about Christie. I know I love her, but how much? We're so different. In a way, that makes it better. She forces me to confront ways that I am that I just took for granted before. She's from Louisiana, you know. From a religious family. Protestant, that is. She went to a community college. And, me? You know 180 degrees difference. Grew up in New York City, went to a private school, Ivy League college, Jewish—by family tradition—even if we weren't practicing or anything. It's a cultural thing. She's kind of wild; I was always extremely uptight. She's good for me."

"Sounds like she encourages you to look more carefully at who you are and where you come from."

"No question about that. Also no question about the fact that I *need* to look at myself more carefully, because I barely have a clue about who I *really* am."

"*Really* am—as opposed to . . . ?"
"I feel like an impostor half the time. I don't know what I
want, who I am, where I'm going."

Nathaniel's relationship with Christie did aid him in thinking
more deeply about who he was and where he came from. He
questioned his beliefs, his plans, his feelings for her and his
relationships within his family. Ritvo's (1971) suggestion that relationships like these serve to bring the late adolescent more in
contact with object relationships is borne out, as is Adatto's (1991)
that relationships at this time help the late adolescent to define what
intimacy is about and what is wanted in a close involvement with
someone else.

External relationships with love objects serve the very important functions that Ritvo and Adatto describe, particularly in the
realm of furthering individuation. External relationships of the type
that I have described with non-parent adults permit late adolescents
to decathect further from their early objects as sources of love and
approval. Like intimate relationships with peers, they thereby further the separation process initiated at the time of puberty. Adolescents also gravitate toward older peers to give them a glimpse of
what is to come in the near future. From talking to these older
peers, they are able to imagine what the adult world may have in
store for them.

Alison

"I was really close to my resident advisor in college. She talked to me
about what it was like to be in graduate school: what was required
academically, what it was like socially, all that stuff. It made a big
difference to me. I compared myself to her, I kind of imagined myself
in her place. I think it helped to prepare me for what was to come."

My relationship with Alison helped her in forming more
positive images of adulthood, generally, but her relationship with
the graduate student who was a resident advisor in her dorm gave

her a more immediate sense of what was to come in the next few years. Both contributed to her moving ahead developmentally with relative comfort. These relationships with the graduate student and me aided her in separating from her family of origin and in individuating. She formed important and strong attachments outside the family that felt real, which supported her separation process. She also compared herself to both of us, and was able through these comparisons to get a better sense of her capabilities, academically and socially; this supported her individuation process.

The kinds of relationships that have been described, ranging from those with adults, to older peers, to peers, all contribute to the forming of positive identifications that move the adolescent toward adulthood. These are based upon a wish to be like the person with whom the adolescent is identifying. Some identifications, however, are based more upon a wish *not* to be like someone than a (positive) wish to be like them. This most often happens within families; adolescents have strong, conscious wishes not to be like their parents or siblings in ways that they dislike.

Elizabeth

When Elizabeth came for treatment, she was 28 years old, but looked much younger. She was thin, dressed in faded blue jeans and a T-shirt, and somewhat nervous.

"I'm so unhappy, but I really can't do anything about it. I feel paralyzed. I hate my job. It's boring. I have no social life. I barely have friends. I talk to my mother every day. It's ridiculous. At my age, I should be married with kids."

As treatment progressed, certain elements of Elizabeth's family life and upbringing rose to the surface. She was from an upper middle class Italian family in which she was the second oldest of six children. The siblings on either side of her in birth order were married with children. Her older sibling was a sister who had been a sexually active teenager. Elizabeth's Roman Catholic parents were furious at this older sister. She was a voluptuous middle adolescent who screamed back at her parents when they criticized her. Elizabeth said the entire house would shake during their fights.

In response to this situation, Elizabeth formed a negative identification with her sister. She was *never* going to be like Rosemarie. Indeed, when she arrived in the consulting room for treatment, she was virtually Rosemarie's opposite: she was waif-like, looked and acted younger than her years, and was completely asexual. She felt that she was abnormal, and was very unhappy about it.

"It doesn't make sense. Everyone I know is with somebody . . . except the ones who are younger. They talk to their boyfriends; I talk to my mother. Something is wrong with me. I know it."

"What kind of something?"

"I don't know. Maybe I'm confused about sex or something."

"What about it?"

"Whether it's okay to have it or not. I mean, I know it's okay. I just mean, I'm not sure that I *really* think it's okay. All that Catholicism growing up."

It took some time before the stories about years of turmoil in her household emerged. Six months into a treatment that was conducted on a three-sessions-a-week basis, Elizabeth mentioned that these fights at home between Rosemarie and her parents were the worst moments of her life. She felt that she hated her sister, whom she had idolized throughout her childhood. She was frightened by her parents' anger at this sister. She was baffled by her sister's appearance and behavior, and somewhat in awe of it, It was overwhelming.

Elizabeth said she did not choose to be this way, she just *was* this way. Her negative identification with Rosemarie was not a conscious choice on her part; it was an unconscious compromise. She was completely unlike Rosemarie in the ways that made her parents enraged: she was asexual in appearance or behavior, and she was accomodating and polite with her parents and other adults. She was even a devout Catholic.

Elizabeth had become "Not Rosemarie," defined more by who she was not than who she was. She identified with her (formerly) adored older sister, but the upheaval of those years led the identification to be a negative one. In particular, the family chaos of Rosemarie's middle adolescence threw Elizabeth's sexual development into turmoil. Her parents' rage at Rosemarie, and Rosemarie's at her parents, left Elizabeth in tremendous conflict. She felt disloyal to both Rosemarie and their parents. She formed a negative identification with Rosemarie, a partially positive one with her parents, and a partially negative one with her parents.

The negative identification with Rosemarie was in the area of sexuality. Rosemarie was the sexual one; she was the nonsexual one. The positive identification with her parents was in hating Rosemarie for being sexual and being aggressive. This hatred, however, ended up being self-hatred, because Elizabeth's pubertal development brought these sexual and aggressive instincts into consciousness.

Their being brought to consciousness meant that Elizabeth became aware of her own sexuality. This awareness brought her into direct conflict—the conflict arose out of the conflict between Rosemarie and her parents, and between Elizabeth's childhood representations of Rosemarie and her adolescent images of Rosemarie.

The confluence of these conflicts overwhelmed Elizabeth. Being overwhelmed, traumatized, kept Elizabeth from being able to use the full range of organizational capacities available to her. She was unable to view the situation in all its complexity, and resorted to a childlike global identification. Identifications usually become more and more differentiated, because they are rooted in cognitive and emotional capacities that become more and more complex over time.

Instead of being able to sort through what constituted her own moral beliefs, Elizabeth ended up simply identifying with her parents and totally rejecting Rosemarie. She simultaneously rejected her parents, because they wanted her to date, get married, and have children. Ultimately, she was unable to move into adulthood; basic aspects of adolescence were impossible for her to resolve on her own. She was riveted to the point in time when her family seemed to fall apart.

The integration and consolidation of adult identifications is what permits late adolescents to feel more like adults. This happens over time, and usually in a piecemeal fashion. Areas of the late adolescent's life, one by one, are experienced in a way that feels more adult. Anna Freud (1958) describes this in terms of outmoded aspects of self and object representations that must be altered and existing object relationships that must be revisited and revised.

The first sexual relationship, which is not necessarily the same as the first sexual experience, is an example of an area in an adolescent's life in which there is such a revision. Late adolescents often become aware of the fact that a sexual union in a relationship of emotional intimacy is an adult experience, in a way that differs from prior sexual encounters. This awareness is possible because of identifications with significant adults (such as parents) who were seen as sexually engaged with each other.

The most important areas for adult identifications are relationships within the family, intimate relationships outside the family, and the adolescent's work life. Each of these must come to feel different (and more adult) to the late adolescent, not like it did in adolescence or childhood.

The end of adolescence, because it involves this host of integrated and synthesized identifications, is extremely hard to define—for the adolescent and for those around the adolescent. Development, as always, is very uneven. Thus, it is likely that adolescents reach adulthood at different points in each of the areas. Only gradually, and often well into their twenties or later, do these individuals feel themselves to have fully entered the adult world. The last area in which adulthood is felt to be reached is often within the family of origin.

The family of origin is the area of greatest conflict because the longings to be wholly dependent, to have someone to rely on completely, are great. It is difficult to leave such wishes behind. They must be replaced by more differentiated dependency wishes—wishes that are satisfied by knowing that there are people who can be relied on, even if those to be relied on are not omnipotent. This kind of awareness corresponds to adolescents' growing capacity to look at themselves more realistically. When they are able to view themselves more realistically, adolescents' ego ideals can mature.

ESTABLISHING A MATURE EGO IDEAL

An ego ideal is that to which an individual aspires. As the individual's behavior approaches the ego ideal, self-esteem rises; when behavior falls short of it, self-esteem drops. The self and object representations that form the ego ideal first derive from what children feel their parents want them to be. When caregivers offer love and affection, children experience a sense of well-being. Maximizing this sense of well-being is a driving force for children's behavior; they seek to comply with their best sense of what their caregivers wish for them.

Their more advanced perceptual and emotional capacities enable adolescents to examine the sources of their self-esteem and their goals, that is, their ego ideals. The disengagement from the parents of childhood creates a situation in which these prior sources of self-esteem, those which derived from pleasing their parents, are no longer as highly valued. The separation process throws adolescents into conflict. They cannot feel as comfortable unabashedly pursuing the love and approval of the parents from whom they are also disengaging.

At times, adolescents look outside their families for ways to derive a sense of self-esteem, and to stretch and test themselves. In the service of separation and individuation, they will define areas of expertise that are markedly different from those that are enjoyed by other members of their families, for example, athletic or artistic endeavors, or areas of intellectual or social focus. This supports their finding value in being different from their families, which facilitates separation, and having their own particular strength (in comparison to other members of their families), which facilitates individuation.

Michael

Michael was a middle adolescent, and the middle child in a family of three adolescent children. The oldest, the only female, was a highly successful student and athlete. The youngest, a male, was also very successful in school and took pleasure in the role of being the youngest. Michael was extremely bright, but somewhat more uneven as a student.

During the latter part of his early adolescence and into middle adolescence, Michael became absorbed in an area that distinguished him from the rest of his family: ichthyology, the study of fish. He pursued the study with vigor, both in his reading and his collecting of fish. He soon became quite expert.

The effects on his family's response to him and his to himself were unmistakable. Each regarded him with a new respect, even admiration, and he looked and seemed more proud.

Michael had chiseled out his own area of expertise. He clearly knew more about fish than anyone else in his family, or even in his large extended family. Others in and outside the family, peers and non-parent adults alike, turned to him with questions about fish in general, and experiences or problems they were having with their own aquariums. Mastering a body of knowledge to a very high level was an empowering experience for Michael, generally, and specifically contributed positively to both his separation from his close-knit family and his individuation.

The pursuit of knowledge and experience outside the life of the family is often an important step in the direction of the maturing of the ego ideal. When adolescents realize that they can define such areas for themselves, they feel less rooted in the family and thus less dependent upon them for affirmation.

In their farewell to childhood (Jacobson 1961, Kaplan 1984), adolescents lose a strong source of ego support, both in terms of ongoing external validation from their caregivers and a detachment, internally, from prior representations of their caregivers. Freud (1905a) describes the detaching from parental authority at this time; Spiegel (1961) notes that there is an estrangement from the superego, which is the inner representation of how parental authority was exercised with the child. The superego combines inner representations of actual interactions with caregivers, the meaning the child infers from the interactions, and the fantasies the child attaches to the interactions.

It is most important to grasp the dual nature of the burden adolescents face. They lose two prior sources of self-esteem: one that comes from the parents themselves in the present, and one that comes from the internally represented versions of their parents. This is the estrangement from the superego to which Spiegel (1961) refers and also demonstrates that the ego ideal has not yet become self-derived. The reliance on the parents as a source of self-esteem is greatly diminished when the ego ideal is mature. Before this maturation has taken place, adolescents may feel somewhat bereft; they have lost important sources of self-esteem and not yet developed viable alternatives.

Some, like Michael, develop an area of expertise outside the family domain that becomes a real source of self-esteem. By developing an area outside the family's interests, he opened up a new channel for potential admiration. He thereby was able to sustain his family's interest in him and respect for him, but for characteristics different from those that evoked attention and appreciation in childhood. He evoked their appreciation for a capacity that developed in adolescence. At the same time, he respected himself for his independent choice and the development of a new strength.

As previously noted, other adolescents turn, sometimes desperately, to people outside the family of origin for such support. Their source of self-esteem primarily remains external to them. When they turn outside in this fashion, their peers—both same age and older—and adults who are not their parents become much more important sources of feedback and objects of comparison and identification. These relationships aid adolescents in redefining their goals for themselves; indeed, sometimes they are defining their goals for the first time. As children, without real awareness of it, they pursued goals that were implicitly and explicitly laid out for them by their caregivers. As adolescents, they ultimately seek to define these goals for themselves.

The importance of caregivers during childhood cannot be overstated. Stemming from the experience of these caregivers as sustainers of life, children develop a sense of need for them that changes only slowly. A period of monumental change takes place in adolescence, for it is during this period that a major shift must occur. Self-esteem moves from deriving primarily from external sources to deriving primarily from internal sources. The sense of need that children have for satisfying the wishes of their parents shifts to a need to satisfy their own goals and desires.

This shift is represented in the changes that occur in the ego ideal during adolescence.[1] What once derived from caregivers must now derive from the late adolescent's more mature cognitive and emotional capacities. Late adolescents' capacities to view their parents and the world at large more realistically and with more complexity need to be applied to the ways that they view themselves. Insofar as they have successfully separated from their families of childhood, they are able to use these capacities on behalf of themselves. When they remain overly involved with the family of childhood, and still use their capacities to evoke expressions of love and appreciation from early caregivers, they often have difficulty moving on in life.

Nathaniel

Nathaniel continued to live with his parents for several months. He remained indecisive about whether to move in with Christie or not, as well as about his vocational aims. What began to emerge in treatment was the way he had shifted his need for love and approval from his parents to a need for love and approval from Christie. He had not been able to focus inward on his own feelings and aspirations. His ego ideal primarily remained unconsciously tied to his parents' wishes for him, and his estimations of what he could

---

1. Some of the most influential psychoanalytic writers on the development of the ego ideal are Blos 1967, 1972, 1974, Esman 1975a, Jacobson 1961, 1964, Ritvo 1971, and Sandler et al. 1963.

accomplish remained tied to his earliest fantasies of his parents' capabilities (i. e., they remained over-idealized and grandiose).

"I want to be great at *something*, at least. After fooling around with one thing or another for all this time, I have to come out of it with something truly great or I'll look like a complete jerk."

"So, if it's not 'truly great,' is it nothing at all?"

"Sounds pretty extreme, I guess. But it *is* how I actually feel about it. If I don't come up with something incredible, everybody's going to be really disappointed in me."

"Who's the 'everybody?'"

"Christie. Mom and Dad."

"Sounds like you feel like you are being watched pretty carefully."

"Maybe I just think that. Maybe I'm the only one with these high expectations of myself. Maybe they're out of whack with what's possible altogether . . . but that doesn't stop me from thinking that I *could* really be something."

"What kind of 'something?'"

"A writer, maybe. But what do I have to write about? What have I experienced of life? I'd have to make it all up. My whole life is like that—I feel like I'm constantly putting on a show. I'm not really being myself, whoever that is."

"Seems like you rely on others to define 'whoever that is' much of the time. Probably makes it harder for you to feel comfortable just 'being.'"

Nathaniel's face tightened, and he squeezed his eyes shut. "It literally hurts to even *think* of 'just being.' I have lived my whole life waiting for other people to tell me how terrific I am. To admire me, love me, whatever. What a waste."

Nathaniel was paralyzed by his need to find love and support outside himself. He had derived so much of his self-esteem from these outside sources throughout his life that his ego ideal remained rooted in what his parents wished for him, rather than what he wished for himself. The usual developmental path for the maturation of the ego ideal had not been followed: Nathaniel's sense of who he wanted to be had not become more and more self-defined, and his gratification did not derive from meeting goals he had set for himself. Instead, unconsciously, his parents remained over-idealized and his expectations for himself remained rooted in both their appreciation of him and goals for himself that came from over-idealized identifications with them.

Most of those who write about the ego ideal describe it as narcissistic in origin.[2] Jeanne Lampl-de Groot (1962), for example, writes that the ego ideal is a need-satisfying agency within us that makes four major moves. First is the wish-fulfillment stage of infancy, a period of development during which inner and outer are not distinguished. Second is a stage in which fantasies of grandeur and omnipotence dominate, after the infant distinguishes inside and outside. Next is a stage in which there are fantasies of the parents as omnipotent, and the child shares in that omnipotence by being loved by them. Finally, there is the formation of independent, realistically attainable ethics and ideals.

Nathaniel had not reached this last stage when he began treatment. His narcissistic development had been compromised by his need to retain the attachment to his parents that stemmed from childhood. His parents had always been laudatory toward their only child. They said they never needed to have more children, because he fulfilled their every dream. Such unabated praise and sense of importance was difficult to leave behind. It also contributed to Nathaniel's having unrealistic expectations for himself.

These unrealistic expectations can be reflections of general adolescent narcissistic development (though the longstanding, un-modified nature of Nathaniel's unrealistic expectations exceeded what is generally found among younger adolescents). The capacity to assess one's abilities realistically and the place they may have in the world usually takes some time. Heinz Kohut (1966, 1971) thoroughly describes how an awareness and acceptance of the realistic

---

2. Examples of prominent psychoanalytic writers who see the ego ideal as a narcissistic institution are Blos 1972, 1974, Esman 1975a, Jacobson 1961, 1964, Lampl-de Groot 1962, Reich 1960b, Sandler et al. 1963, and Schafer 1967.

limitations of the self increasingly replaces the need to maintain equilibrium by an investment in grandiose self-images. This process is tied in with the gradual decline in the need to see the real parents and the internalized parent images in over-idealized terms. As an offshoot of the process, there is a growth of ego autonomy.

In addition to his compromised narcissistic development and undeveloped ego ideal, Nathaniel was burdened by a too harsh superego. His superego had not been modified by the influences of the more developed ego functioning theoretically available to him (A. Freud 1952). His superego remained rooted in the experiences of prohibition with his parents of childhood: it had the absolute, black and white quality of a child's superego. Things were definitively right or wrong, or good and bad. There were no greys, no ambiguities, no complexities in the moral domain. He was, thus, very hard on himself for what he perceived as his failure. Both the harshness of his superego and the lack of maturation in his ego ideal kept Nathaniel from moving into young adulthood.

Late adolescence brings with it a modification in the superego and a maturation in the ego ideal. Many others have written extensively about the functioning and changes in these intrapsychic structures.[3] In working clinically with late adolescents and young adults, I find it especially useful to have a working understanding of what the superego and ego ideal are, how they evolve, how they operate, and what the interrelationships and the distinctions are between them. Many of those who come for treatment at these ages are struggling with issues in self-definition and focus that arise from problems with superego functioning and ego ideal maturation.

The ego ideal, as Blos so aptly describes (1972, 1974), is an agency of aspiration. To approach it is to feel pride; to remain far from it is to feel ashamed. The superego is an agency of criticism;

---

3. Superego and ego ideal development during adolescence have been extensively discussed by Beres 1958, Blos 1972, 1974, A. Freud 1952, Freud 1914, Jacobson 1961, 1964, Kohut 1966, 1971, Lampl-de Groot 1962, Laufer 1966, 1968, Reich 1960b, Sandler et al. 1963, Schafer 1967, and Steingart 1969.

the criticism may be benign or harsh (Schafer 1960). In either case, the action of the superego leaves us feeling guilty; how guilty, with what sense of a need for punishment, is idiosyncratic to the individual. Both the ego ideal and the superego originate in infancy and early childhood, and the relationship between children and their caregivers forms the foundation for each of them.

As noted earlier, the ego ideal evolves from our wish to feel the sense of well-being that comes from emotional and physical satisfaction in the early years. This satisfaction comes from admiring, being admired by, and being well cared for by caregivers. Initially, children believe that their omnipotent, omniscient caregivers have the power to grant them this satisfaction. The desire to feel this sense of well-being as much as possible is strong; thus, the wish to comply with the parents' wishes for the child are strong. Further development leaves children more aware of the conflicts between what parents may wish for them and what they may wish for themselves.

In adolescence, a high degree of such conflict is ushered in by the onset of strong sexual and aggressive urges, and the subsequent need for separation and individuation. In the context of these differentiation processes, much of what the adolescent has aspired toward comes into question: Whose goals are these? Are they realistically attainable? Do they feel real to the adolescents themselves, or have they been imposed by the caregivers?

Nathaniel's goals were neither attainable nor self-derived. His ego ideal representations were relatively unexamined until he came for treatment. In the context of treatment, we were able to sort through his goals, which were highly perfectionistic and grandiose. Coming to terms with his actual abilities and objectives was difficult for him, and involved some real sadness and disappointment, but in the end he was able to make decisions for himself and choose and sustain a suitable career path.

Superego development has a two-pronged result. First, a conscience develops: a personal sense of what is right and wrong. Second is the way we respond when we have either acted in keeping with our superego demands or violated them. An overly harsh superego is one that sustains ideas that are too absolute, as are the ideas of children. The power of the guilt that someone with a harsh superego sustains is great. Indeed, as was true for Nathaniel, it can paralyze a person. Not only did he disappoint himself over and over again by starting but never continuing in his career, he also felt absolutely awful whenever he gave something up. The disappointment was an ego ideal manifestation; the awful feeling resulted from conflict that arose from the workings of the superego.

The distinction between the ego ideal and superego is important not only for understanding development, but also for making clinical interventions. Knowing how a feeling develops, for example, will give a clinician a starting point for intervening. Ego ideal pathology needs to be addressed by looking with patients at: what their expectations for themselves derive from; whether they are realistic; whether they take into account who the patient is at this time; and what are the patient's actual capacities. Superego pathology must be addressed by looking with patients at: how they come to see what they are doing as so right or so wrong; why they feel as badly as they do; and what makes them assess the situation as warranting such a harsh response. In both cases, early representations of caregivers and identifications with them will be unearthed in the treatment relationship, especially in the transference.

Elizabeth

After a year of psychotherapy on a three-session-a-week basis, Elizabeth and I decided that she needed to be in psychoanalysis. Her suffering was great, her difficulties were highly complicated, pervasive, and rooted in childhood and adolescence. A psychoanalysis would permit the level of regression in the transference that she needed to fully reexperience and explore the important childhood and adolescent relationships within her family that still so dominated Elizabeth's psychic life. One of the significant and recurrent aspects of the transference relationship that developed between us in the ensuing months was a tremendous hostility that she directed alternately toward herself and toward me.

"I *hate* you. You have everything. You're so perfect. And I have nothing. Nobody. What good is all this analysis going to do for me? It's not going to change *anything* . . . and you know it."

"I wonder how you have become so convinced of something that has not yet taken place."

"Nothing ever helps. Nothing has ever helped . . . and this won't be any different."

"Perhaps you're so convinced because you are actually referring to something that has already happened."

"Bullshit. Nothing has ever happened. That's the problem. Nothing ever has and nothing ever will. This is my life. It sucks. And that's the way it goes. I don't even know why I'm here. It's just not going to do anything."

"Though I know that you are here because you wish for things to be different, perhaps there is also some way that you don't wish for them to be different."

"Go to hell. What kind of thing is that to say? Do you think I *like* living this way? I'd have to be crazy to like living this way. You don't get it. You just don't get it. This is the worst. I hate living like this, being like this. I can't believe that you think I *like* it. That's sick."

"There is a difference between having a wish for things to remain the same and liking the way they are."

"Why would I want things to be this way?"

"What comes to mind?"

"Fuck you." Elizabeth fell silent. She remained that way for several minutes.

"So, maybe you're very angry at someone—and, maybe, particularly angry about something related to sex. And you want them to suffer with your unhappiness."

Elizabeth had built up an enormous amount of rage: at Rosemarie, her parents, and herself. Her childhood idealizations of her sister and parents, and then the sudden sense of tremendous disappointment with each of them that she felt during her sister's adolescence, left her feeling alone and enraged. There was no gradual deidealization process that took place through her adolescence, no real modification in her superego identifications or ego ideal representations. She remained dependent upon appreciation from her parents, and never developed a set of images for who she wanted to be that felt personal and authentic to her.

What developed instead was a moral, masochistic position that left Elizabeth in a state in which she needed to suffer to feel a sense of self-worth; in fact, her suffering even made her feel superior. She also wished to let those who cared about her know she was suffering (and have them suffer along with her) as a way to vent some of her accumulated rage. Her parents made it clear that they suffered over her not being married.

My role in this component of the transference was to be the externalized version of some particular aspects of the representations of her parents and Rosemarie from childhood and adolescence. In each instance, I was the parent or sister that she adored, but also hated both for disappointing her in so acute a fashion and having a sexual life (while she had none). Elizabeth's sexuality had become infused with an inordinate amount of aggression, making it especially difficult and dangerous for her to imagine having her own actual relationships. Her sexual desires also were riddled with guilt, both conscious and unconscious.

On a conscious level, she could not imagine pursuing a sexual relationship because she feared her parents' rage. Even though she knew that she was much older than Rosemarie had been when all the turmoil erupted between her and their parents, and she was not living with her parents, she was convinced that having a sexual relationship outside of marriage would be anathema to them. Unconsciously, she was paralyzed by the rage and disappointment she felt, guilt at harboring such feelings, and guilt over the pleasure she took from causing others to suffer over her.

In the course of the time that Elizabeth was in treatment, she was able to see that I had no particular designs for her present or future life, other than a wish that she feel freer to define a life for herself. Identifying with this attitude aided her in valuing her own sense of herself, and, ultimately, in defining a more mature ego ideal. Included in this ego ideal was a wish to have a partner with whom she could share a sexual and emotionally intimate life.

Her treatment helped Elizabeth to become more autonomous. She was able to define an ego ideal that was based upon her own real desires for herself, regardless of whether her desires coincided with those of her parents or were different from them. The development of an ego ideal that feels self-derived and real aids a late adolescent in having relationships in and outside the family that feel consistent and cohesive. They develop a way of *being* that feels consistent and cohesive: an "I."

There are distinct steps along the way to real autonomy that are illustrated in the case examples presented in this chapter. Alison, for instance, was able to relate more comfortably with her parents because she had a clearer sense of where she was going, in part from her relationship with her resident advisor. The experience she had relating more openly to adults outside her family, such as Laura's mother and me, made more direct communication with her parents possible as well. Michael's plunge into ichthyology gave him an anchor outside his close, loving, and competent family, which would make dipping in and out of the family in the years following middle adolescence more possible. Nathaniel's involvement with Christie was all too similar to his involvement with his parents, but was a step away from them that gave him a glimmer of awareness of what living outside his family would be like. He finally was able to become more autonomous when his sense of who and what he wanted to be developed from knowing how *he* actually felt about himself and the world, rather than paying more careful attention to those around him than he did to himself. Treatment helped him enormously in this regard, because of its exclusive focus on *his* perspective.

To be fully engaged with another person, emotionally and sexually—to, therefore, have achieved full genitality—requires true autonomy. Such autonomy derives from identifying comfortably as an adult and having developed a sense of who to be that feels self-derived and authentic, that is, a mature ego ideal.

An outgrowth of both the synthesis of adult identifications and the maturation of the ego ideal is what Jacobson (1961) describes as a *weltanschauung*, a worldview. This is a set of values, ideals, and ethical standards. It may involve opinions on nature and culture. A worldview encompasses a wide range of subjects, including the sexual, social, racial, national, religious, political, and general intellectual realms.

Having a worldview empowers late adolescents to move forward into adulthood. In contemporary American society, how one identifies oneself in a multicultural context plays a significant role in the development of such a worldview. The next chapter defines and describes the development of an ethnocultural identity, an aspect of how we see ourselves that gives us a self-derived sense of place in the world.

Brian Wilson's lyrics from the Beach Boys' song "When I Grow Up To Be a Man," as excerpted in the epigraph of this chapter, give us a glimpse into late adolescents' preoccupations with entering the world of adults. He aptly identifies some of the most important areas of focus: What will be the sources of pleasure? What might be the regrets of the future? What will it be like to be a husband? Or a father? The words bring to mind the fears, the dreams, and the desires that late adolescents share as they move toward adulthood. There is an excited and anxious anticipation of a future filled with commitments and responsibilities. These are the major conflicts of late adolescence, and these are the problems that those of this age must address to achieve full genitality successfully.

5

Mature Ethnocultural Identity: Leaving Home, Belonging, and Finding a Place

It takes a whole village to raise a child.
African tribal saying

There is an important aspect of adolescent identity formation that falls outside the rubric of genitality: mature ethnocultural identity. In moving out of their families of origin, adolescents seek a sense of belonging in the larger sociocultural world and a sense of connection to traditions that precede them and will outlive them. Developing a mature ethnocultural identity satisfies these needs.

In a world of 5.4 billion people, in a country of 255 million Americans, we actually see and describe ourselves as belonging to smaller, ethnocultural groupings. These are defined by some combination of factors such as religion, class, ethnicity, national origin, geography, activity, and/or sexual orientation. These groupings—working-class Irish, New York Jewish, African-American attorney, white Southern Baptist, gay San Franciscan—provide an essential context for adult life and identity. Ethnocultural identity is a person's sense of connection to such groupings.

Ethnocultural identity consists of a cohesive set of mental representations that begin to develop in early childhood and coalesce in late adolescence. The maturing of ethnocultural identity is a critical component of the adolescent developmental process. To move out successfully from the family home, literally and figuratively, the adolescent needs to feel a sense of belonging to some defined sociocultural group. Feeling rooted in the sociocultural world provides each adolescent with an anchor during the years of transition from childhood to adulthood.

In childhood, a sense of ethnocultural identity derives from two sources. One is the context in which early caretaking occurs, the place in which and to which children belong. As the world of children develops, what they perceive becomes more and more complex, both internally and externally. The other source is the external world, as perceived by children through the ways in which it is brought into their homes. At the juncture between the inner worlds and the external worlds is ethnocultural identity, the aspect of identity that eventually links them to ethnocultural groups.

Ethnocultural identity permits people to feel the sense of belonging that was once reserved for their homes in situations other than home and with people other than members of their families. What children perceive in concrete terms (a place in which they belong), adolescents perceive in more abstract form (a group to which they belong). This occurs in tandem with and is made possible by the fuller development of the capacity for abstract thought in adolescence.

The earliest representations that form ethnocultural identity derive from the relationship between the infant and caregiver as colored by the context in which the relationship forms. The representations then become images of relationships and experiences that place the family in a larger sociocultural context, for example, religious observances or specific ethnic practices, such as those related to foods, holidays, or healing. Eventually, ethnocultural identity crystallizes into differentiated mental representations, including abstract ones such as beliefs or ideologies. These representations, like those of the mature ego ideal, form during the last stages of the adolescent identity formation—the consolidation phase. Culture also influences the development of other components of intrapsychic structure: in addition to the ego ideal, the ego and superego have important roots in the sociocultural world that are modified when adolescents turn their attention so vigorously to the world outside their families.

Particularly in the context of a multicultural society, adolescents turn to specific sociocultural groups with which they feel a sense of belonging in order to separate comfortably from their families of origin. In early and middle adolescence, these are transient groups that adolescents choose; these groups may be characterized by a clothing style, a type of music, or a sport. By late adolescence, fundamental characteristics such as ethnicity, religion, sexual orientation, and national origin become central organizers in an adolescent's identity. The choice of these as central organizers for the individual adolescent signals the formation of a mature ethnocultural identity. The fact that the adolescent has made such a choice, that there is a self-derived sense of ethnocultural identity rather than one that simply is given through familial custom or authority, is a significant factor in assessing the maturity of ethnocultural identity.

Those adolescents who come from families in which ethnocultural distinctiveness is de-emphasized or even negated can find the adolescent developmental process more difficult. Adolescents who have moved from their cultures of origin, whose ethnocultural identity formation processes, therefore, have been thrust into conflict, also may have difficulty in this late adolescent consolidation phase. It is especially hard for adolescents whose personal histories have left them in a state of cultural loss or confusion to find a comfortable niche for themselves in the multicultural world in which they live.

This chapter first describes the nature and development of mental representations of culture. Cultural influences are rarely thought of in terms of how they are internally represented. I, therefore, trace some of the history of psychoanalytic thinking about how the world outside the home is brought into the home and recorded by the developing child. It is these representations of culture that coalesce into what I have called ethnocultural identity. I place particular emphasis on the maturation of this aspect of identity during the second individuation process of adolescence. How the definition and elaboration of ethnocultural identity aids in normal adolescent development and how circumstances of cultural loss or confusion may become central for a patient will be emphasized. Case examples will show why it is important to establish an ethnocultural identity in adolescence and what happens when there has been interference in its development.

Culture is here conceived of in its broadest sense, as in one's sociocultural context or one's nation of origin. It is represented by the objects, sights, sounds, smells, and practices of home as they are developmentally perceived. Ethnoculture is an even more inclusive term. It encompasses such varied aspects of the sociocultural world as religious or ethnic tradition, sexual orientation, or geographic location, all of which have a profound impact on the way someone lives and sees the world. In the increasingly diverse, complex world in which we live, it is more difficult to feel at home in the larger sociocultural context; it is a necessity to achieve an inner sense of ethnocultural cohesion. This is what will be elaborated as mature ethnocultural identity.

THE ROLE OF CULTURE IN IDENTITY FORMATION

The sense of identity begins with babies' images of their bodies and bodily sensations (Greenacre 1958) and proceeds with the development of progressively more differentiated, symbolic, and continuous mental representations of the self, and of animate and inanimate objects (Jacobson 1964, Mahler 1968, Schafer 1968). Infants react to seeing and touching their bodies by forming images of self and non-self, body and environment (Hoffer 1950). They also take in real features of the environment during periods of alert wakefulness, which form an important part of their ability to test reality (Pine 1986, Wolff 1959). Thus, from the very beginning, identity critically involves an awareness of what is in the environment.

The earliest reciprocal relations with the primary caretaker, which ultimately lead to object constancy, are also significant in the first identity formation process (Fraiberg 1969, Mahler et al. 1975). These caretaking experiences take place within a particular setting, a setting which itself becomes familiar. The setting alone (that is, one's room or home) will come to evoke comfort through its association with the caretaker (Levy-Warren 1987). That sense of comfort allows the infant, and later the child, to feel a sense of belonging in the home, even in the absence of the caregiving person (or persons). Comfort is also associated with patterns of care involving language and other vocalizations (such as lullabies or nursery rhymes), ways of handling, and smells. These are precursors to the cultural norms of that child's future.

The mechanism of association that permits a setting to evoke the sense of comfort that derives from the reciprocal relationship with the primary caretaker is similar to that which is described by Donald Winnicott (1971) when he writes about the child's use of transitional objects. He sees the baby's play with the transitional object as occurring in a place that is exclusive neither to the baby nor to the caretaker. He conceives of culture as "the potential space between the individual and the environment, that which initially joins and separates the baby and the mother when the mother's love, displayed or made manifest as human reliability, does in fact give the baby a sense of trust or confidence in the environmental factor" (p. 121). Winnicott suggests, but does not quite state directly, what I see as critical: the environmental factor, culture, is *internally* represented. Without such representation, the baby would not be able to develop this sense of trust or confidence. Before there is constancy in these environmental representations, babies often have difficulty settling down or sleeping in new surroundings.

Calvin Settlage (1972) extends Winnicott's transitional object thesis. He sees past and current experiences as contrasted, compared, and refined in the potential space between the individual and the environment. These experiences (as well as images or ideas) are played with in the mind's eye. He suggests that early interferences in children's playing serve as potential disruptions in the process of internalization of cultural values that takes place in late adolescence.

I see these early representations of the surrounds (the environmental factor) as the first form of what later become mental representations of culture. As the child's world expands through the maturation of both emotional and cognitive apparatuses (Hartmann 1939, Werner 1957), these cultural representations become more complex, more differentiated. The representations eventually (during adolescence) must come to encompass both the environment of the home and that of the external (sociocultural) world.

The idea that what is represented internally is not restricted to relationships with the significant people in one's life has precedence in the psychoanalytic literature. Freud, for example, in "Mourning and Melancholia" (1917), writes that mourning can occur in reaction to the loss of an abstraction (which takes the place of a loved one) such as "one's country, liberty, an ideal, and so on" (p. 143).

The influence of the sociocultural world also is represented in the values and standards that constitute the superego (Freud 1933): it is a container of cultural tradition, one in which generations of assumptions about what is right and wrong and good and bad are represented within each individual. He notes that the superego includes "not only the personalities of the actual parents but also the family, racial, and national traditions handed on through them, as well as the demands of the immediate social milieu which they represent" (1940, p. 146). Thus, parents introduce both the culture of the present and the cultures of the past to their children.

Transcultural psychiatrist Ari Kiev (1972) writes that human beings are distinct from other members of the animal world because they live in social groups whose actions and feelings are determined by ethnocultural patterns handed down from generation to generation. In formulating the concept of the superego, Freud provides us with a way of understanding how these ethnocultural patterns are recorded and transmitted down through the generations intrapsychically.

Anna Freud (1936, 1965) and Heinz Hartmann (1950) emphasize the value of looking at another of the intrapsychic structures, the ego, and its defensive and adaptive functions in relation to the external environment. Beginning with Hartmann's *Ego Psychology and the*

Problem of Adaptation (1939), the issue of the relative autonomy of the ego from the surrounding culture became a major subject of theoretical work (Erikson 1950, Rapaport 1958). David Rapaport proposed that the ego takes in various nutriments from the environment that work to help it sustain defensive and adaptive structures. Hartmann and his colleagues (1951) noted that cultural conditions shape the opportunities for egos to function in a conflict-free sphere, and that they may also shape possible conflict situations.

The critical importance of adaptation, the necessity for dealing with sociocultural conditions, is underscored by Mahler and colleagues (1975) and Werner Muensterberger (1968). Mahler and her colleagues focus on the ever-present need of the infant to shape itself to and be shaped by the environment. There is a reciprocal nature to this shaping process, that is, there is an internal pressure (from within the individual) to accommodate and an external pressure (from the sociocultural world) to conform.

As previously discussed, particularly in the contexts of overall adolescent development and the development of gender and sexuality, certain aspects of the first period of separation–individuation, according to Blos (1967), are recapitulated during adolescence. He describes this as a second individuation process. With the upsurge of instinctual energy initiated by pubertal changes, there is a significant force driving the youth to the culture outside the family of origin. Turning to the now incestually charged parents for comfort is impossible; thus, there is interference in the adolescent's feeling of belonging in the family home. Engagement with new physical, social, and intellectual experiences is intensely sought. People outside the family have the potential for becoming significant in ways not previously possible. Social and physical experiences provide the adolescent with opportunities for testing out newly acquired capacities; the world of ideas offers opportunities for testing out the growth in their intellectual abilities, that is, being able to think abstractly (Inhelder and Piaget 1958).

Adolescents become aware of the sociocultural world at this time in a way that is very different from the ways in which they have seen it before. They become aware, for example, of political ideology, religious ideas, philosophical concepts, sociocultural differences, and the influence of media. What it means to be an adult, what it means to be female or male, what it means to be part of an ethnic, religious, or other ethnocultural group, all become extremely important at this time. Even (or, perhaps, especially) their own families are seen in more distinct sociocultural terms, in these larger contexts, rather than as unitary, given phenomena. The engagement in considering these abstract elements of culture and the formulation of a personal set of values, beliefs, and ideologies (i.e., a mature ego ideal) are critical components of the adolescent process.

The adolescent needs to find a way of fitting into the sociocultural world. This is a major aspect of the identity formation process of this time (Erikson 1956, 1959, Lewin 1939, 1951, Ritvo 1971). The earliest sense of belonging, which develops in the home of origin, is brought into conflict with the adolescent's need for greater autonomy. This motivates the move outward, into the sociocultural context in which the adolescent lives. It is at the juncture of this inner need for belonging and the turn outward that ethnocultural identity coalesces.

Mental representations form as the adolescent interacts in the world outside of the home; when these interactions provide the adolescent with the comfort, the sense of belonging, which was once associated with the family home, an awareness of ethnocultural identity emerges. The choice of groups with which to belong is significant in the formation of a mature ethnocultural identity.

Adolescents first choose to belong to sociocultural groups that form around types of music, sports, or styles of dress. These are the early form of adolescent ethnocultural identity. At times, the absence of such groups in an adolescent's life can interfere in the development of ethnocultural identity. Beth provides an example of someone whose early and middle adolescence lacked the experience of feeling that she belonged in groups such as these.

Beth

Beth grew up in a family that she described as Jewish by family tradition, but completely nonobservant. She said that her parents were quite assimilated into the small Christian community in which she was raised. As a child, she used to accompany her friends to church on Sundays from time to time. She was fascinated by the rituals and the air of solemnity in the services. She remembers feeling envious.

When Beth was an early adolescent, her family moved to New York City. She was both excited and overwhelmed. The diversity of the environment was extremely stimulating to her, but also seemed foreign. She was aware that there were other kids who looked more like her than the kids with whom she had gone to school in her previous community. They, too, had curly hair and dark complexions. Some of these peers were practicing Jews. They seemed to her to assume that she was Jewish as well. She felt like an impostor. She was reluctant to bring her school friends home. She felt that non-Jewish kids, to whom she felt more similar, regarded her as coming from elsewhere. Jewish kids, who regarded her as like them, seemed very different to her. She was sure that either group of kids would find her home life to be too revealing of her differentness.

Beth entered treatment at the age of 21. She felt depressed, isolated, and lost. She did not feel that she could define a professional direction for herself, nor even settle on a place to live. She felt embarrassed about moving back to New York after college, back to where her parents lived. She just "didn't know where to go"; she did not feel that she belonged anywhere.

She described her early home environment as "sterile." Everything was "just so." There were no actual plastic coverings on the living room sofa, but "there might just as well have been." She did not feel that she was permitted to play anywhere but in her room, and she did not feel that either of her parents really enjoyed playing with her. She most preferred visiting her best friend's home, where she remembers the smells of baked goods, the toys all over the house, and the warm, affectionate greeting of her friend's mother.

Beth's mother was "tailored." Just as the house was "just so," so was her mother. The attractive, well-dressed woman was someone whom Beth admired, but from whom she felt estranged. Her father was the more affectionate and playful parent, but was very busy establishing himself as an attorney. He had long office hours and frequently had to work over the weekends.

The birth at the age of 3 of a sister was difficult for Beth, because the already limited attention of her parents felt further diminished, but also welcome because of the anticipated presence of a new playmate. The sister did prove to be a playmate for Beth but, much to her dismay, seemed to be the apple of her mother's eye as well. Her sister, an adorable blond-haired, blue-eyed little girl, in Beth's words "was exactly the kind of daughter her mother wanted to parade around with in the community. That way she could pass for WASP—her life's dream."

Beth felt marginal at home, marginal in school, and marginal in her community. Her sense of belonging was interfered with from an early age; indeed, she never quite felt that she was a daughter of whom her mother was proud.

In the course of her twice-weekly psychotherapy, Beth joined a health club, which she began to attend regularly. Soon, it became clear that she was utterly involved in the "culture" of the club. Each person she came to know there was talked about in the treatment; even her athletic routines and choice of gym clothes became significant topics for discussion.

She stopped describing herself as socially marginal. She began to talk about how important the gym experience was to her, how much she looked forward to going there, how much she missed being there when she was away. "It's the first place I've ever felt I really belonged," she reported. "People like me there. They accept me for who I am, even in the sweaty, smelly state I'm in."

The change was dramatic. Beth seemed to move quickly into establishing herself on a career path, with friends from the gym and elsewhere. She even sought out people she had known in high school. Her relationship with her parents, which had always been strained, was more easy-going. She presented herself to them and others as fit, high-spirited, and involved in her work and social life.

Beth came into treatment still struggling with the issues of early adolescence, which stood in the shadow of her childhood experiences of feeling unwanted, unaccepted, and unappreciated. In the context of psychotherapy, she was able to see her parents and herself more clearly, and to live more fully in her present life. The involvement in the health club permitted her to make a transition into a middle adolescent ethnocultural identity formation; she has yet to contend with more fundamental issues about her place in the world. She has begun by establishing a career path, which is one possible segment of a more mature ethnocultural identity formation.

Beth exemplifies how early interferences in a sense of comfort and belonging dovetail into an adolescent experience of not fitting into the sociocultural world, which, in turn, makes a late adolescent consolidation of identity virtually impossible. Feeling rooted in the "culture" of the gym, with its attendant acceptance of her physicality, helped Beth to see the possibility of having a place in the sociocultural world. Thus, she could move more fully into a second individuation process.

Late adolescence brings with it the personal consideration of fundamental aspects of social organization such as culture of origin, ethnicity, religion, or sexual orientation, with particular focus on where and with whom a late adolescent feels a sense of belonging. When late adolescents choose to see themselves as members of these groups, a mature ethnocultural identity forms. Where there are obstacles in a late adolescent's path, problems in the maturation process may occur.

Raiz

Raiz, a 19-year-old college student at a highly prestigious university, came for treatment complaining of feelings of estrangement from her family, marginality among her contemporaries, and conflicts about a relationship she was having with a young man at the same university. She was so preoccupied that she was having difficulty completing her classwork. She was concerned that her grades would drop. She said that she felt frightened and nervous much of the time. She had never felt this way before.

Raiz came from an ethnoculturally mixed family. Her father was an olive-skinned Muslim from the Middle East, her mother a white American Catholic, whose own parents were Italian Catholic on one side and Polish Catholic on the other. Raiz was dark-complected and regarded herself as a non-practicing Catholic.

Her arrival at college was, in her own words, "an experience in culture shock." She was surrounded by "fair-haired, fair-skinned, bright, rich, prep school WASPs." She was overwhelmed. She had grown up in a lower- and middle-middle-class neighborhood, attended the local public high school, and felt very much a part of her peer group. She was distinguished by her academic achievements among her peers, but not by any aspect of her family background. Many of her friends were from multi-ethnic or mixed ethnocultural backgrounds.

At college, most of the peers who gravitated toward Raiz were from what she referred to as "the minority groups." The young men who sought dates with her, the young women who shared confidences with her, were primarily from African-American and Latin American backgrounds. The social groups that invited her to join them were similarly constituted. This was markedly different from her experience in high school. Though her friends there were of mixed background, few identified themselves as anything but white.

Her first steady boyfriend in college was African-American. When she introduced him to her parents, they were extremely upset about and critical of the relationship. Raiz was baffled. She had never had a serious conflict with her parents; they never before had attempted to interfere in her social relationships in any fashion.

Her boyfriend was furious. Her new friends were more sympathetic to him than her. Raiz felt absolutely lost. She described herself as feeling as if "she had no place to go, no shoulder to cry on." She thought that no one understood how torn apart and confused she felt. She did not know where to turn.

Raiz responded quickly in a once-weekly psychoanalytically oriented treatment. She saw that she felt caught between her parents' expectations of her and her own partially formed ones, her new friends' ethnocultural sense of her and her own ethnocultural sense of herself. She recognized her struggles around separation and individuation, and began to contend with them. She realized that she felt an enormous amount of loss, especially in her relation-ship with her parents and in her peer group. Allowing herself to feel the intense pain and sadness, to understand why she felt what she did, freed her up to move on developmentally.

She began to talk to her new friends about her actual family background and how different she felt from some of them. She described the shock that she felt upon arrival in college, and was relieved to find that many of them shared her sense of alienation. She broke up with her boyfriend, but not until they were able to have an extended conversation about her disappointment in him for not being more sympathetic to her about the painful confron-tation with her parents. She began to attend some of the Catholic students' community action meetings, and found that a new social group was open to her. Her relief was palpable.

Raiz arrived at late adolescence with a reasonably stable sense of ethnocultural identity, but not one that felt as self-derived as a mature ethnocultural identity needs to be. Her early life and adolescence had left her feeling competent and happy. Her arrival at college, however, with the subsequent (in her words) "culture shock," demonstrates that an internal sense of ethnocultural and emotional stability had not yet been achieved. When her contem-poraries regarded her ethnoculturally in ways that were dramatically different from ways in which she had been perceived before, and her parents seemed to be unaccepting of the world in which she was living, her capacities and spirit began to flag. She no longer felt comfortably rooted in the sociocultural world.

Feeling comfortably rooted in the portion of the sociocultural world that they have chosen enables late adolescents to develop a mature sense of ethnocultural identity. This, in turn, aids them in the last stages of adolescent separation–individuation process. Raiz was disrupted in this late phase by the cultural shifts of her college experience and her parents' rejection of her college ethnocultural life. Coming to terms with her personal sense of ethnocultural identity and being able to present herself socially and familially in accordance with that personal sense permitted Raiz to feel more firmly established ethnoculturally. She was thus able to proceed with

the development of a mature ethnocultural identity and an overall
late adolescent consolidation.

Isaac

At times, adolescents are aware of a wish to feel a sense of belonging,
may even long to belong, but do not feel at home in the groups that
they are most intimately connected to by family history. Isaac is an
example of such an adolescent.

Isaac grew up on the Lower East Side of Manhattan, on the
border between a primarily Jewish neighborhood and Chinatown.
His family was Jewish, but not observant of religious customs. He,
nonetheless, was sent to an Orthodox yeshiva for his schooling. His
parents thought that he would receive a better education at the
yeshiva than he would in the public elementary school.

He felt out of place in the yeshiva, for he was surrounded by
students whose households were far more religious, and they,
therefore, were far more knowledgeable about Jewish tradition and
the laws of Jewish practice. By the time he reached high school, he
hated the school. He never felt that the other students accepted him
and never felt that he belonged there. He switched to the local
public high school, where he felt more comfortable. The comparative diversity in the student body provided him with more social
opportunities. He found that he was drawn to his Chinese-American
peers, who were most often second generation and shared his sense
of straddling ethnocultural worlds.

Isaac came into treatment at the age of 20. His father had
insisted that he enter the family business, in which Isaac had been
working since he was 14. He said that he felt like he was "bursting at
the seams," then began to laugh. The family business involved
selling goods to tailors and clothes manufacturers; the reference to
"seams" struck him as particularly appropriate.

Isaac thought easily in psychological terms. He described
himself as trapped in his family and by his life. He felt that he had
not had any opportunity to explore the world. He did not know
anything other than the Lower East Side, but knew that he also was

afraid to look outside of it. His aging father expected him to take over the business; he was worried that looking outside his current life would make him so frustrated that he would not be able to assume that responsibility.

His parents could not understand why his friends were Chinese. They had sent him to a Jewish school, they said, so that he would feel rooted in Jewish culture. It did not seem to them that he was at all interested in it.

Isaac had a difficult early life. His parents fought continually with each other, and both were highly critical of him. His mother was very intrusive. In his words, "she interrupted me on the toilet, in the bathtub, or while getting dressed. There was no such thing as privacy."

Shortly after he began treatment, Isaac's parents separated. Their eventual divorce took place after a tumultuous series of negotiations. Isaac's father became depressed, his mother rageful and vindictive.

Isaac felt bombarded. Both parents sought his allegiance. His mother frequently called him and criticized his father. He lived with his father in the apartment in which he had grown up, worked in his father's store as he had since early adolescence, and spent every day listening to his father's sighs and seeing his father's tears.

Isaac used his treatment both to air his concerns and to break out of his very circumscribed life. Even coming to a different part of Manhattan for his weekly psychotherapy visits was a source of some comfort to him. He often used his sessions to discuss his observations of the world as it was revealed to him through the magazines he read, the movies he saw, even the people he noticed.

He began to date a soft-spoken, accepting Chinese woman who was working in a store in his neighborhood. She introduced him to her friends and customs. He began eating primarily Chinese food and wearing silk shirts hand-sewn by Chinese tailors. Over time, their relationship intensified and solidified, and they decided to get married. Isaac felt at home with her, he said, and with her world. He looked forward to their having children who would span the Chinese and Jewish worlds.

Isaac never felt quite at home in his familial home; he never

quite wanted to belong in it. He was uncomfortable both with the
religious hypocrisy that characterized it and the very circumscribed
life that his parents led and that they expected him to lead. He felt
marginal at home and at school. He looked longingly at the
adjacent Chinese community, which he felt was characterized by
greater cohesion.

The opportunity to choose to go to the public high school was
very significant for Isaac. The fact that there were Chinese students
who accepted him, though he looked different from them, and that
they saw him as a neighbor—a member of their community—was a
very powerful boost to his self-esteem and sense of efficacy. His
effective use of psychotherapy to continue both his internal and
sociocultural journey permitted him to articulate his view of himself
as a cultural straddler, which then contributed to feeling strong
enough to separate from his parents and to choose and pursue a
marriage partner who consolidated this sense of himself.

Carmela[1]

Cultural straddling may arise for other reasons. Carmela's difficulties in consolidating a mature ethnocultural identity stemmed from
several sources. Two that were especially important were the act of
moving from her culture of origin as an adolescent before her
ethnocultural representations were fully defined and internalized,
and her feeling a sense of belonging with very varied places, ideas,
and people.

Carmela, a 28-year-old from Central America, came into treatment confused about whether to continue in a long-standing
relationship, whether to pursue the career she had chosen, and
whether to stay in her current job. She could not resolve her
indecisiveness and felt guilty and anxious much of the time.

Carmela had left her culture of origin at age 17 with the

---

1. This case was first discussed in an article entitled "Moving to a New
Culture: Cultural Identity, Loss, and Mourning" (Levy-Warren 1987).

intention of attending college in this country and then returning home. Her close-knit family remained there. After college, she attended a trade school, then she took a position in a training program in her field. While in the program, she met the man with whom she was now in a relationship. They talked periodically about getting married.

At no point in time had Carmela truly determined whether she was going to return to her culture of origin or stay here. By maintaining the belief that she might return, she kept active her connection with that culture, which seemed to make it more and more difficult to participate fully in the life she had established for herself here. There had been no mourning process for her culture of origin, for she had never allowed herself to leave. "I feel like I have been living for eleven years as a permanent temporary," she noted, "neither here nor there. I have made a life here but never committed myself to really living it."

Carmela described her life as a child and adolescent as rather carefree. She was from a well-to-do family in which she was much loved and somewhat overprotected. Only her school life posed difficulties for her. She was sent to a strict Catholic girls' school that she found overbearing. She became a ringleader among the girls in the school who fought with the nuns about rules regarding dress codes and lunch hour privileges. Her parents were distressed about the school behavior reports, but her high academic achievement and acceptable behavior at home led them to conclude that Carmela's wish to leave this school upon graduation from high school and go to an American university was one they would grant.

There were many ways in which Carmela's cultural background and sense of ethnocultural identity played a role in the dilemmas she brought to treatment. She spoke early on about having no feeling of being firmly identified with either American culture or that of her origin. It seemed as if she had moved before choosing to be identified ethnoculturally, that is, before a mature ethnocultural identity formation had taken place. She also had moved at a time when an important part of her sociocultural world—school—posed real conflicts for her.

The middle adolescent sociocultural group identifications had taken place before she relocated to America, but not her late adolescent consolidation. When she entered treatment, this process had been suspended by not having made a decision about whether to stay in or leave this culture. She therefore neither mourned her culture of origin nor made an affirmative choice to identify herself with it. Either decision would have aided her in establishing the personal significance of culture. In order to participate more fully in her current life, Carmela had to exercise some choice with regard to where she felt the most sense of belonging, ethnoculturally speaking. She, thus, had to continue the second individuation process, which had been interrupted in the move from her culture of origin, and form a mature ethnocultural identity.

Adolescents are deeply concerned with issues of sameness and difference. They focus on ways in which they are the same and different from what they were like as children, ways they are the same and different from their peers, and ways they are the same and different from their families. Their second individuation process (Blos 1967) critically involves delineating these areas of sameness and difference.

In order to make these comparisons, adolescents must first have some stable sense of themselves. In contemplating the highly complex world in which adolescents live and find ways to feel part of it, Erikson (1956, 1959) describes the need for a psychosocial moratorium. Adolescents need time to explore and feel connected to sociocultural groups and to feel rooted in the sociocultural world. They need time and experiences in the world to develop a mature ethnocultural identity.

In early adolescence, in the context of deidealizing the parents of childhood, adolescents move out into the sociocultural world to form best friendships and relationships with adults (other than their parents). These relationships are often at extremes of the sameness–difference spectrum; they are based upon feeling very much like or very unlike those individuals toward whom the adolescents gravitate. Middle adolescence brings with it more of an orientation toward groups in the sociocultural world that feel the same and different. These groups often define ways of dressing, types of music, kinds of athletics, or ways of having fun. In late adolescence, more fundamental aspects of the sociocultural world and the adolescent's place in it get negotiated and integrated, that is, a mature ethnocultural identity forms.

The patients presented here all suffered from disruptions in the formation of their ethnocultural identities, which served to interrupt their overall development. Needless to say, perhaps, ethnocultural identity is only one of many elements that could be (and were) examined in each of these patients. For the purposes of illustrating the formation of a mature ethnocultural identity, this is the element that has been discussed.

All four case illustrations demonstrate how disruptions in the formation of a mature ethnocultural identity can interrupt the overall late adolescent consolidation process. They show that there are instances in which specific attention must be paid to this very important feature of the internal and sociocultural lives of those who enter treatment.

Establishing a personally derived, mature ethnocultural identity is a significant organizer for aspects of sameness and difference in adolescents' lives. It is always important from a developmental point of view, and particularly critical now. Our culture continues to become more and more diverse, and there is a greater and greater emphasis on ethnocultural integrity and cohesiveness. This differs from the ideal of assimilation that characterized earlier periods of American immigration. All of us must be mindful of this changing multicultural world and place ourselves within it. It is in this context and because of it that we form a mature ethnocultural identity.

3

Psychotherapy

Clinical Considerations

6

Adolescent Psychotherapy:
Beginning, Middle, and End

Even a thought, even a possibility, can shatter us and transform us.

Nietzsche, *Eternal Recurrence*

Beginning treatment with an adolescent is akin to embarking on a new adventure. There is little that can be expected (except that having expectations is a problem) and trouble spots are inevitable. The therapist must be prepared for surprises. The best training would probably include a wilderness survival course, a bout of moshing at a rock concert, a nose or naval piercing, a visit to a vintage clothes store, and a shot of hormones. Yet these activities would only begin to convey the experience of being an adolescent, which is what the therapist must attempt to grasp.

What is particularly tough is grasping this experience when even the adolescent is unlikely to know what is going on. Adolescents feel a great deal and act on what they feel, quite a bit before they can frame the experience enough to think about what they are doing. For this reason, one of the more important objectives of treatment is to aid adolescents in seeing and understanding all that they experience. Adolescence itself is a time of creating a psychic structure that embraces the whole of what adolescents feel, think, imagine, and sense. Children have a tendency to see things in absolute, black-and-white terms; it is only in adolescence that the capacity to see shades of gray develops.

In a sense, then, adolescence is the perfect time for an individual to be in psychotherapy. The treatment process parallels the developmental process. Adolescents must look within and outside themselves in a more complex fashion, taking into account the full range of human activity and human nature. This serves their developmental needs of separation and individuation. They ultimately come to see themselves, their families, and the world in more realistic and differentiated terms.

When there is interference in adolescents' capacities to develop in these ways, psychotherapy is in order. The goals of psychotherapy are defined by adolescents' developmental need to see themselves in these more realistic and differentiated terms. The therapist functions as an extra pair of eyes, a mind, and a heart, thus aiding adolescents in coming to know their thoughts, feelings, and motivations.

Adolescent development does not proceed in an even, predictable manner. It is, therefore, difficult to know how to gauge the level of the adolescents' knowledge and the perspicacity of their judgment in a multitude of situations, particularly those in the social realm. It is difficult for adolescents themselves to know and it is difficult for the adults in their lives to know.

While in the throes of developing a greater autonomy, adolescents inevitably have false starts, make mistakes, and take what might often appear to be foolish risks. The adults around them, whose life experience is more varied and longer, struggle to deal with these trials and tribulations. Their strong desire is often to actively intervene, to keep the adolescents from heading down dangerous paths. These paths have a very wide range, from intentional risk-taking, such as playing chicken in cars or scaling high walls without protective devices, to self-destructive acts that involve self-denial, such as substance abuse or physical fights. Both parents and therapists may find themselves feeling frustrated, fooled, bewildered; and concerned. When they try to leave enough room for the adolescents to grow, they may find that they have left so much room that the adolescents lack a sense of direction or support; when they try to guide their charges, the adolescents may feel intruded upon and infantilized. The image of an obstacle course comes easily to mind.

This chapter attempts to create a map of that obstacle course. It describes the way an adolescent treatment is structured, what can be accomplished, how the relationship between the therapist and the adolescent patient evolves, what its ending looks like, and how unresolved adolescent issues may appear in adult treatment. The first consideration is establishing the structure of the treatment.

SETTING UP THE TREATMENT

How to set up a treatment structure poses a number of problems. The therapist begins with a decision about who to meet first, the adolescent or the parents. This choice may convey to the adolescent whose point of view has priority to the therapist: that of the parent (or school or court) or that of the adolescent. This consideration tends to be more significant as adolescence proceeds. Early adolescents often expect therapists to meet with their parents first; late adolescents expect therapists to meet with them first (and sometimes not at all with their parents). The particular situations of middle adolescents have to be thought through on a case by case basis. Indeed, each adolescent case must be thought through in its own terms. What is described here is meant to be understood as what occurs most frequently; exceptions to general practice are common.

The way treatment is presented to adolescents is important. Whether it is required of them or suggested to them, for instance, has direct relevance for their growing sense of autonomy. There are situations in which outside agencies, such as schools or courts, require the adolescent to be in treatment. It also is quite common for parents to demand that treatment be pursued. It is least common for adolescents themselves to request treatment.

In writing about the introduction of therapy to pubertal adolescents, Fraiberg (1955) suggests that clinicians must be mindful of whether adolescents feel that there is a punitive tinge to coming for treatment, whether they fear others' knowing, and whether they feel they are being made to come. These concerns apply to adolescents of all subphases. It is, therefore, incumbent upon the therapist to make treatment directly relevant to and interesting for adolescents, rather than something adolescents feel is being imposed for the purpose of changing them in ways that others want them to be changed but they themselves do not. It also is important to let the adolescent know that confidentiality is one of the therapist's rules for treatment, that is, that others will not know about the treatment unless the adolescent chooses to tell them.

Parents of the adolescents who come for treatment, generally speaking, are extremely concerned about their children. They want to know what is going on with them, including in the therapy. Being financially responsible for the treatment often gives them a belief that they have a right to know what is happening. How to present the issue of confidentiality to the adolescents and to their parents is critical. Parents must be informed of the necessity for the adolescent to have access to a private relationship, with the proviso that if the therapist is concerned about the adolescent's safety or well-being then the parents will be told. The adolescent must know this as well. There are times when parents are insistent upon knowing more about the content of the treatment; in these cases, the therapist should consult with the adolescent and present to the parents an agreed-upon set of issues and problems.

What kind of contact to have with parents is of enormous consequence for both the adolescents and the parents. One of the most common reasons that adolescent treatments suddenly end is complications arising out of parent contact. Parents may want more or less contact than they have; adolescents may want the therapist to have more or less contact with their parents. Therapists must find ways to ally themselves with parents as adults who are concerned with the welfare and well-being of the adolescents, and simultaneously to ally themselves with the adolescents, remaining particularly aware of the adolescents' wishes to become more autonomous and self-aware. It is a bit like walking a tightrope without a net; a slip in either direction can be disastrous.

Whether parent contact takes place with the adolescent present or not is another consideration. This must be assessed, as well as whether family therapy or group therapy is preferable to individual therapy, both in the beginning and after an initial period of treatment. The main criterion for making this decision is what will most support the adolescent's autonomous growth. Sometimes the family is so entangled that family therapy is necessary; the family interaction may so impede the adolescent's independent growth that focus on this interaction must be first on the therapist's agenda. Sometimes problems with peers are paramount; in this instance, group therapy may be the treatment of choice.

Individual therapy with collateral parent contact is, however, the most common choice for adolescent treatment. This orientation encourages a particular focus on the refinement of the adolescent's independent ego functioning, an important element of adolescent treatment. Alone with the adolescent, the therapist is able to point out aspects of how the adolescent sees or operates in the world in a neutral context. When other members of the family are present, it is often harder for the adolescent to hear and absorb such comments, for they are distracted by how their parents may be reacting to the therapist's observations. As adolescents mature, they become far stronger in their capacity to stay within their own emotional and cognitive frameworks. Initially, however, in development and in treatment, what their parents think or feel is often more important to them than what they think or feel.

How often to meet with the adolescent is another significant question in setting up the treatment. This must be determined on the basis of therapeutic need, financial considerations, and the inclinations of both the adolescents and their parents. It is often advisable to establish in the beginning that the initial setup will be reconsidered after a predetermined time, so that the therapist and the adolescent have an opportunity to review their first decisions about what treatment structure makes sense. Most adolescent treatment experts mark the importance of this initial period in treatment.[1] This is a period in which an assessment of the form of treatment is made, as well as one in which early direct contact with the adolescent must be achieved.

The adolescents themselves, who are most often in their first treatments, rarely understand the need for treatment or its purpose; thus, it is unusual for them to understand the need for more than once-weekly treatment. It is only after they have some greater involvement in the therapy that the value of increased frequency may emerge for them. If they do wish to increase the frequency of their sessions, this often has to be counterbalanced by fears of regression and dependency.

When and/or whether psychoanalysis is indicated in adolescence is a much debated subject in clinical circles (Blos 1962, Eissler 1958, Sklansky 1972). Some feel such treatment is extraordinarily difficult, for the adolescent has little energy for getting attached to the psychoanalyst, much like people with narcissistic neuroses, those in the midst of unhappy love affairs, or those in mourning (Adatto in Sklansky 1972). Others feel its difficulties outnumber its successes, but it is called for at times (Friend in Sklansky 1972).

I believe that psychoanalysis is called for in circumstances in which the adolescent has come to a grinding halt, developmentally speaking. In these instances, the back-and-forth sense usually conveyed by adolescents, the progressive-regressive movement, is not present. These adolescents in need of psychoanalysis are highly symptomatic and seem almost frozen in time. Only the mobilization of the regressive forces that become available through psychoanalysis provides the energy they need to move forward. Most adolescents evoke a much greater sense of energy flow, of being in flux. They do not need the time-consuming, intense experience of psychoanalysis to contend with the difficulties they present in treatment and face in life.

Decisions about the structure of treatment include not only

---

1. Some of the foremost psychoanalytic writers who underscore this point about clinical work with adolescents are Blos 1962, Evans 1976, Geleerd 1957, Harley 1970, and Meeks 1971.

those about type of treatment and frequency of contact, but also what financial arrangements are to be made. The issues of who pays for the sessions, how the bill is transmitted, and whether there is a charge for missed sessions are all potential trouble spots. In families in which parents are divorced, for instance, which parent assumes responsibility for payment may become a sore point, often mirroring larger problems about responsibility and control over the adolescent child's life. If there is a charge for missed sessions, adolescents may come to express their anger at their parents through purposely missing appointments. Whether the bill is sent directly to the parents or handed to the adolescent patient is also significant: sending it directly to parents permits adolescents to deny the fact of payment, while handing it to the adolescent puts the fee and remembering the bill in the forefront of their minds. In any case, these financial arrangements are inevitably drawn into the conflicts that exist within each adolescent and within each family. It is most important to keep open the avenues of communication about these and all other issues involved in setting up and conducting the treatment. Adolescents in treatment must come to see all matters as potential sources of information about themselves, their families, and the worlds in which they live.

OBJECTIVES OF TREATMENT

Making immediate and effective contact, defining the process and function of treatment, framing the adolescent's personal issues, and creating a trusting and open relationship are the most important objectives of treatment in its initial phase. Each of these must be negotiated in order for an ongoing working relationship between the therapist and the adolescent patient to be established.

When adolescents first present themselves for treatment (or are presented for treatment), there are a multitude of factors which must be taken into account to assess their needs and the specific objectives of the psychotherapy. The initial period of treatment is the time this assessment is made. Many who write about adolescent treatment highlight the importance of this early contact, not only for the reasons related to setting up the treatment structure but also for reasons related to the nature of the connection with the adolescent.[2] This period is critical for the establishment of a working relationship between the therapist and the patient.

Once a working relationship is established, the primary objective of treatment is to get the adolescent back on a suitable developmental track (Adatto 1958), in which separation and individuation are in process and there is a clear focus on increasing the complexity and reach of the adolescent's psychic structure. In particular, the observing ego must be able to contain the experiencing ego; the overly harsh and self-punitive superego of early development must give way to more benign superego action; and the parent-defined and unrealistic child's ego ideal must be subordinated to a self-defined and reality-based mature ego ideal.

What is important in making an effective initial contact is both to be aware and to let the patient know that the therapist is aware of how the adolescents perceive the situation in contrast to their parents, the school, or the family court system. The early connection to adolescent patients is dependent upon the therapist's ability to convey that the adolescents' point of view is critical to the therapist's understanding of what has happened and what is happening in the adolescent's life. If the therapist presents a point of view that is highly influenced by the adults around the adolescent, it will be difficult for the adolescent to form a working treatment relationship.

In the initial period, adolescents must come to appreciate the ways in which treatment can aid them in their everyday lives. The therapist must, therefore, perform an educative role. What the adolescent needs to learn is what therapy is and what it can be used for, in particular how the adolescent can use it to develop a more autonomous life both at home and in the community. Sometimes the only way an adolescent who feels forced into treatment will be able to engage in it is if the therapist suggests that it might be worth

---

2. Aichhorn 1925, Blos 1962, Geleerd 1957, Harley 1970, and Meeks 1971 highlight this issue.

the adolescent's while to discuss what it is like to live with parents who demand that the adolescent be in treatment. One way or another, the therapist must assist the adolescent patient in seeing treatment as useful, interesting, and enlightening. Without this sense, the adolescent may attend sessions but not really be engaged in the treatment process.

Leah

Leah, a bright fourteen-year-old, was failing several of her ninth grade subjects. She had been a straight-A student before this year. Both the school personnel and her single-parent mother were alarmed, and required Leah to be in psychotherapy. Leah, however, claimed to be indifferent about her grades and totally uninterested in treatment.

"What's the point?" she queried. "Ninth grade doesn't mean anything. No one looks at these grades."

Her mother came to see me first. A number of the school personnel called next. I counseled Leah's mother to tell Leah that I had heard from her mother and heard from her school, but really needed her point of view to understand what was going on.

Leah breezed in a few days later, five minutes late for her appointment.

"Am I late?" she asked, as she sauntered in, plugged into her Walkman.

"A few minutes," I responded, as I showed her into the consulting room.

"So, what's up?" she said, as she plunked herself onto the chair, folding her feet under her body as she sat down.

"I was just about to ask you the same question."

"My mother thinks I have to come here; my school is on my case, too. Personally, I see no reason for it."

"Well, what's it like having people pressing you this way?" I asked.

"It sucks. It's claustrophobic. I feel like screaming when I think about it. . . . I don't really know what to talk about."

"You can talk about anything you want here—and it's just between us. The only exception would be if I were concerned about your safety for some reason."

"Oh, I'm fine. I'm just really bored in school and really sick of everybody being in my face about my homework and grades."

"That sounds like a good place to start."

And so treatment began. It started with Leah's late arrival and her announcement to that effect. She was signaling both of us that she felt behind the times. Though as old as many girls entering middle adolescence, this daughter of 1960s throwbacks was in no way ready to be part of her peer group's dating, parties, and school focus. She was late developmentally, and trying to put a halt to her forward progress.

Leah had been brought up on a commune in which sexual promiscuity, chaos, and alcohol and drug use were commonplace. Her father, whom she adored, left the commune with a 22-year-old daughter of friends when Leah was 8. She and her mother left soon after. Leah had never heard from her father again. Rumor had it that he left the country; he sent a copy of a Mexican divorce decree to her mother via mutual friends at the commune.

It seemed clear from our first contact that Leah needed to talk to an interested, dependable, informed adult about what her life was like. Her mother harbored tremendous antipathy toward her father, which she voiced to Leah with great regularity. Her mother also let Leah know that there was a great father–daughter resemblance: both were bright, funny, music lovers. Leah's mother had come from a very different background from her former husband. He was an upper-middle-class, college-educated man who grew up in a city; she had been from a poor, rural family and had received a high school education.

Leah had never been able to mourn her father comfortably, identify with her mother, or relate to her peers. It was clear that treatment had to aid her in these processes of mourning, separation, and individuation. She needed to be able to see herself as having a history in order to live in the present; she needed to come to a better resolution of her early adolescent tasks in order to move into middle adolescence.

The form of the treatment took hold early on: I saw Leah once weekly and periodically saw her mother or spoke to her on the phone, usually at intervals of three weeks. Both mother and daughter agreed that sending the bills to her mother was the best way to ensure that her mother received them, for Leah was notoriously forgetful.

Establishing immediate contact with Leah was critical. She needed to see the treatment as something for *her* rather than something that simply was imposed upon her by others. The opening exchange between us succeeded in doing this: Leah was able to continue with an agenda that felt self-defined and responsive to her own needs.

The opening exchange also began an educative process which continued for a number of weeks, in which the function and process of therapy increasingly became defined. In the interplay just described, several ideas were expressed about the nature of treatment: that Leah takes the lead in establishing topics, that *her* point of view is of particular importance, that she can discuss anything she wishes, and that what is discussed will be held in confidence.

During the initial period of treatment, these ideas and others are articulated and underscored. Leah (and other adolescent patients) must come to know what to expect. This is an important building block in the foundation of the working relationship that develops between the therapist and the patient.

ESTABLISHING THE TREATMENT RELATIONSHIP

The therapeutic situation must be both predictable and consistent, and the therapist someone that the adolescent can rely on to be honest, interested, concerned, direct, matter-of-fact, and nonjudgmental.

The predictability and consistency of the therapeutic situation permits adolescents to be more freely in their actual state of flux while they are seeing the therapist. When the therapeutic situation itself is less stable, adolescent patients will feel compelled to be more on guard. A stable situation gives adolescents more latitude in displaying the full range of their development, both their most childlike and their most adolescent and/or adultlike states. Just as adolescents are most likely to show their widest range at home because of its familiarity and consistency, so will they be able to be the most themselves in the therapeutic situation if it becomes familiar. The predictability provides them with a feeling of safety.

Once a full range of development is seen by the therapist, then the stumbling blocks to the adolescent's further development become more clear. In Leah's case, for example, the fact of her father's prepubertal disappearance and mother's fury about it made it harder for Leah to leave her childhood behind, and move from early to middle adolescence. She was too young to have the ego strength to contain the full range of feelings she had about his leaving, and her mother's ongoing rage at her father made it difficult for Leah to express loving feelings about him in her mother's presence. His absence also made it harder for Leah to form a more realistic picture of him, a necessary component of the deidealization process that accompanies early adolescent development. Without the deidealization, adequate identifications are far more difficult to form; Leah's potential identifications with her father as an intellectual and educated person were steeped in conflict.

Therapists are important objects of identification for their patients, not only as non-parental adults in the adolescents' lives, but also as people who look inside at themselves and at their adolescent patients with warmth, understanding, and objectivity. One of the important processes of adolescent treatment is the internalization by the adolescents of this way of looking at themselves. It is conveyed both by the therapists' example of looking within themselves in this manner and looking at the adolescent patients they treat in this manner.

Leah

"You're late," Leah announced as she walked in the door.

"You're right. I'm sorry to keep you waiting."

"Well, if it were me, you'd be asking what happened, and looking for some deep psychological meaning. So, why are *you* late?"

"Good question. I could tell you about the telephone call I had trouble cutting short because of the nature of the conversation, but that probably wouldn't do it as an explanation, would it?"

"Well, for sure it wouldn't if it were you asking me about what happened. So I guess it shouldn't do it for you, either."

"I think I have some trepidation about hearing about what went on at that party you were going to over the weekend. As you probably could tell, I was a bit worried when you told me who was going to be there and what might be going on. The guys sounded like they were on the wild side, and the girls you were going with didn't sound like people with the greatest judgment. I was concerned about your feeling pressured again."

"I can't believe you're telling me this. I didn't think you'd be so honest. I could see you were worried when I was here last week, but I don't think I would have brought it up. But it had a big effect on me. I think you don't get worried that easily, and you seem to have a lot of faith in me, so it made me think more about the party ahead of time. And, you know, you had reason to worry—it was an unbelievable scene. I've never seen so many kids so high before. It was actually a really weird situation. Kind of scary, even."

In this exchange, Leah demonstrated her understanding of the therapeutic process, her internalization of it, and both her regard for and identification with me. She also showed that she felt safe enough to challenge me in the very way I frequently challenged her. My choice to answer frankly provided her with an example that she readily followed.

What also is demonstrated in this snippet from the treatment is a kind of good-humored openness, one which encourages both parties to be honest and nonjudgmental. This is a quality in the atmosphere of the relationship toward which I strive. When it is present, it is easier for adolescents to tolerate the inevitable mistakes, both theirs and their therapists', and to acknowledge vulnerability. This aids in toning down the potential harshness of the childlike superego formation and the possible grandiosity of the childlike ego ideal. Both the adolescents and the therapists can look at themselves in a bemused, matter-of-fact way.

It will become increasingly clear in the case illustrations that I tend to be rather frank in my responses to adolescents and sometimes self-revealing. I do this with the intention of conveying my willingness to be as open with them as possible, in the hope that they will have the strength to act in a similar fashion with me. This differs from the way I work with adults, who generally have greater ego development and identity formation, and therefore a greater capacity both to be real and to tolerate the frustration of my being less self-revealing.

I see the role of the therapist as that of an observer of the adolescent's life, life in general, the therapist's own life, and life in the consulting room. In each instance, the therapist's observations aid the adolescent in the development of ego functioning, particularly those aspects of ego functioning that involve sharpening perceptive and organizational capacities. Leah's trust in me and her awareness of my worrying about the party contributed to her thinking ahead about it and looking more carefully at how she felt and thought about it at the time it took place. Her observing ego, objectivity, and self-protectiveness were strengthened. The fact that we were able to talk about this process in our session permitted her to integrate and frame the experience in a more thought-out manner.

An adolescent's developmental place is highly related to what usually emerges in the treatment dialogue. In the most general terms, early adolescents are likely to talk the most about their family lives, middle adolescents about their peer and school lives, and late adolescents about their intimate relationships and struggles in defining who they are and who they will be. Caution must be exercised by the therapist in making references to an adolescent's past; these references may push an adolescent backwards at a time when they are prepared (albeit fragilely) to move ahead. The past only needs to be evoked when it stands in the way of the adolescent's living fully in the present.

Leah

"This school thing is really starting to get to me. I've been keeping up with my homework for weeks now, but I can't seem to get myself to go back and do the stuff that's overdue. It just feels like there's too much there." Leah looked sad as she spoke.

"Something about revisiting the past, maybe?"

"I don't know. I'm not one for looking behind me or anything."

"Lack of interest, or fear, or what?" I asked.

"Well, in terms of homework—it just feels like it's history already. We're past it in class. I either got the work already or I didn't. It seems pointless to go back and do busywork. But I have a feeling this thing about me looking back is bigger than just the homework thing. Must have something to do with what my life was like when I was little. It all seems so long ago, so mixed up, and so recent, all at the same time."

"I have a feeling that some of it is with you a great deal in the present. It may be part of why it's so hard to look backwards. It may also have something to do with how comfortable you are doing as well in school as you might."

"You mean, doing well like my father did, for instance?" she asked with a big grin.

"Yes, for starters," I responded with a laugh.

"It was one of the things they used to fight about, you know. My mother would say my father was an elitist snob, my father would laugh and say she should go back to school if she's jealous. That really pissed her off."

"I can imagine."

"Don't think I don't worry that my mother will start to accuse me of being an intellectual snob or something."

"Has it ever happened?"

"Yeah, definitely. When I got a good report card last year, she said that I was going to be beyond her any day now . . . and that I better not become a smartass snotnose like my father was."

"What was it like when she said that?"

"It made me really mad. Also, it made me realize how much I wished my father were around. I mean, she can't even help me with most of my homework now—can you imagine what it's going to be like later in high school?"

Leah clearly needed to speak about her past. In particular, she needed to talk about her father, for her conflicted identifications with him stood in the way of her performing adequately in the present. Her mother's difficulty in letting the past remain in the past also contributed to Leah's identificatory problems.

This clinical illustration demonstrates another important function of treatment during adolescence: its role in the differentiation process that is so crucial to development at this time. Separating past from present (childhood from adolescence) and seeing ways in which the adolescent is like others in her family are important aspects of separation and individuation. Pointing out that Leah is capable of doing better than she is doing is another example of therapy in the service of differentiation; providing a realistic assessment of an adolescent's capacities contributes to the formation of a mature ego ideal and the refined sense of oneself that comes from an adequate individuation process.

The relationship between the adolescent and the therapist is one in which there are likely to be strong transference and countertransference reactions, along with ready displacements from the parents (in the present) onto the therapist. I use the concept of transference to mean that the patient is relating to someone in the present in ways that derive from past relationships and ultimately distort or interfere in the present relationship. This implies that a way of relating has been internalized by the patient; there also are reactions that adolescents have in the present toward their parents that are simply and automatically displaced onto the therapist. Both of these must be addressed. Displacements are seen more easily by the adolescent; transference interpretation requires that a therapeutic relationship of some stability and trust be in place. In either case, developing a pattern of discussing the relationship between the adolescent patient and the therapist is crucial to the treatment.

Countertransference, which I see in the same way as Annie Reich (1951a, 1960a), is the flip side of transference: it implies that the therapist is distorting the relationship with the patient because of something that has been evoked in the therapeutic situation or the relationship with the patient from the therapist's past. This may happen because the patient reminds the therapist of someone from the past or a situation has developed that is reminiscent of some prior experience for the therapist. In either case, the therapist is unable to be fully present when such a reaction occurs.

I regard countertransference as different from the therapist having feelings, thoughts, or fantasies in response to the patient. These noncountertransferential responses must be expected and used as part of the way the therapist understands what the patient is communicating. Often, the therapist functions virtually as a container for the patient's strong feelings and reactions: a patient may simply not be differentiated enough yet to both recognize and hold a feeling or set of feelings that are intense or conflicted. In these instances, therapists may find themselves filled with the feelings that the patient cannot quite hold inside.

Leah

"You looked mad just now when I said I wanted to try 'shrooms."

"I'm surprised I looked mad. . . . I wasn't feeling mad at all, just a bit concerned. I was thinking about that kid you mentioned last week who got so sick from the mushrooms that he ended up in the hospital."

"Maybe that's the look, then; maybe it wasn't that you were mad."

"Some people get mad when they're worried."

"My mother is definitely like that. She hates being worried, so she's always getting mad when she's worried."

"This makes me wonder if you expected me to be mad, for some reason."

"Well, my mother would be mad as hell."

"About what?"

"She thinks messing around with your head is really stupid. She says we should all consider our brains to be precious, 'cause once they get fucked up, it's hard to get them back. She also talks about all her friends who got screwed up from drugs in the sixties, how the drugs ruined their lives and stuff."

"Sounds like she's seen some upsetting things happen from drugs."

"Yeah, definitely."

"You ever worry about anything happening to you? " I asked.

"Sometimes. But I'm careful. I never go driving with anyone who's high, for instance. I never smoke up with people I don't know really well."

"Do you feel comfortable saying you don't want to smoke pot if other kids are doing it and you don't want to?"

"Usually. But sometimes I get too intimidated. Then I smoke up just to fit in with the other kids. Like I don't want them to think I'm too straight or afraid or something."

"Let's go back for a minute to your thinking I was mad at you for thinking about trying mushrooms. Maybe, in a way, you wanted me to tell you not to do it?"

"I don't know. Then I would have been mad at you for telling me what to do."

"Yeah, but it would have made you focus on what I thought, rather than what you thought. You would be concentrating more on something happening between you and me than on something happening inside you. I have a feeling that you have your own doubts about these mushrooms."

"Well, that's true. I don't really want to mess up my head, either. Sometimes I feel like it's plenty messed up without adding the drugs to it."

This example contains an articulation of a transference reaction (Leah's thinking I was mad when I was worried), an externalization of a conflict (her thinking I was mad when she was conflicted about trying the mushrooms), and a displacement from Leah's mother to me (her mother would have been mad). In each case, explicating the defensive process aided Leah in coming to terms with what *she* actually thought, felt, and observed. All of these contribute to her differentiation and integration processes, and full experience of the present. The fuller description of her inner experience permits Leah to see, feel, and contain her inner experience. All of this is in the service of achieving a sense of mastery through more self-knowledge.

When Leah mentioned that her mother had friends who had been damaged by drug use, I had a moment of feeling quite frightened. The timing of the feeling and Leah's apparent indifference were what led me to ask her whether she was ever worried about something happening to her. I sensed that it was difficult for her to hold and express this feeling, and asked the question to support her in her capacity to do so. This is an example of my becoming a container for a patient's feelings.

Leah

In the course of treatment, adolescents often speak about ideas, books, or movies. The way this kind of discussion unfolds and its meaning is different from what occurs in child and adult treatment. Adolescents use words in these discussions the way that children use games: for symbolic articulation and exploration of personal issues and themes.

"I saw the greatest movie on video last night. It was called *Smooth Talk*. Did you ever see it?"

"Yes, a while ago. What did you like about it?" I asked.

"I thought that it really portrayed what it's like to be a teenager. I mean, that girl felt so young and so old at the same time. And I could really understand why she wanted to go out with those guys, how it felt so good and everything. And her mother, who was such a bitch. The movie was so good, I even felt bad for her some of the time. The girl was all into her life, and the mother kind of missed her. The girl also missed her mother some of the time, but there was nothing they could do about it. It was, like, too hard to get over it. Maybe they can in a few years. Also, the mother seemed so sad."

"How'd the daughter react to her mother being so sad?"

"She tried to ignore it. She didn't want to deal with it. What kid would?"

"Like it's hard enough being a kid and trying to deal with your own problems—having to think about your mother at the same time is just too much?"

"Yeah, something like that."

Staying within the framework of the movie, encouraging the patient to look from within the plot and from outside it, but not extrapolating from the movie to the adolescent's actual life is often extremely productive. In this instance, Leah explores the feelings and motivations of the central character in the movie and expresses some sympathy for the character's mother. She demonstrates a capacity for observing a wide range of feeling in each of the characters, much wider, in fact, than she has yet been able to observe either in herself or her mother. However, if I had made a comparison between Leah and the movie character, she most likely would have rejected it.

In the context of an adolescent's evolving capacity for self-observation, dealing with movies, books, or ideas in the manner that Leah and I dealt with this movie is a transitional step. It permits Leah to stretch her capacities for observation without pressing her in such a way that she defensively moves away from using these observing capacities. It is much like the way child therapists respond to a child's play: they stay within the play rather than immediately suggesting that the play resembles the child's family's life.

Over the course of treatment, therapists must attempt to move adolescents from observing others carefully and good-naturedly to observing themselves in this fashion. This is often done by a combination of talking about characters in movies and books and using the therapist's self-observations. Both of these pave the way for the therapist and patient to talk more openly about their relationship with one another.

Talking about the relationship between the therapist and the patient provides opportunities for transference interpretation and descriptions of characteristic ways the adolescent acts. These contribute to the adolescent's differentiation processes. Transference interpretation aids particularly in the process of separation from the significant objects in the adolescent's life. Forming a picture of the adolescent's customary ways of interacting helps in articulating both character formation and aspects of the individuation process.

Just at the time when adolescents feel comfortable with the therapist and have formed a relatively clear picture of themselves, including their histories and their current lives, questions about the value of their continuing in treatment often are raised. These questions are raised by parents, the adolescents themselves, and the therapists. Ending with adolescent patients poses challenges to all involved in the decision.

ENDING ADOLESCENT TREATMENT

This section is not entitled "Terminating Adolescent Treatment." The concept of termination is one that suggests a *process* of ending treatment. In most instances, adolescent treatment ends abruptly. Indeed, as adolescents leave consulting rooms for the last time, it is often their therapists who are reeling, while the adolescents themselves seem comparatively unbothered. The adult in the dyad is filled with a wide range of feelings, while the adolescent seems calm and even-tempered. Some of the wide range of feelings that the therapist feels belong to the adolescent, some to the therapist.

The psychic structures of adolescents are in a state of flux. This leaves them with an ever-growing capacity to feel, see, identify, and contain their affectual lives. Along the (developmental) way, adolescents may have difficulty being aware of their feelings. Adults who are close to them, including parents, teachers, and therapists, may find themselves feeling feelings *for* the adolescents. As mentioned earlier, the adult becomes a container for the adolescent's feelings.

What happens inside an adolescent therapist as treatment ends is a prime example of an adult becoming such a container for an adolescent's feelings. As therapy comes to an end, the adolescent is likely to feel a good deal about the treatment, the therapist, and saying goodbye. Where the adolescent stands developmentally will determine how great a capacity is present for the awareness of feelings and how much of an ability is there to articulate them. It is often not until the close of late adolescence that adolescents are differentiated enough to be able to tolerate a wide range of feelings, identify them, and describe them to someone else. Up until this time, they are likely to have only partial views of their inner lives.

Adolescents struggle mightily with their dependency needs. Most seek to be independent, and have greater and greater capacities for being so over time. They become more able to use their cognitive and emotional resources to make informed decisions, live fully in the present, and relate to others in an honest, open, and intimate manner. Their dependency needs often leave them feeling hampered in the use of their personal resources; they end up relying too heavily on the views and wishes of others, especially those upon whom they rely for emotional sustenance.

The adolescent's balance of dependence and independence is critical to the decision whether or not to end treatment. It is time to end treatment when an adolescent is on track in terms of the significant features of their subphase development. The most important of these features is the balance between dependence and independence.

Early adolescents need to be independent enough to see their parents with greater objectivity than they had in childhood. They must have the capacity to be realistic about when they need their parents and when they do not. They also should have formed a sense of personal history, a childhood that they have left behind. Finally, they need to be able to form satisfying, reciprocal friendships among their peers. If this describes an early adolescent, then this is an adolescent who does not need further treatment.

Middle adolescents need to be able to choose freely among their peers, in terms of forming friendships and physically and emotionally intimate relationships. They have to think of themselves as owning their bodies, and thus be independent in caring adequately for them. Personal hygiene, eating habits, and physical protectiveness (i.e., not taking unnecessary physical risks) are examples of adequate independent physical care. They also need to be sorting out a personal sense of morality and ethicality, one that includes thoughts about sexual and aggressive behavior. If a middle adolescent is dealing competently in all these areas, then this adolescent is ready to leave treatment.

Late adolescents need to have a self-defined set of ideas about who they want to be, how they want to be, and what they want to be. They should view their parents as other people, and not invest them with powers beyond adult human capacity (as children do, and as developmentally younger adolescents are still feeling disillusioned about). They should be able to choose intimate partners and pursue reciprocal relationships with them that are both emotionally and sexually satisfying. Treatment is no longer necessary when a late adolescent patient is conducting life in these ways.

The decision to end adolescent treatment is not based on behavior; it is based upon how ensconced an adolescent is in the subphase development that is age-appropriate. It is not necessary (nor possible, in most instances) to wait for adolescents to be well-formed as people; this really does not occur until the end of adolescence. Among other considerations, it is not clear that the end of adolescence can be reached while an adolescent is in treatment. Most of the time, adolescents must consolidate their identities on their own. Treatment may actually impede this last aspect of the adolescent developmental process.

Adolescents sometimes know instinctively that they cannot integrate their identities while being scrutinized by someone else (as is the case in psychotherapy). They need to develop a strong (personal) observing ego more than they need to have an adult auxiliary ego (in the form of a therapist). This kind of instinctive knowledge often leads adolescents to act; they attempt to figure out why they acted after the fact. At times, adolescents act as a way of ascertaining what they think or feel. This must be distinguished from acting out, in which patients put some affectual or cognitive experience into action rather than words; they act instead of remembering (Blos 1963). Leaving treatment may be an acting out or one of those instinctive acts of adolescents in which they take an action without fully knowing why.

An abrupt leave-taking may be precipitated by adolescents or by their parents. It may be difficult for parents to have their children in treatment for a host of reasons. Having their adolescents talking frankly to another adult at a time when they may not be speaking so openly to their parents, for example, may create conditions for competitive feelings between the parents and the therapist. Having their intimate lives revealed to a stranger leaves some parents feeling quite uncomfortable, especially when they are often having only very limited contact with the therapist "stranger." Adolescents' external lives may dramatically improve when they are in therapy, thus leaving parents questioning the need for further treatment, given its attendant financial and time commitments. In any case, parents may feel that it is time for their adolescent to leave treatment before the therapist or adolescent feels ready to end. They may exert pressure on the adolescents, by asking whether they still really need treatment or by raising concerns about the finances or time constraints entailed in continuing.

The various reactions parents may have to their adolescent's treatment make clear the importance of the therapist's sustaining a working relationship with the parents of their adolescent patients. Therapists may need to convey to parents the importance of continuing treatment; to do so requires that there be a solid relationship between them. The relationship is often built around their joint objective of serving the best interests of the adolescent.

At times, however, parents may want adolescents to remain in treatment when both the therapist and the adolescent feel it is time to end. The parents may feel overwhelmed by having an adolescent child, or overwhelmed in their own lives. Single parents, for example, sometimes welcome the presence of another adult in their adolescent's life. They see the therapist as a person to whom they can turn when their child is difficult for them to understand, and they fear being left alone to contend with their adolescent when treatment ends. In these instances, a good working relationship with the parents is important as well. More often than not, compromises are formed among the therapist, parents, and patient about when ending makes sense.

Adolescents often link ending treatment to external circumstances, such as graduations or summer vacations. They rarely have enough internal structure to gauge when they are "ready" to end; they are far more likely to look for some external structure within which they can plan an ending. Jack Novick (1976), who wrote one of the very few articles about the process of termination in adolescent treatment, notes that adolescents often enter treatment with a pre-established unilateral termination in mind. Such an ending permits the adolescents to feel safer, because it gives the treatment a shape that aids them in containing their dependency needs. He also suggests that active leave-taking helps adolescents in contending with these needs.

Leah

Leah was now 16. A year of once-weekly sessions was followed by almost a year of twice-weekly psychotherapy. She was now coming in once a week. At this point, Leah was doing well in school, and was satisfied with her relationships with her friends and mother. She had traced her father and had spoken to him over the telephone and written him some letters. She also had been involved with her first boyfriend, and was pleased both with what had happened and how things were left when they broke up.

"So, Levy-Warren. Maybe it's time to say goodbye. Don't you think I'm all better?"

Although I had been thinking about talking to Leah about ending treatment, I still felt somewhat taken aback when she said this. "I certainly feel like you're doing well these days. I'm not so sure what 'all better' means, though. What were *you* thinking?"

"Oh, you know. My grades are fine, I'm getting along with my mother and everything, I like my life. I even like myself. Can't get much better than that, right?"

"Definitely truth to that."

"So, what's the problem?"

"There really isn't one. I guess I was just thinking about how it would be to say goodbye."

"Well, that's the hard part. But it'll be okay. You won't get rid of me that easily—I'll call you, stop by, whatever. Anyway, my mother will be happy."

"What makes you say that?"

"She's been on my case about the money. She asked me the other day how much longer I was going to need this; said that it was a lot for her to deal with. Made me feel bad. But then I realized that I would come forever, just because I like it. And maybe I don't really need it anymore. You know, it just made me think more about this whole thing. Don't you think I'll be okay?"

"Actually, I *do* think you'll be okay. And I'm glad you said you'd be in touch. I would hope that you would want to be, and I would always be happy to hear from you."

"So, is this it, or what?"

"I would pick the 'or what.' I think it makes sense to live with this idea for a little while before we take action on it. So how about if we choose a time in the future to stop meeting regularly and see how it is to know that this is the plan?"

"Okay with me. You have a time you think would be good?"

"I would rather leave that up to you, with the understanding that you can change your mind if you want to. I don't want to make assumptions about what you're thinking or feeling."

"This sounds heavy to me. But, all right. Let's see. How about the end of this month?"

"That gives us three more weeks. I can live with that."

In the ensuing weeks, Leah spoke very little (directly) about ending treatment. What she focused on was a project she was working on in school that involved her setting up a tutoring program for homeless kids in her neighborhood. She described how daunting the responsibility felt and yet how excited she was about doing it. She looked forward to helping the kids and to running the program. The message I inferred was that Leah was ready to be on her own.

Leah remained relatively light-hearted throughout the month. I felt sad at times, and pleased about who Leah had become at other times. In our last moments, I was the one who spoke about how I would miss seeing her. Leah acted as if that were not an issue for her:

"Don't worry. I'll be around. You won't have to miss me."

It was many months before I heard from either Leah or her mother. Toward the end of the following year, however, I got a message from Leah on my answering machine.

"Hey, Levy-Warren. It's Leah. Remember me? I just got into Wesleyan early. Pretty good, huh? I'm psyched. Wanted to let you know."

Adolescents or their parents sometimes have contact with therapists after treatment ends, but not in the majority of cases. Treatment often seems to become associated with a past that both want to leave behind. Therapists are left wondering how their former patients are and who they are, and quite conscious of the fact that treatment ends before the adolescent process ends. Thus, inevitably, adolescents leave treatment unformed in many ways. The best result that treatment can reap is that the adolescents ending therapy are merely as unformed as others are at this time of life.

Treatments ends as treatment begins, with a host of questions, negotiations, and contacts with both the parents and the adolescents, and a therapist who is attempting to look to the adolescent's past, present, and future. In looking, the therapist will at best see an adolescent who has a clear sense of a past, firm family and peer connections in the present, an ability to make good use of personal cognitive and emotional resources, and a capacity for balanced self-observation that will serve to stave off future crises.

ADOLESCENCE IN ADULT TREATMENT

Many adolescents in need of treatment are not able to obtain it until later in life. They may then be left with a multitude of adolescent issues to resolve as they move into adulthood. A chapter on adolescent treatment, therefore, seems incomplete without some mention of how adolescence may appear in the treatment of adults. Many chronologically young adults enter treatment unable to leave late adolescence behind and fully enter into adult life. Some of the patients discussed in this book fall into this category. They often present themselves with highly unrealistic ideas about their capabilities, are very self-critical, and feel paralyzed. They cannot progress in their adult lives by consolidating and synthesizing adult identifications, establishing mature ego ideals, and forming mature ethnocultural identities.

Older adults may come into treatment with what appear to be age-appropriate developmental concerns: difficulties in their primary relationships, concerns about their parenting capabilities, problems with faltering ambition or other aspects of their work lives. These adult patients may later reveal certain conflicts that stem primarily from adolescence, even though the conflicts have roots in earlier development.

Adults who come into treatment with eating disorders, addictions, or other substance abuse problems are a common example of those with adolescent conflicts. Though these difficulties most often arise from deprivations in relationships with their caregivers during early childhood, the problems usually erupt and take hold in adolescence. They most often reflect significant differentiation conflicts related to bodily ownership and self-regulation: these are adults who never took over the capacity to care adequately for themselves. Mental representations of their bodies have often not been modified to incorporate changes that they have undergone.

Adults who are prone to acting out in treatment are another group who are often signaling that they have critical unresolved adolescent issues. Taking action rather than putting experiences into words is standard fare during adolescence, because of the relative lack of ego development in the presence of intense sexual and aggressive impulses. Adult patients who need to express themselves in this fashion are frequently recreating circumstances from their adolescent lives.

Barry

Barry entered treatment with significant concerns about his capacity to sustain an intimate relationship. He was 35, and had never been married or in a relationship that lasted for more than a year. He felt lonely and bitter much of the time.

He had been in treatment several times in the past. In each instance, the treatment lasted for less than a year. He had little hope that he could be helped, but said he "had to try once more—just to prove to myself that I've exhausted my possibilities." He seemed driven to prove that he could not be helped.

He appeared to be bored when he talked about his rather chaotic childhood. His father was charming and philandering, a salesman who traveled a great deal. His mother was a depressed, critical housewife who complained about her absent husband and "disobedient children." She began to drink when Barry was an adolescent.

He also had a brother two years older, and a sister three years younger. His brother was a superstar: athletic, handsome, and an excellent student. He teased Barry mercilessly for being short, undeveloped, and "dumb." Barry's sister was quiet, sweet, unassuming, and frightened of her brothers and mother. She also was "Daddy's little girl," a position that evoked intense jealousy from everyone else in the family.

Barry's father treated his girlfriends better than his wife. He bought them expensive gifts, sent them flowers, and called them when he was at home. He made little effort to shield his wife and children from these affairs. When Barry's mother complained, her objections were met with sarcasm at some times, outright cruelty at others. He would often scream at her for being incompetent as a wife and sexually inadequate. He said that he was entitled to his "dalliances."

After five months of being in twice-weekly treatment, Barry seemed quite engaged in the process of looking at what expectations he brought into relationships, and what problems typically arose in them. He attended sessions regularly, was punctual, and arrived eager to talk. It was completely out of the ordinary when he did not show up for an appointment one day and did not call either before or after the time he was due. The next session brought the following exchange.

"I didn't realize that I had forgotten our last appointment until this morning. I can't really believe it happened. You know, I went to get lunch that day and bumped into an old girlfriend of mine. I hadn't seen her for years. It was great to see her. She looked good, was happy to see me. We ended up having lunch together. We talked and talked. It was one of those things. You know, one thing led to another." Barry looked away. He seemed very uncomfortable.

"You seem so ill at ease."

"Yeah, well, you and I . . . we've never talked about sex or anything. Well, that's not completely true. We've talked about my father—and all the women he had affairs with. . . ."

"But not so much about *your* sexual relationships."

"True. She's married now . . . and we . . . well, you know."

"Seems hard for you to talk about this."

"Well. I don't know about how you feel about these things. I assume you're married. And, well . . . I generally don't screw around with married women or anything. But I guess this was different."

"Different?"

"You know. I mean, we had already had sex before and everything."

Barry had never been so faltering in his speech. He had always talked with far more ease and self-assurance. He clearly was uncomfortable.

"This is so strange. I feel like a kid or something."
"How old a kid?"
"A teenager, maybe. High school age, definitely. I even feel like that at the moment."
"Anything in particular from that time come to mind?"
Barry looked at me, then looked out the window. The silence that followed was deafening.

"This seems like a silence filled with thoughts and feelings that are disturbing for you," I said, looking directly at him.

"I can't believe what happened," he said slowly and evenly. "Something came over me when I was with her. As I'm sitting here, I'm suddenly beginning to remember that it's happened before . . . but it was a long time ago. I think when you asked me 'How old a kid?' I was . . . it struck me . . . funny that I put it that way."

I looked at him quizzically.

" 'Struck me.' My father beat the shit out of me for this. . . . When I was 16, my sister walked into my room while I was masturbating. She kind of froze and stared. She must have been all of 13. . . ." He set his jaw and almost seemed to grit his teeth as he continued. "I made her put her hand on my penis and masturbate me. I put my hand over hers. . . . We never talked about it, but she must have told my mother. When my father came home the next day, I heard him fighting with my mother, for a change. Anyway, I guess she told him. All I know is, he stormed into my room, called me a scumbag and a pervert, and hit me with his belt. . . . In a way, he's right. I am a scumbag and a pervert." Barry was visibly upset. He had grown pale and was perspiring.

I started to speak, and he held his hand up as if to signal that I should stop.

"There's more. The other day, I basically grabbed Marilyn's [former girlfriend's] hand and shoved it down my pants. I had an erection. I kind of forced her to hold me—hold my penis. She was clearly rattled. She said, 'Not here'—we were in the park. Anyway, that's when we went back to my apartment. And the sex was kind of rough. I wouldn't say I forced her, exactly, but I was pushy. There was a kind of intensity—it reminds me of that time with my sister."

The experience with his sister that Barry related was a turning point in his life. His missing his appointment and recreating some of the circumstances of that earlier experience was an acting out in the transference relationship that was developing in his treatment. Instead of putting the memory into words and connecting it with me, he had put it into action. What emerged over the next few weeks in our work was that he had been having passing stirrings of sexual excitement when he was in the room with me. These feelings disturbed him; he felt they were "incestuous." The feelings touched upon the repressed memory of the sexual incident with his sister and his having been beaten by his father. The memory was pressing into awareness simultaneously with enormous guilt and shame pressing to keep it out of consciousness—and out of our dialogue. Missing the appointment and the incident with Marilyn were evidence of the growing necessity for Barry to be aware of the earlier incident.

The harshness of his own reaction made it possible to look at how unmodified his superego was and how he was afraid of the deepening of relationships, for fear of what would emerge from him. He feared the eruption of the kind of aggressive sexuality that appeared in his action with his sister. There also were significant conflicts related to the violent reaction of his father, both in terms of an identification with his father and Barry's (oedipal) wishes to retaliate against his father.

His development was, in many respects, arrested during adolescence, although based on even earlier conflicts. Barry was unable to clarify his sexuality, modify his superego and ego ideal, or permit himself to pursue an intimate, reciprocal, and committed relationship. These kinds of difficulties inevitably have (and had) a foundation in early life, but the particular nature of Barry's problems took form during middle and late adolescence.

Adult patients who act out are frequently reenacting split off adolescent conflicts. Adolescents typically take action when full awareness of feelings and thoughts has not yet been achieved. Acting out in adulthood is often a memory of this action-oriented form of encapsulating and expressing experience; the particular enactment expresses the individual's adolescent conflict. The use of defenses such as intellectualization and asceticism, which become available during adolescence, may similarly signal the presence of adolescent conflict in an adult patient.

The issues highlighted here are a sampling of those that stem from adolescence and often appear in adult treatment. I include them to alert clinicians who work with adults to the ongoing presence of such issues and their roots in adolescent life. We are all too inclined to think immediately of the earlier foundations of difficulties adults present to us; it is important that adolescent manifestations be appreciated as well. It is with the quote from Nietzsche that begins this chapter in mind, "Even a thought, even a possibility, can shatter and transform us," that I include this sampling of issues. At times, the awareness of the critical importance of adolescent experience can help in transforming adult treatments that have ground to a halt to be set in motion once again, or illuminating issues that seem inevitably to recur and, thus, resolving them.

7

Considering Subphase: Early vs. Late Adolescent Outbreak of Bulimia

Every age has its pleasures, its style of wit, and its own ways.
Nicolas Boileau-Despréaux, *The Art of Poetry*

Conducting adolescent treatment, or for that matter any treatment, requires that the clinician come to some formulation about the root and the nature of the symptoms being presented by the person seeking psychotherapeutic intervention. In this puzzle to be solved, one important piece is often neglected: deciphering psychopathology requires a careful consideration of *when* in a person's life symptoms develop. The same symptoms, erupting at different points in life, may have quite different meanings. The developmental issues particular to the stage of life in which the symptoms emerge must be evaluated in order to develop a full understanding of their etiology.

I describe adolescence not as a unitary phase of development but one more aptly divided into early, middle, and late subphases. This chapter demonstrates why and how the subphase in which symptoms first occur must be taken into account to develop a full understanding of the nature and meaning of those symptoms for a particular adolescent patient. In effect, the developmental issues of the subphase are the straw that breaks the back of this adolescent's psychic structure. The conflicts associated with this subphase are so strong that the adolescent cannot contain them within the psychic structure that has evolved up until this time.

To illustrate the impact of the time of outbreak of symptoms on their etiology, this chapter will discuss two adolescents who became bulimic, one in early adolescence and one in late adolescence. Even though those who have written about adolescent bulimia have described it almost exclusively without regard to the specific developmental subphase in which the bulimia appeared, the subphase in which bulimia emerges is crucial to understanding its etiology. Indeed, some of the controversies in the field about etiology can be clarified by looking at the subphase in which bulimia emerges. The degree of pathology is often related to the subphase as well: in general, the earlier the onset of bulimia, the more severe the level of pathology involved.

Bulimia (as described in *DSM-III*) is characterized by repeated episodes of rapid ingestion of large amounts of food in a discrete period of time, usually two hours. Typically, consumption is of high-caloric, easily ingested food. Eating is stopped by abdominal pain, sleep, or self-induced vomiting. Bulimics are prone to severely restrictive diets and the use of laxatives or diuretics for the purpose of weight control. They are at or above normal weight, and have weight fluctuations of at least ten pounds. Bulimics know their eating pattern is abnormal, but feel unable to stop eating voluntarily. They are depressed and self-deprecatory after bingeing.

The families of bulimics often are disengaged, highly conflicted, chaotic, and show a high degree of life distress and contradictory communication patterns. There are strong tendencies for suppression of negative feeling and double-binding of daughters with regard to control and autonomy issues. There is generally a preoccupation with food and dieting in the family. Mothers are usually described as domineering and physically distant, fathers as somewhat seductive.

In this chapter, bulimia is regarded as an entity that primarily afflicts adolescent girls (even though there has been a recent rise in the incidence of male bulimia). It is regarded as separate from anorexia or obesity (although there are many patients for whom these entities are on a continuum with one another). It is clear that there are also many people who suffer from more than one of these conditions.

Bulimia involves disturbances in both body image and the sense of autonomy, primary aspects of adolescent development. The particular ways in which body image and autonomy develop during the adolescent subphases are critical when considering the meaning of the onset of bulimic symptoms.

The early adolescent is faced with the task of assimilating the vast changes of puberty. She must move from seeing her body as that of a sexually undifferentiated child to that of a young woman. This involves an identification with her mother as an adult female, at the same time as the adolescent is separating from her mother as a parent of childhood.

This move out of childhood involves the taking over of the nurturant functions of the parent. These nurturant functions include eating, dressing, and personal hygiene practices. The girl who becomes bulimic at this state puts a halt to this growth process. In a sense, she is announcing—albeit secretly—that she cannot comfortably identify herself as an adult female, nor can she take over the nurturant functions of the parent of childhood. It is a "secret" announcement because there are often no outward manifestations of the bingeing and purging that is going on, in contrast to both obese and anorectic girls.

These girls have most often been left wanting by their mothers: wanting of more clarity of self-definition, wanting of physical affection, and wanting of empathy. They feel that they have not been attended to enough, nor accepted for who they are and what they feel. The dyadic relationship with their mothers (or other primary caregivers) did not feel reciprocal. Their mothers seemed to demand more than they were able to give.

These early adolescent onset bulimics are outwardly compliant throughout childhood in an effort particularly aimed at pleasing their mothers, much like the "good girls" Hilde Bruch (1978) and Salvador Minuchin and his colleagues (1978) describe in their studies of anorectics. They are afraid to lose what little caring is available. They turn to their fathers (Schwartz 1988) for satisfaction of the needs of early childhood, the preoedipal supplies, that were not forthcoming in sufficient quantity from their mothers. These physically and emotionally close relationships with their fathers feel too charged, often overeroticized, as they get older, especially in the oedipal phrase. Faced with this dilemma, and unable to engage in comfortable (and adequate oedipal) relationships with their fathers, these girls retreat to developmentally earlier ways of interacting in their families and of looking at themselves (e.g., oral and anal resolutions). Whatever tentative resolutions they achieved in early childhood (during the oedipal phase) are sustained throughout latency; the inner pressures of puberty then overwhelm their early, fragile foundations.

These early adolescent onset bulimics cannot assimilate the changes of puberty. Their deep longings for the comforts and nourishment (both emotional and physical) that caregivers offer in the early years are enacted in the bingeing; their unacceptable repressed rage toward the early mother and the intolerable over-sexualized relation to the father are expressed in the purging. What is taken in must be cleaned out, for it is tinged with conflicted rage toward the mother and a sexual connection with the father.

The inner dramas of these young bulimics seem to be consistent with the dynamics of the bulimics that Alan Sugarman and Cheryl Kurash (1981) describe, whose psychopathological roots are in the practicing subphase of the first separation-individuation process. According to Mahler and her colleagues (1975), the practicing subphase is the time in which children are having a "love affair with the world." It is a period of narcissistic investment in one's own functions and body, no full awareness of separateness, and a relative imperviousness to pain.

Sugarman and Kurash note that interferences in the practicing subphase lead to disturbances in self–other boundary differentiation and the capacity for symbolization. This fits these early adolescent bulimics, who put food in and get rid of it without any clear sense psychologically of who is being fed, who is having something taken from them, what is being put in or taken out, and for what purposes these activities are taking place. For example, they cannot distinguish whether it is their mothers, fathers, or themselves they are feeding and/or taking food from, or what the (so-called) food really is for: sustenance, control, or power. They are ultimately terrified at the prospect of becoming more grown up, for they are in no way finished with being young children.

Erin

Erin was referred to me by the consulting psychologist in her school. Several of her friends had talked to the psychologist, expressing concern that Erin was going to damage herself. They said they had heard Erin vomiting in the girls' room in school and that they knew that she was very down on herself about her weight. They said that she had not verbally acknowledged the vomiting when they confronted her about it, but had burst into tears. They didn't know how to help her.

The consulting psychologist spoke to Erin about her friends' concerns. Erin again cried, but did not either confirm or deny what her friends had said about her. When asked about whether she was willing to see a therapist, Erin nodded in the affirmative.

The school's psychologist called me when Erin was in the room. She told me about Erin's friends' concerns, and Erin's willingness to see me. She then put Erin on the line. I was struck by how young this ninth-grader sounded. I could easily have been talking to an 8- or 9-year-old girl. We made an appointment for later that week.

Erin arrived for her appointment early. She looked younger than her 14 years. She was overweight, and dressed in an oversized man-tailored shirt over black pants. She had green eyes and very long, light brown hair and bangs. She spoke clearly and intelligently, but very quietly and only in response to direct questions. The few times she made eye contact, she looked on the verge of tears. Her intense neediness seemed just under the surface. She expressed very little outward emotion.

Erin had never acknowledged before—even indirectly—her problems with binge eating and vomiting. Neither of her parents knew anything about it. In response to my asking how she felt about this secret being known, she shrugged her shoulders, but looked at me with eyes brimming with tears. When I told her that I would like to meet her mother, because it was my custom to meet with the parents of new patients her age for the purpose of making arrangements for payment and giving them an opportunity to meet me, she said, "You're not going to tell her, are you?" It was clear that my keeping her secret was a critical component in forming an alliance with Erin.

It took Erin two years to put her bingeing and purging practices into words. She would only make very indirect references to experiences of arriving home from school to find no one there, rapidly eating pints of ice cream and candy bars, and putting her finger down her throat to make herself vomit. She was both profoundly ashamed and protective of the experience. It was her way of making the time between her arrival home and her mother's arrival home disappear.

Erin's parents had separated when she was 3½ years old, and divorced a year or so later. She had only very sporadic contact with her father since that time. She and her father would occasionally meet for what she called "dates." Usually, they would have meals together in restaurants. He would make promises about seeing her in school meetings with her teachers, but, more often than not, he would arrive very late or not at all. According to both Erin and her mother, he had not kept up his child support payments. Despite the facts that there were obvious ways in which her father and his relationship with her were somewhat marginal and that he repeatedly disappointed her, Erin became more animated when she talked about her father than she did at any other time. She treasured her moments with him.

To Erin, life with her mother was a series of contradictions. Erin had been arriving home to an empty house for a number of years. Yet, when her mother was at home and Erin was planning to go out, her mother demanded to know where she was going, with whom she was going, whether the parent of the friend she was visiting was going to be at home when they arrived, when Erin was returning, and so on. She saw her mother as overprotective but distant. Her mother was very efficient about making appointments with doctors and teachers but withholding of any support or warmth; she was more apt to point to ways in which Erin could be better at her schoolwork than she was to recognize Erin's obvious achievements.

There was no question that Erin's bulimia derived from intense difficulties with both her bodily changes and the processes of separation and individuation into which she felt she was thrust. She clearly suffered from having conflicted identifications with both her mother and father, repressed rage and disappointment with each of them, and terrible early longings. All of these had to be secret, like the bulimia itself. Her growing ability to put into words her mixed feelings about her parents and her wishes both to be a child and to be more grownup led to her being comfortable talking specifically about her bingeing and purging practices. These practices then moved from being daily occurrences to being infrequent, usually related to particular frustrations or disappointments.

This is a somewhat different picture from that of late adolescent onset bulimics. In general, they are struggling far more with issues related to their peers and their appearance. They have taken many more steps out into the social world than have the early adolescent onset bulimics, who primarily live in their families, both literally and figuratively. Where the early adolescent breakdown is in the realm of the body and the family, the late adolescent bulimic breaks down primarily in the social realm. In each case, these are very much in keeping with subphase issues.

John Sours (1974) and others look to problems in the rapprochement subphase of the separation–individuation process of early childhood for gaining an understanding of bulimia. Mahler and her colleagues (1975) describe this as the peak of the separation–individuation struggle, when there is an awareness that neither their mothers nor the world are totally at children's omnipotent command and disposal. This is a period in which frustration tolerance disintegrates. The rapprochement subphase seems to be particularly important for these late-adolescent-onset bulimics: they are venturing out, sometimes for the first time, into the social and sexual worlds.

The social and sexual worlds hold a great deal of danger for these late-adolescent-onset bulimics, for they are not at all clear about what it is that they are seeking from their peers. This particularly seems to be the case in sexual relationships. Though drawn to the male world, they are often terrified by both the quantity and quality of need that they feel. They have a mix of early developmental (preoedipal and oedipal) needs that overwhelm them. Both oral and anal psychosexual components are present, but phallic components predominate in these late adolescent bulimics. They focus strongly, for example, on who dominates and who is submissive in relationships, and often seem more interested in conquest than they do in having ongoing relationships with their sexual partners.

In late adolescent bulimic patients, the food that they take in is frequently representative of the forbidden paternal phallus, of which they must then rid themselves. Early on in treatment, the late adolescents present both conscious and unconscious pregnancy fantasies (often oedipal in nature). At times, their bingeing unconsciously represents paternal impregnation that they must then vomit out.

Melissa

Melissa was a blond-haired, blue-eyed, tall, slim 22-year-old recent college graduate. My first impression was that of a very attractive, well-dressed, athletic-looking young woman. Her manner was direct. In the first session, she virtually announced that she had been bulimic since her freshman year in college. It was at that time that she consulted with the therapist who had now referred her to me. She said that the bulimia had been under control until now, but that recent events in her life had caused her a great deal of stress, and she was again bingeing and vomiting. She seemed almost impatient as she described her bouts of overeating whatever was in her apartment and forcing herself to vomit afterwards.

The recent stresses included moving to a new city, starting a job in which she was in constant conflict with a female superior toward whom she felt contempt, not finding any young women with whom she could form friendships, and being infatuated with a young man who seemed to be losing interest in her. She pressed me directly about what she could do about all this. The message seemed to be: what could she do about all this *right now?*

Melissa felt that she could deal with the job stresses and being in a new city, but she could not handle being without a man in her life. She wanted to have a boyfriend and wanted to get married. She could not understand why men were so fickle and why they so easily used her—by parading her around as if she were something they could wear, having sex with her, and then dropping her.

As her life story unfolded, it became clear that Melissa felt that her mother was well-intentioned but really did not understand her. Melissa was the youngest by several years of five children, and Melissa felt that her mother was tired and uninterested by the time she came along. She had very little respect for her mother. She felt that both of her parents were more apt to provide her with material supplies than emotional supplies, but that her father was the more openly affectionate and involved with her. He would often take her out alone for food treats. She would often confide in him about her troubles with her peers.

Melissa had many sexual encounters with young men, but never had a relationship of more than a few weeks duration. She often had sex with a man on their first date. She said that she liked sex, and liked being desired. She also said that she felt that men had very little sense of loyalty.

Her bingeing and purging episodes almost always followed her disappointments with men. She said that she hated waiting at home for the telephone to ring, and would binge "to take up the slack," then vomit so that she "wouldn't get fat from all the eating." When she was home, alone and waiting, she said that she felt weak. She said that she would eat, angrily, and that it soothed her in some way that she could not understand. She knew she felt empowered by it.

Melissa's bulimic symptoms ebbed and flowed with her social/sexual life. Her rage at being denied what she sought from men was apparent. She had made the adolescent transition from her parents to her peers, but found herself with needs to be satisfied from her peers that were greater than any one person could satisfy at that point in her life.

Erin and Melissa are typical of the many adolescents whose bulimic symptoms are linked to the failures of subphase resolution. Both are also fat-phobic, a characteristic present in most eating disordered patients, which has been extensively and articulately discussed by C. Philip Wilson and his colleagues (1985, 1992). There are, however, important differences between Erin and Melissa as well.

Erin is an early adolescent who is passive and secretive. She cannot tolerate being alone, because her intense and conflicted early (preoedipal) longings leave her feeling infantile and fragile. She did not feel adequately cared for by her mother in those early years, but—especially in the absence of her father—needed her mother desperately. She feels hungry for the kind of affection, attention, and nurturance that very young children need in order to feel loved and to feel that they have a substantial place in their parents' lives, and, therefore, in the world.

She symbolically binges on these early emotional supplies; her purges are motivated by conflict over preoedipal rage and oedipal guilt. She is ashamed of her sense of greed (Boris [1984] discusses the important role of greed in eating-disordered girls.) Putting her experience into words is difficult, because speaking implies a higher level of differentiation than she has as yet achieved. She has very little sense of bodily integrity.

Though rooted in experiences of early childhood, her disturbance has crystallized around early adolescent issues. The need to assimilate her pubertal changes, and thus accept that her body is her own, for example, is not yet possible, for her body is intrapsychically intertwined with her mother and father. The early adolescent's need to deidealize the mother and father of childhood as she moves through the separation and individuation processes of adolescence is interfered with by Erin's intense disappointment and frustration with each of her parents: the greater the disappointment, the greater the need to idealize them and sustain that idealization. Erin's need to continue to get symbolically everything she can from her internalized idealized parents of childhood makes it extremely difficult for her to make the necessary early adolescent moves out into the world of her contemporaries.

Melissa is clearly in a different place, developmentally. She is actively involved in the world of her contemporaries, though evidencing real difficulty in negotiating the late adolescent task of achievement of intimacy. She has trouble liking and respecting her female peers, and is both needy and competitive, particularly sexually, in her relationships with the young men she so desires. Unlike Erin, who kept her body and her bulimia as shameful secrets, Melissa virtually flings both of them out into the world. Needless to say, her rage is much more on the surface, as is her competitiveness. She cannot bear having her vulnerability noticed, but is otherwise very interested in being seen and admired. Rather than idealizing the adults around her, particularly the women, Melissa is contemptuous and demanding of them.

Though her problems also began in early experience, Melissa presents very much as a late adolescent. In the formulation of her more mature ego ideal, she has established that both attractiveness and intimacy are important to her. She is unhappy with the failures in her capacity to achieve these self-formulated goals. In the consolidation of sexual identity that is part of the late adolescent identity integration, Melissa has come up against obstacles that overwhelm her. She does not understand what it is that she seeks in relationships, and how it is that she interferes with achieving her desires. Unlike Erin, Melissa is very much attuned to the social world. She has turned to the new world of her peers to satisfy old longings.

Both Erin and Melissa binge, but the meaning, timing, and substance of the binge is different. Erin binges on the forbidden sweets of early longings, and then must purge herself of the indulgence. Melissa eats anything that is around, in an effort to fill herself up and to stave off feelings of emptiness and powerlessness. She must then rid herself of these (unconsciously stolen) phallic substances. Erin binges while waiting for her mother to return; Melissa binges when she feels deprived of the phallus that she feels she deserves in her oedipal triumph.

DISCUSSION

Needless to say, each of these cases is far more complex than a brief case illustration can indicate. It is my intention to alert those who treat adolescent bulimics to the special significance of the subphase of adolescence in which the bulimia emerges. Indeed, it is my intention to alert clinicians generally to the significance of the timing of the outbreak of any symptomatology.

In adolescence specifically, an awareness and appreciation of subphase onset will help both in assessing the importance and meaning of the bulimia in the patient's life history and in anticipating the course of treatment. Adolescent girls whose symptoms appear around the time of early adolescence, for example, are more fragile than those whose symptoms emerge later. They are building upon a foundation with weaknesses that may well stem from difficulties that arose as early as the practicing subphase of the first separation-individuation process. Later adolescent onset bulimia is generally more accessible to treatment. The fault in the foundation in this group seems to arise later in development, particularly in the rapprochement subphase of the first separation-individuation process.

I also wish to emphasize the role of their fathers in the etiology of the bulimia. The fathers of these adolescent patients have had a profound influence on the development and psychic meaning of their bulimia. The early adolescent bulimic often turns to her father for preoedipal supplies of which she has felt deprived to her relationship with her mother. She then flees the oedipal situation and heads back to the safer, more easily regulated oral/anal stages. The late adolescent bulimic seems more often to be riveted to the phallic/oedipal stage, in which she feels a conflicted triumph over her mother. She treasures her special relationship with her father, but its persistence makes relationships with other men extremely difficult. It also contributes to her feeling contemptuous of women.

When comparing those whose onset of bulimia is in early adolescence with those whose onset is in late adolescence, the nature of the bulimia is qualitatively and quantitatively different. The adolescents with early onset often enter treatment with the bulimia intertwined in their character. They have come to use the symptom complex in a manner that is emblematic of their defensive styles and personalities. They are often secretive and have difficulty putting their experiences into words, particularly experiences related to their bodies and family relationships. The bulimia looms large in their self-concepts.

Later onset bulimics are not as dominated by the symptom complex. They resort to it in the face of dealing with frustration and anxiety, especially in the realms of their social and sexual lives. It almost seems as if it is an adjunct to their personalities, rather than central to it. While the early adolescent's rage is difficult for her to identify and express, the late adolescent is often quite aware of her rage and even quick to articulate it.

It is noteworthy that bulimia tends to emerge at the beginning or end of the adolescent process. It is a way for the early adolescent to hold onto childhood; it is a way for the late adolescent to barricade herself against entering adulthood. In either instance, it is inextricably intertwined with the critical issues of the adolescent process. The adolescent bulimic is fending off the central purpose of this period of development: making the transition from childhood to adulthood.

Case Studies

8

Frozen at the Brink:
An Early Adolescent's
Wish Not to See

None so blind as those that will not see.

Matthew Henry,
Commentaries, Jeremiah : 20

The case examples presented in the book up until now have been designed to illustrate particular theoretical points. The three that are presented in this and the next two chapters are meant to demonstrate more fully the technique I use in working with adolescents: my stance; the way I understand what I hear and sense; and the degree to which I reveal my own thoughts, feelings, and experiences. I also try to show how the treatment process shifts during the three subphases of adolescence. To this end, I present three cases, one from each subphase.

Moving from childhood into adolescence, from the world of the family into the world of peers, is the primary task of early adolescence. Disruptions in the family during childhood, particularly those that involve children being exposed to aspects of parents that disturb or frighten them, make the transition out of childhood more difficult for the young adolescent.

Such was the case for Maggie, whose home life was so consuming that she could not take part in the social life her contemporaries enjoyed. She felt young and scared, in no way ready to join her friends at their junior high school parties and dances. She felt frozen at the brink of adolescence, unable or unwilling to take the necessary plunge into the social world. Her attention was more focused on her past than on her present life.

Maggie was in twice-weekly psychotherapy for three years, then shifted into a once-weekly treatment for another year. What follows is a brief description of her history, a report of her treatment, and a discussion of her struggle out of childhood into a full early, then middle adolescent life.

THE TREATMENT

First Visit

Twelve-year-old Maggie bounced in, flipping her long, light brown hair back with an easy motion of her wrist. She was slight, though showing signs of pubertal development, of fair complexion, and quite adorable.

"Hi. How are you?" she said with a big smile.

"I'm fine, thanks. How about you?"

"I think I'm a little nervous. I've never done this before, you know. I mean, everybody else in my family sees someone . . . but I have no idea what I'm supposed to do."

"Any idea why you're here?"

She looked around the room nervously. Suddenly, she looked up and spoke very quickly: "I get spooked really easily. My parents fight with each other really badly. I mean, you know, they get really mean. Well, especially my mother. My father just tries not to get crushed by her or something. I don't even remember the last time they hugged each other." Maggie fell silent. Her eyes opened wide, and she blinked several times.

The blinking proved to be an important symptom. At moments, it almost seemed as if Maggie were in an hypnotic state. She was unaware of me or her surroundings. She looked like a deer frozen in the headlights of a car, but one who blinked rather than remained open-eyed. When it happened around her peers, they alternately felt estranged from her and made fun of her for "odd habits." When she blinked around her family, they harangued her, laughed at her, or pleaded with her to stop.

History

Maggie was the oldest of three children. She had two brothers: one three years younger and another six years younger. She lived in a well-to-do suburb outside of New York City and attended the local public school. She had friends at school, though she often said that she did not really like most of them. She felt that they were superficial and catty and would be quick to betray her if it would suit them to do so. She said that she felt close to her family, especially her next younger brother and her mother, though her mother's fierce temper scared her at times.

"I love my mother so much," she would often say. "I just wish she didn't get so mad sometimes."

Her parents fought a great deal. They had for as long as she could remember. After they fought, Maggie often went into their bedroom in the hope that she could make peace.

"I would try to make nice," she said with a slight smile. "Not that it worked or anything, but at least I tried. . . . I was always worried that it would upset my brothers."

Maggie frequently couched her own concerns in terms of worries about her brothers. She was very protective toward them, and saw herself in a maternal role. "I love them to pieces," was her usual refrain. It almost seemed like a chant Maggie used to keep any other thoughts or feelings about them and her role in relation to them out of her consciousness.

Years before, when Maggie was 9, she had witnessed a very upsetting event. Her parents were fighting, "about money, as usual," and the fight escalated. Her mother, who drank too much too often, had been drinking. As her anger mounted, her mother screamed, "I hate you so much—I'd like to kill you" to her father. Maggie ran to the doorway of the kitchen, where the fight was taking place. At that moment, her mother picked up a plate and threw it in the direction of her father, though not directly at him. The plate hit the wall, shattered, and several shards pierced Maggie's skin: one in her thigh, one in her upper chest near her left shoulder, and one in her arm.

Her parents rushed her to the hospital. Her thigh and arm wounds required stitches, her chest wound was more serious. The shard had pierced her lung, and required surgical removal and repair. There was an air of tremendous urgency surrounding the operation, which proved successful. Maggie completely recovered from a medical standpoint, though the emotional wound remained.

The experience led Maggie's mother to seek psychotherapeutic intervention. Her alcoholism and marital problems had never before moved her to take this step. It was the horror of injuring her own child that frightened her to such a degree that she knew that her difficulties were more than she could contend with on her own.

At the time Maggie entered treatment, her mother had not had a drink in three years. Her parents still fought, but much less frequently and with no attendant violence. The incident also had led Maggie's father to seek treatment.

Maggie's father was a quiet man. He had been brought up in a very wealthy family, with a dominant, successful, self-made father. His mother catered to him. She had been unable to have any more children after he was born, which made her depressed and overly concerned with her son's safety. He was overprotected and given everything he ever wanted. He grew up without a realistic sense of the world, especially what it meant to be a parent and what it took to make a living. Maggie's mother was initially charmed by his sweet, unassuming manner and apparent lack of concern about the material world. This soon gave way to disappointment about his lack of personal ambition and general passivity.

Maggie's mother grew up as the middle child in a family with three daughters. She idolized her older sister, who was an extremely attractive, bright, high-achieving person. This older sister tended to be critical of herself and others, especially Maggie's mother. The youngest sister was a very cute, small, funny child who charmed everyone in her family. She was the youngest by six years, and had come at a time when both parents thought that they could not still have children. She was described as a "gift from the heavens." Maggie's mother was neither "the cute one" nor "the smart, pretty, one;" she looked up to her older sister and looked after her younger sister. She felt bitter, unattended to, and uncared for growing up.

When Maggie's parents met, they were initially very happy. Maggie's father was very generous with her mother, and extremely supportive. She pursued a career in public relations, in which he helped her emotionally and financially. At the time, he worked for his father and made a very good living.

Marital difficulties began with two events: the father's family business was sold and Maggie was born. Maggie's father was content to stay at home to work on various computer projects and write poetry, while his wife remained in the business world. At first, she enjoyed this division of labor, then she became increasingly resentful. She felt that "it was abnormal." She would tell her husband that, as a man, he should be out working and that she should be at home with Maggie.

This history emerged quickly in the early meetings with Maggie's parents, but also in sessions with Maggie. She knew the story quite accurately, for it had been told to her by both parents. She told it matter-of-factly, almost as if she were describing the plot of a movie or novel. She seemed older than her 12 years at these moments.

At other times, Maggie seemed quite young. She giggled easily, and talked in a baby voice about various aspects of her home life. "My little brother is so-o-o cute. He has the eeny-weeniest little nose. I love to play baby with him. I can't believe he's already 6! I still feel like he's my little baby brother. I still make him let me cradle him in my arms." Maggie's wish to stay young was palpable; at these times, she appeared to be no more than 8 or 9 years old.

In the beginning of treatment, Maggie talked more about her home life than any other part of her life. At times, it was easy to forget that she was already in junior high school, where her peers were beginning to have parties and, in some instances, even pair off with one another to be "going out." Occasionally, however, this social phenomenon would emerge in Maggie's sessions. "Susie and Rick are going out. I think it's so stupid. It doesn't really mean anything. They're just showing off, trying to be big shots."

In the middle phase of treatment, there was a shift of attention to her girlfriends. Toward the end of treatment, school and her social life with both female and male friends were her topics of choice.

Treatment Process: Beginning Phase

In the first part of Maggie's treatment, it was as if she had no life outside the family. Each session was spent describing the details of her life at home.

"When my mom got home today, she brought in Chinese food. It was so good. I love it when she does that. The boys don't really like Chinese food, but Mom and Dad and I like it a lot. Sometimes it feels like there are two different families in our family. One with the boys and my parents, and one with me and my parents. Well, and then there's the one with me and my brothers. They definitely see me as another parent figure or something."

"What kind of parent are you?"

"I'm really nice to them, especially my baby brother. Jesse [her older brother] and I are really more like brother and sister most of the time. Bobby [her younger brother] is almost like our kid. But when Jesse is upset, like when Mom and Dad fight or something, I comfort him."

"So who comforts you?"

"I can handle it." Maggie stared straight ahead of her and began to blink. This went on for a few moments, then she seemed to wake up and she became silent.

I let a few moments pass, then asked: "What happened just now?"

"I spaced out."

"What does it feel like when you space out that way?"

"I get sort of blank. It's almost like I'm looking right in front of me, but I can't see anything. It's weird, isn't it?"

"I wasn't thinking that it was weird, but I *was* thinking that it must mean something."

"Other kids think it's weird. And my family thinks it's weird."

"And you?"

"Well, I don't really know what it looks like to other people. I only know what it feels like. . . . I guess it feels kind of weird. Not like it hurts or anything. It's just, like, nothing . . . nothingness."

"Maybe it happens when it feels better to feel nothing than it does to feel something else."

Maggie looked thoughtful. "Maybe. I don't know . . . but what kind of something else?"

"Maybe something that feels worse than nothing."

"Lots of things feel worse than nothing, I guess." Maggie looked a bit upset.

"Well, if we just look at what happened before, we have an example of something that might be worse than nothing. When I asked about who comforts you, you said that you could handle it . . . and then you spaced out. So maybe something about having to comfort yourself feels bad."

Maggie fell silent and looked down at the floor. In a voice hardly above a whisper, she said: "Yes. I think so. It hurts. Sometimes all I really want is a mother like I am to Bobby—and sometimes Jesse, even." Her big brown eyes, filled with tears, looked at me longingly. I felt a strong desire to gather her up in my arms and hold her. I decided that I could not act on this desire, because it might press Maggie back into a more childlike position in her life. These feelings, however, led me to be acutely aware of the depth of Maggie's longing.

"It must be so hard to want something so much that you feel you don't have."

A tear rolled down Maggie's face. "I guess you can't have everything."

Sessions during this time in Maggie's treatment seemed to alternate between those that identified painful aspects of her home life and those that presented her home life in its rosiest form.

"I love my mommy. She cuddled with me last night after we watched a scary movie. She said I made her feel better."

"And what about you? Did she make you feel better, too?"

"Ummmm . . . yes. It was so nice to get some hugs. It was almost worth seeing that movie to get them."

"Almost?"

"I hate scary movies, really. But I would never tell my mother, because she likes them. And if I act like I like them, too, then I get to watch them with her. And then we cuddle, afterwards."

"Special moments with your mom?"

"You know, she's the best. It's like she's my mommy and my best friend all rolled into one. I feel so lucky."

During this time in her treatment, Maggie barely mentioned her father. Her life seemed to revolve around her mother and brothers, even though it was her father who was there when she arrived home from school. Occasionally, however, she would make passing reference to an interaction between her parents.

"Mom and Dad went out last night and left me home to baby-sit. It was the first time they ever let me do that. It made me excited and scared at the same time. I mean, they were only down in the mall. But I was still in charge. . . . They almost never go out, you know."

"How come?"

"Sometimes I think it's because they don't really have any friends, sometimes because they just like to be with us. Other times I think it's because they just don't like being alone together very much." Maggie looked uncomfortable. She looked around the room a bit, tapped her foot on the floor, crossed her legs, then uncrossed them.

"Something made you uncomfortable just now, didn't it?"

"They're not like other kids' parents."

This was an important moment in Maggie's treatment. It was the first time she ever indicated that she compared her family to the families of her peers. Up until this time, which was after six months of meeting, she spoke about her family as if it existed in a vacuum. She never even compared it to families she read about or saw on television. The world outside the home was beginning to become more salient to her. She was getting ready for her first forays into adolescent differentiation.

"I dropped Jesse off at his friend's house this afternoon after school. His friend's mom was there and offered all of us cookies and milk. I thought it was so nice. I mean, I know it's corny and everything, and I'm too old for that now, but that kind of thing *never* happened at our house. You know, Daddy was there. But he never baked cookies or anything. And anyway . . . I know you're not supposed to say this or anything . . . but Daddy's not a Mommy." Maggie looked at me and then became quiet. It was clear that she had suddenly become extremely uneasy. I saw her eyes move away from me and she began to look around the room, then out the window, then stared straight ahead and began to blink.

I waited a few minutes to see if she would spontaneously emerge from this state.

"I just did that thing, didn't I?" she said, with some timidity.

"Yes, you did. Any guesses about why it might have happened just then?"

Maggie looked uneasy again. She seemed to be struggling to stay with me, rather than slipping back into the altered state of consciousness that she had just been in. She looked at me in a way that seemed almost like she was pleading, but did not speak.

"How about if I give it a try?" I said.

She nodded.

"I think you were talking about some of the disappointments that you have had about how your family works. It's never been easy for you to identify those disappointments. I guess it makes you feel like you're being bad, or betraying your parents in some way. I also had the slightest hint that maybe you were thinking something about me, or wondering something about me just now—and that, too, made you uncomfortable. Sort of a double whammy. The kind of thing that can be awfully hard to talk about."

"Well, do you have kids?"

I smiled. "I don't mind telling you the answer to that question, but I certainly don't want to miss out on the full meaning of the question and answer for you. I have a feeling that there's a whole lot behind it, and that it's too important to miss. When something affects you so much that you get into one of your spaced-out states, it usually is full of all kinds of thoughts and feelings. When we figure out some of those, I'll be more comfortable simply answering your question."

"I was wondering whether you ever made cookies for your kids," Maggie blurted out.

This began a phase in Maggie's treatment in which I became more and more important as an object of transference. Was I like her mother? Her father? Her idealized mother? Her idealized father? Or someone else entirely? There were times that I represented each of her parents, in their real and idealized forms. She saw me as an idealized version of her friend Emily's mother as well, and a teacher at school who had taken Maggie under her wing many years before.

Maggie also was interested in how I coordinated working with having children. Maybe I didn't have children, she concluded at one point. She did not directly ask me questions about this again for months. Indeed, the next time she brought it up, it was stated in the declarative.

"I've decided that you *do* have children, and that they're older than me. And that you didn't used to work when they were little." Her voice sounded nearly triumphant as she told me this. It was as if she had figured out the answer to her question on her own, and no longer needed to know the actual facts.

This took place a bit over a year into treatment. Maggie's involvement in the transference relationship aided her enormously in moving out of the family home, figuratively speaking. She began to talk much less about her mother, father, and brothers, and more about some of her friends in school. She became particularly focused on a group of three girls with whom she had become quite close. This began a new phase of treatment for her, in which early adolescent issues predominated and issues of childhood faded into the background.

Treatment Process: Middle Phase

"I can't believe that Emily told Rachel what I said about Wendy. It makes me so mad. She has no sense of loyalty!"

"Sometimes it's hard to know who to trust?"

"I guess so. You never know who you can tell what, who they'll tell, how they'll react."

"I wonder if that's an old issue, too. You know, one that comes from growing up in a family and keeping things in a family private."

"Well, there's certainly plenty of things I would never tell anyone about my family . . . at least, any of my friends." Maggie became quiet, then looked directly at me. "You know, after all this time, I don't think I've ever told you some things that happened in my family."

"What do you have in mind?"

"Well, I know you know about that thing that happened when I was 9, but I don't think we ever *really* talked about it."

"I think you're right. Or, at least, I think that there's lots of things we could say about it now that we couldn't have said before, lots of things we understand about you and your family now that we didn't used to know."

"Yeah, like my mother has a mean temper. Not as bad as it used to be, but that's because she doesn't drink anymore . . . well, and maybe her therapist has helped her. And Daddy stands up for himself more now. I guess in general they don't fight as much as they used to. And the boys aren't as scared. Jesse doesn't have those awful nightmares, and Bobby doesn't wet his bed all the time. And I don't space out as much. And I'm not as afraid of boys." This last statement was said with a shy grin. It was the first mention of a concern of hers that had been brought up when she first came to see me, but not since that time.

"Boys? Did I hear 'boys'?" I asked with a smile.

"Oh, come on. I'm in eighth grade already. You know what it's like."

"I have some idea."

"Well, let's put it this way. Rachel is going out with Jonny, Wendy has a crush on Michael. And me? I feel like I ought to like someone, but I really don't. I just don't feel as scared of it all as I used to."

"You know, we got into this because you mentioned the incident at home from when you were 9. I have a feeling that incident is related to a number of other things that you've just talked about, like the spacing out, and the early fears about boys. What do you think?"

"I've always wondered about it."

"Do you feel like talking about it? Or would you rather think about it and talk about it another time?"

"I want to talk about it now. That's why I brought it up. I've been thinking about it a lot lately. I was even thinking of talking to Emily about it. I'm just not sure I can trust her to keep it to herself. . . . I think that whole thing between my parents made me scared of relationships with boys. I don't know whether I was scared I'd be like my mother, or scared I'd be like my father. I also think that. . . ." Maggie's demeanor suddenly changed dramatically. Her face contorted as she fought off tears. "She could have killed me! Did you ever think that? My own mother could have killed me!" She burst into tears and sobbed deeply. I had difficulty containing my own very strong feelings. I wanted to hold her, and felt very much like crying. I did not act on these feelings; instead, I tried to use them in framing my response to Maggie. I felt that she needed to know she could safely and independently feel and express these emotions. I let her cry for a few minutes, then said:

"I know what courage that took for you. I'm so glad you could say this with me."

This was another turning point in Maggie's treatment. We were able to talk about her wish not to see what was in front of her and inside of her, and how overwhelming it was for her to face it all. She described repetitive nightmares, in which her body fell apart from being stabbed repeatedly. We put together how she may have been reacting to feelings and fantasies about the pieces of plate that had entered her body, the stitches, and the pierced lung. She spoke of her fear that her body was only fragilely sewn together, that it could fall apart. We recalled her early repeated use of the phrase "I love them to pieces," and related it to the sewn-together version of herself.

This was a tremendously productive time in her treatment. Over many months, into the third year of her treatment, the multitude of issues related to bodily integrity and ownership were articulated and discussed. Her profound fears of sexuality were most deeply rooted in early sadomasochistic oedipal fantasies, enhanced by the terrible fights between her parents that she heard during her early years. They were further elaborated by the fighting that continued into her pubescence, when her early adolescent oedipal fantasies formed. The world of sexuality was one that terrified her, for it evoked deep concerns about her body falling apart, rage, and death.

"Emily and I talked about sex yesterday," Maggie announced one day in the middle of her third year of treatment. "I decided

that I had to ask her what she thought. I mean, we're turning
15 already. Some kids have already had sex at this age!"

"So, what did you two decide?"

"Well, it's not like we really decided anything. But I was
really glad to find out that she's scared of it, too."

"What kinds of things scare you?"

"You and I have talked about a lot of it, I guess. But I really
am scared of it hurting. I mean, a lot."

"Are you scared about other kinds of sexual experiences,
or just intercourse?"

Maggie blushed. Then she grinned widely. "Well, here's
something I haven't told you. You know that boy I told you
about—Jamie?"

"Absolutely."

"Well. Turned out he liked me, too. And he was at that
party I went to the other day. We talked the whole time.
And . . . he kissed me goodnight!"

"You seem so happy about it—I'm really happy for you!"

"Well, we have a date for Friday night, too. I am *so* excited.
I know this sounds funny, but I finally feel so normal."

"Certainly doesn't sound funny to me. I know what you
were feeling before and how much you've worked to get here."

"Seems strange to call this work. But I know what you
mean. It certainly isn't easy to talk about the things we talk
about, sometimes."

The change in Maggie was unmistakable. Though a bit slower
socially than most of her friends, she was sounding and acting very
much like an early adolescent moving into middle adolescence. It
was, therefore, not very surprising to me when, late in her third year
of treatment, she said the following.

"I've been thinking. I really want to join the newspaper. It's a
big commitment. I have to be there at least three days a week
after school. If I come here twice a week, it doesn't leave me any
time to do anything else. Would it be okay if we met only once
a week?"

"I wouldn't object to it. How do you think you'd feel about it? It would certainly be different."

"Yeah, I know. I'm so used to seeing you every Monday and Thursday, ever since I was little, practically. I can hardly imagine it just being once a week. But I feel like I'll be okay."

"Let's just think about it for a couple of weeks. Kind of live with thinking we'll make the change. See how that feels. Then, if it seems fine, we'll give it a try. But let's just assume that if you're not comfortable, you'll tell me, okay?"

"Yeah, definitely."

And so it went. Maggie did decide to come once a week, and did become very involved with her school newspaper. This change precipitated a strong reaction, however, from her mother. "I'm very worried about Maggie," she said over the telephone. "I'd like to come in and talk to you about her."

Over the years that Maggie had been in treatment, I had periodically met with Maggie's mother, her father, and her parents together. I tended to meet with them together once in the beginning of the school year and once at the end. I met with each parent separately during the year as issues arose that seemed particularly related to one of them. In general, I had met with Maggie's mother far more often than with her father, especially for the first two years of treatment. Maggie began to talk more about her father toward the end of her middle phase of treatment. Her relationship with him had improved dramatically. Her descriptions of him seemed more real. She seemed to see both his strengths and his foibles.

The meeting with her mother proved to be about her concerns over these changes in Maggie's relationship with her and her father.

"I feel like Maggie hates me these days. She seems to adore her father . . . and you . . . which makes me jealous. And then of course she despises me. Don't get me wrong, I see that she's generally in good shape—and I'm very grateful to you for your help. But this is hard to bear. She doesn't want to be alone with me anymore, she's constantly on the phone with her friends, and she's always cheery with her father and kind of tolerates me. I suppose this is normal, but I can't stand it. It wasn't allowed in the family I grew up in. Of course, nothing much was. I guess I should be happy that she's got friends, is doing well in school, has interests. I don't know what it is, but I know I'm worried. Do you really think it's okay for her to see you only once a week?"

"I actually think it's fine. Maggie seems to be getting on track, as far as her development is concerned. And she seems happy. I see that you're feeling a bit distressed, but I know that you can see that she's doing pretty well, at the same time."

"Maybe I just don't know what normal teenagers are like. I know they have to be more independent and everything. But I hate the fact that she and I used to be so close, and now she barely gives me the right time of day."

"Patience definitely helps. When kids have been close to their parents, if the parents can just tolerate a couple of years of greater distance from their kids, a time for the kids to explore their social and intellectual lives—especially with their contemporaries—then there is usually a reconciliation in the future."

"That's comforting. I only hope she doesn't hate me so much for what I was like when she was growing up that she *can't* reconcile with me . . . and it really bothers me that she's so close to my husband all of a sudden."

"Kids need mothers *and* fathers, when they're lucky enough to have both available."

"I suppose that's true. It just burns me up. He was never there for me."

"And now?"

"We're working on it. There's some improvement. We certainly don't fight as much as we used to. Not that there's any real intimacy."

The relationship between Maggie and her mother was definitely more distant and more tense, and her relationship with her father *was* closer.

"Dad said he'd teach me to drive when I get my learner's

permit. I can't wait. Mom, of course, is all pissy about it. She makes it seem like he doesn't know how to drive well enough to teach me. It's ridiculous."

This was a period in which my relationship with Maggie's mother was a lightning rod for the tension that kept rising between them. From Maggie, there was: "I hate her. It's so hard being in the same house with her. We had the worst fight last night. Can you believe that she actually got on the phone when I was talking to Jamie and said that I had too much homework to do to be talking on the phone for so long? Jesus Christ!"

From Maggie's mother came: "Soon it's going to be either her or me! She's unbearable! Is it really supposed to be like this?" When I told her that sometimes the tension between adolescent daughters and mothers was in direct proportion to how close they had been previously, she was somewhat comforted. But the flare-ups continued for some months.

Treatment Process: Final Phase

Notwithstanding the tension between Maggie and her mother, Maggie's relationships at home were generally absent in her sessions. Her focus was almost exclusively on her relationships with her peers, especially the entanglements that took place between the females and males. She also discussed various school projects, anxieties about academic performance, and what she saw as her own talents and weaknesses.

> "I think Roberto is really mistreating Angie. He flirts with everybody in sight when she's not around, but then gives her a hard time for remaining friends with Jimmy. And she and Jimmy really are just friends. I don't know what he does with the girls he flirts with—some of them are definitely attracted to him and they're the types that fool around with anything in pants. Although he even had the nerve to hit on me!"
>
> "Presumably, he knows that you're going out with Pete?"
>
> "Definitely. He just doesn't care. I'm telling you, he's just

into coming on like the hottest thing around. He has no respect for Angie, himself, or anyone else. . . . I feel like telling her, but I don't want to hurt her."

"Tough call—which hurts more, finding out later, knowing your friends knew all along, or finding out from your friends while it's happening?"

"Yeah, I know. This is really hard to decide. It's all about your values. You know, what kind of person you want to be, and all that. Loyalty. Friendship. Sometimes everything seems like it's about everything else. Or maybe it just seems like everything is so important."

"Only when you let yourself really think through things."

"Seems like I can't help myself these days."

"Getting older, I guess."

Maggie's eyes sparkled as she said with a big smile, "Don't say that. Soon we'll be plucking out my grey hairs."

"*Whose* grey hairs?"

"Oh, God. I can't believe I said that. I'm sorry."

I smiled and said. "Hey, look. Everybody gets older. We've known each other long enough that you've noticed that I'm getting older, too. Why be sorry about that? It's life, right?"

"True. I just didn't know if you were sensitive about it or anything."

"What would have been your guess?"

"No. You don't seem the type. But half my friends' parents dye their hair . . . including the fathers! My mother doesn't have any gray hair yet. Wonder what she'll do when she does."

The relationship that existed between Maggie and me was a warm, open one. I had become an object of identification for her in a number of ways, and she felt free to speak of them.

"I've been working out lately, can you tell?"

"You do look quite fit, if that's what you mean. As far as weight is concerned, you've always looked trim to me."

"I think I have to work at it. As you know, both of my parents are overweight, and nobody pays any attention to what they eat at home. And the boys, well, they don't have to worry about it. They're growing so fast these days, they could eat junk food all day and nobody would be able to tell the difference."

"These things have a way of catching up with everybody."

"Well, you've always been thin and you've always looked the same, the whole time I've known you. You look like you watch what you eat and get regular exercise."

"I know this may sound a bit corny, but I do believe that it's important to try to be healthy of body and healthy of spirit."

"I like that. And I guess I knew that about you before you even said it."

Acknowledging the reality of Maggie's observations about my personal commitment to physical health is an example of how, in adolescent treatment, it is important to allow yourself to be an object of identification. This is especially true in the context of becoming such an object in areas in which the adolescent is struggling to differentiate herself. In her family, eating and exercise were areas of conflict and difficulty. Maggie was focusing on me and what she saw as my habits as a way of bolstering her own commitment to remaining healthy and fit. Acknowledging the reality of her observations, both about herself and about me, also underscored her reality testing, another objective of adolescent treatment.

At this time, Maggie was more and more open about what she thought about me, the treatment, and herself. She talked about our past together and a future in which I would not be present.

"It won't be long before I go off to college. I can't believe I'm going to be a junior next year. Then it's one more year . . . that'll be weird." She became quiet for a few moments. "It's going to be really strange not to see you."

"Seems like something you've given some thought to."

"True. I actually have been thinking that I really love talking to you, but I don't know if I feel like I really have any big problems anymore."

"I would agree with that."

"But I can't imagine still living at home and not seeing you."

"What strikes you as unimaginable about it?"

"What if I got into one of those horrible fights with my mother?"

"I'm not trying to play games or anything, but what if you did?"

"I don't know. I guess I could handle it. I could talk to Dad about it, or Emily." Maggie looked at me, but seemed unable to say what was on her mind.

"You have that look—like you want to say something, but are having trouble spitting it out."

"I mean, could I just call you or something? Could I come in and talk to you if I needed to? Would I have to be seeing you every week for you to talk to me?"

"I would always want to hear from you . . . and I would always try to see you as soon as possible. You know, sometimes my schedule gets kind of tight—so it might take a few days—but I would always work it out so that I could see you."

Maggie grinned. She looked visibly relieved. "I thought so, but I was almost afraid to say anything . . . just in case I was wrong."

This began our ending process, which took place over the next two-and-a-half months. We talked about the treatment, Maggie's current life, both at home and in school, and some of her thoughts about the future. There was some discussion of her feelings about me, and mine about her. We both acknowledged that we would miss each other when we were not in regular contact.

"So, I guess this is it, huh?" she said in our last session.

"Guess so."

"I sort of can't believe it."

"Well, we've known each other for a good long time—and certainly all of your time since childhood."

"I'm going to miss you so much."

"Thanks for telling me so. I will certainly miss you, too."

"Well, I'll definitely stay in touch. Maybe I'll write. Would that be okay? I love to write to my friends."

"I'd love to hear from you. And if you write, I'll write back."

It was time for the session to be over. I told Maggie, and she said: "Would it be all right if we hugged goodbye?"

"By all means," I responded, as I came forward to hug her. Hers seemed a request that arose from a middle adolescent firmly rooted in the present.

Maggie did not call, but she did write to me, nearly a year later. She wrote to report that she had done well on her college entrance exams and was doing well in school. She also mentioned that she had been elected editor of the school newspaper for her senior year. She said that things were going well at home, or, as she put, "as well as can be expected."

Her most important news, however, was that she had a steady boyfriend. "I really think I'm in love. I know you'd really like him. He's so sweet, he's really good-looking, and I love talking to him. He's perfect. I only wish you could meet him. Who knows, maybe someday you will." She signed her letter "I still miss you, but in a way you're with me. I still talk to you in my head. Love, Maggie."

DISCUSSION

Maggie was an extremely engaging young adolescent, who immediately—seemingly instinctively—latched onto the treatment. The traumatizing incident that took place when she was a pubescent 9-year-old kept Maggie frozen at the brink of adolescence. She could not go on, for she could not fathom what had happened, what she had seen, and what she felt about it all. Therapy provided her with a place to look at the incident, her reactions to it, and the layers of feelings and fantasies that accompanied and later were constructed over it, in the company of someone who supported her in this process. The moment when she told us both that her mother could have killed her was an extraordinarily moving one; there was a distinct sense of release of long-held emotion that she had struggled to keep from awareness. It virtually reverberated in the room.

Carrying the idea inside her that her mother could have killed her made the deidealization process of early adolescence difficult to initiate. She had to retain a highly idealized version of her mother until she was strong enough to face the unusually non-ideal feelings that existed beneath the surface of her awareness.

It was, therefore, very difficult for Maggie to leave childhood behind. To leave it behind required that she fully face that childhood. Once she was able to begin to do so, early adolescent issues began to enter the discussions in the consulting room with great regularity. Her first descriptions of the intricate interactions with her girlfriends actually reflected many family issues and conflicts, such those related to loyalty and betrayal. Discussing these in the context of her friendships segued into talking about them in relation to her family.

Facing the actualities of her childhood and the real characteristics of her parents in treatment reduced the need for Maggie to avoid looking and seeing. She was, therefore, able to give up her blinking symptom. What she once had needed to "space out," she was now able to fill in with memories, thoughts, and feelings.

Her fear of adolescent life, particularly involvements with boys, derived from larger fears about developmental progression and bodily integrity. Moving on, leaving childhood behind, meant giving up on a fantasy of having someone else take care of her. It was hard for her to give up what she never felt she had adequately received.

Seeing her body as something she owned and was precious was made more difficult by the life-threatening incident with her mother and the surgery that followed it. She had profound fears about bodily integrity and questions about whether it was safe to be intimately involved with other people.

The opening up of these topics for discussion led to a gradual change in her attitude and behavior. She began to take greater pride in her body, which ultimately permitted her to feel more comfortable dating. She also developed an independent way of eating and caring for her body, which helped to distinguish her from the rest of her family and made her feel more at home with her peers.

There were aspects of the psychotherapy with Maggie that were somewhat out of the ordinary. Throughout most of her treatment, for example, Maggie maintained a highly positive relationship with me. Her negative transference was suggested only slightly and intermittently. One example emerged around her fantasies of whether I could possibly have children, and if I did, how adequate could I be as a mother, given that I worked so much. These critical allusions, however, were rare. I had some concern about this very consistent positive transference. Given her life history, I assumed that she had to have some very angry, indeed enraged feelings, fantasies, and thoughts stored up. I was concerned that these might emerge in transformed, self-destructive ways.

The self-destructiveness did not appear at any point in her treatment, nor did any other apparent transformations of her anger. Instead, slowly but surely, she was able to be openly angry toward her parents, especially her mother. This, as noted in the case report, caused her mother to become quite upset, but it was important for Maggie's development and effective in facilitating it. For her to risk being critical of a mother that she felt had threatened her life, both psychically and physically, was tremendously helpful. Through the expression of this anger, she was able to release aggression that she utilized to progress in her development. She seemed to need to retain me as a positive object to aid her in this process.

Though it is common in adolescent treatment for the therapist to become an object of identification for the patient, Maggie's use of me for this purpose was far greater than is usually the case. It seems that she felt that the adults in her life so needed her that she immediately and hungrily turned to me when I provided a safe, non-needy, adult presence. Without my offering direct advice, she used me repeatedly and consistently for guidance about how to live her life, how to formulate values, and how to relate to other people. She carefully took note of everything from how I looked, to how I thought, to how I joked, and incorporated these into ways that she was in the world. She could not rely as much on her parents in these ways because she constantly felt that she had to protect them. Instead, she modeled herself on an idealized image of me, permitted by her sense that she did not have to take care of me.

The consulting room provided Maggie with a truly safe haven for self-examination. It was the only place that she felt free to look inside and out; at home, she was too busy looking out for her brothers and parents to be able to look at herself. Indeed, the whole issue of looking, seeing, and processing what she saw was crucial in her treatment and in her development.

Forming a relationship with me aided her in building up the strength needed to proceed in her development. She saw me as a person who did not need to change herself to suit others, as exemplified by her assumption that I was not the type to dye my gray hair. She also saw me as someone who took care of herself physically; thus, I did not need to turn to others to take care of me. In each case, she saw me as independent and strong, characteristics she needed to form in herself to have the strength to face what had happened to her, how she saw her parents, and how she actually felt about all of it.

Maggie entered treatment still a child, but ended treatment a middle adolescent. Her ending was another of the unusual aspects of her treatment. It is remarkable that Maggie had the ego strength to tolerate what was, for middle adolescent psychotherapy, a protracted ending process. As described in Chapter 6, such endings tend to be far more abrupt.

Maggie ended treatment, however, as she began it. Her sense of connection to me was deep and consistent, her honesty extraordinary in one so young.

9

Inside Out:
A Middle Adolescent's
Wish to Stay at Home

Home is where one starts from. As we grow older the world becomes stranger, the pattern more complicated . . .

T. S. Eliot, *Four Quartets*, East Coker: V

A turning away from the family and toward the world of peers is critical to middle adolescent development. An adolescent of this age who is preoccupied with issues in his family is likely to find such a move outward difficult to negotiate. Kevin is an example of someone with this kind of stumbling block in his middle adolescent development. Though he came into treatment chronologically at the age of a middle adolescent and (physically) looking like a middle adolescent, he still regarded himself as much younger and still struggled primarily with the issues of early adolescence.

What is presented here is a twice-weekly treatment that took place over a period of twenty-seven months. First there will be a brief description of Kevin's history, then the treatment process. The discussion will focus on how his treatment permitted Kevin to feel more rooted in his appropriate development subphase, and, thus, to move from early into middle adolescence.

THE TREATMENT

Kevin began treatment at the age of 17. At first glance, he was a tall, thin, muscular, square-chinned, dark-haired, handsome young man. Upon further study, his averted glance, slumping shoulders, and general air of nervousness made him seem somewhat boyish and timid.

A court ordered Kevin to be in psychotherapy. A couple of months before, he and a friend had broken into a department store. They tripped an alarm system and were caught on the way out. When I asked him if he knew what this incident was about for him, why he might have done it or what it meant for him to have done it, Kevin first said he "really didn't know." A few moments later, he continued by saying, "My friend Billy wanted to do it. He asked me if I was too chicken to do it with him, and I guess I just kind of wanted to see whether I was or not."

Kevin seemed to look at himself from the outside in; he would take an action, then try to infer what his feelings and motivations were from that action. It was very difficult for him to think ahead, to make a plan, or to know what he was thinking or feeling. He often went along with what others wanted to do. By both his own description and his father's, he felt moody, detached, and depressed much of the time. He rarely applied himself at home or in school. Kevin felt that he was a shell of a person. He had little or no sense of inner drive, feeling, or thought. He looked to those around him whom he admired to supply him with self-definition.

History

Kevin's parents divorced when he was 3 years old. Their relationship afterwards was usually amicable, though, according to Kevin, quarrelsome when it came to making arrangements for him. When they divorced, Kevin moved from New York City to southern Oregon with his mother. He lived there with her until he was 10, at which point he came to New York to live with his father for two years. He then returned to Oregon, where he lived until he was 17. At 17, he came back to New York City, where he planned to remain until he went to college. Summers and Christmas were always spent with the parent with whom he was not living.

In describing his history, Kevin tended to focus on the relationships in his parents' lives and his own acts of unexplained violence. His father remarried when he was 5, and divorced when Kevin was 15. His mother began to live with someone when he was 8, whom she married when he was 16. His father currently had a steady girlfriend.

The acts of violence included breaking into his school when he was 8, getting into numerous fights with boys his age, and kicking his father's second wife in the shins. Kevin reported that his father was more effective in controlling him than his mother, but that neither of them was able to understand the roots of his behavior and help him to stop it. Each of these incidents was followed by his being sent to the other parent's place to live. As he put it: "They just got sick of me after awhile. I was too much to deal with, and, anyway, they had their own problems."

Kevin described his mother as a loving, overprotective, somewhat childlike person. She taught pre-school, which Kevin felt was "the perfect age for her. She could be affectionate and playful, and wouldn't have to deal with any serious behavior problems." He said that when he was growing up, his mother was more concerned with finding a new husband than she was with anything else. She didn't understand him very well back then, but she "definitely didn't understand him at all now."

Kevin felt his mother had allowed her boyfriend (now husband) to dominate her and ("even") to dictate to her how she should bring Kevin up. As a child, Kevin had always been frightened of this man. He was subject to bursts of temper, and occasionally "smacked" Kevin "around." To Kevin's knowledge, his stepfather never hit his mother, but he bellowed at her with some frequency, especially when he drank. Kevin often felt enraged at his stepfather, but impotent to take any actions that would protect either him or his mother.

When he was 12, Kevin walked into the living room after school and found his mother and stepfather naked on the couch in an embrace. He felt embarrassed and frightened. Despite the fact that it was obviously quite upsetting to Kevin, the incident was never discussed. At the point that he entered treatment, Kevin vowed never to talk to his stepfather again. He noted that it would be quite a while before he talked to his mother, either.

Kevin's father sounded like a perennial adolescent. He loved fast cars, sports, dating different women, and talking to his son about "scoring." He was multitalented, according to his idealizing son. He could "sing, play the piano and guitar, hit a mean tennis ball, and charm the pants off anyone he bumped into." He and Kevin were pals. Kevin described his father as his idol; he "was always on top of things."

Kevin had two best friends, one on each coast. The one on the West Coast, Billy, was "bad," into drinking, troublemaking, and doing poorly in school. He tried to get away with whatever he could at all times. He came from a family that was "more messed up" than Kevin's. The friend in New York, John, was a more serious student, less into getting into trouble, and from a family that Kevin admired for its stability and "family feeling." Family feeling was noticeably lacking in Kevin's life.

Kevin felt that his own persona changed when he went from one coast to another, based upon who his best friend was and with whom he was living. He believed that living with his father and being around John would insure better school performance and less getting into trouble. He also felt that his father treated him as if he were older and more responsible, and that "made him" act more responsibly.

Treatment Process: Beginning Phase

My first contact was a telephone call from his father, who set up an appointment for Kevin after telling me about the department store incident, how Kevin had always gotten into scrapes with the boys at school, and how he had lived a bi-coastal life. Neither Kevin nor his father thought it necessary for me to meet with anyone but Kevin.

Although Kevin first seemed rather shy, he took quickly to the treatment situation. Within the first few sessions, he began to talk easily and openly about his fears and concerns.

"Life is hairy," he noted. "I'm 17 and I feel like a little kid a lot of the time. I sure as hell—sorry—don't feel ready to be 18, 19, you know, go to college. I don't know where things went wrong with me, but they did."

When I inquired about what he felt was wrong with him, he responded that he had no mind of his own, and that he was "lazy" and "stubborn." He knew he hated "being forced" to do anything, and that it was a matter of pride not to give in when someone tried to force him to do something. He said that this attitude had created serious problems for him in school.

In school, he said that he could only do well if he liked the teacher. He also said that he couldn't talk to girls. He was most successful athletically, but only in team sports. He said that it was easiest for him to make real efforts when it was for the team; individual performance sports were "not his thing."

Individual performance was something Kevin knew was a problem for him. Early on, he told me he could not even lift weights unless someone was in the room with him. This led to our talking about what he needed other people for and what he did not need others for, and how his feelings changed when others were in the room. It became clear that he was easily embarrassed, and that he all too quickly came to the conclusion that he was perceived as "showing off" in situations of individual performance.

Kevin showed real interest in looking at himself in treatment. He said that he was not used to being with an adult who paid such attention to him. It was hard for him to believe that I did not have a personal agenda.

Raising the issue of adults with personal agendas gave Kevin the opportunity to talk about what the major adults in his

life were like, both in the present and in the past. He acknowledged feeling loved by his mother, but noted that he felt it was
a kind of generalized love. "She only loved me because I was her
kid. She never seemed to get very involved in who I was or what
I was doing. As long as I didn't flunk out of school or act fresh
with her boyfriend, everything was okay. As soon as I stepped
out of line in some way, she would cry and plead with me to
behave."

We came to frame these experiences as being about Kevin's
feeling both too important and too unimportant. He felt too
important, because he "made" his mother cry so easily (and so
frequently); too unimportant, because she seemed so uninterested
in who he really was. His "importance" led him to want to tone down
his presence, which we saw as one of the reasons individual
performance was such a struggle for him. His "unimportance" was a
view of himself that he came to see he shared with his mother. Until
beginning treatment, he placed very little value on knowing himself.

The degree to which he relied on others to help him in
establishing what to do was a prominent issue in this first phase of
treatment. He realized that he had never valued his own feelings,
thoughts, and attitudes enough to pay much attention to them. The
fact that I was paying attention and seemed genuinely interested in
him felt like something new to Kevin. When I pointed out that we
might suffer the same problem, in that, once again, perhaps he was
following someone else's (that is, my) lead in looking at himself, he
responded: "Yeah, I thought of that. But this is different. I can use
this to figure out what I really do think and feel, then I can make
up my mind about things. And, anyway, you don't tell me what to
do."

The last part of Kevin's statement was a particularly telling one.
He was seeing something about our working process that he
had not acknowledged before. In general, he had (up until this
time, which was about three or four months into treatment)
often asked me what I thought he should do about one
situation or another, usually related to a school problem (e.g.,

a late homework assignment) or minor disagreement with his father (e.g., a household chore he disliked). My consistent response was to press him about *his* thoughts on the subject, with the explanation that it did not make sense for me to become still another person who would tell him how to lead his life, and that I thought he was quite capable of figuring this one out on his own.

"That's what you always say," was Kevin's smiling response.

"That's what I really think," was mine, also said with a smile.

This was a typical kind of interchange in the first year that Kevin and I worked together. There was a good deal of warmth and humor between us.

After the first few months of treatment, Kevin began to think that his father also had a personal agenda. His first descriptions of his father were practically blemishless: his father could do anything, knew everything, and was (almost) always right. The sole source of conflict between them, from Kevin's point of view, was the unequal distribution of household chores that his father demanded. His father required that Kevin both cook *and* clean up, since he "was the breadwinner." This struck Kevin as unfair and, in his most critical moments, manipulative. "He's the father, I'm the kid. It's ridiculous. I'm not supposed to take up all the slack. I'm not his wife or something. He's jerking me around, just because he doesn't want to do this stuff."

These were the first hints of what became Kevin's growing dissatisfaction with his formerly idealized father. He began to see more and more of his father's self-involvement. Even the nature of his interest in Kevin's life came into question.

"So, big deal . . . he comes to all my games. I think he gets off on it. He likes having a son he can brag is on varsity teams. He sure never makes me feel good about playing. He acts like he's my personal coach or something, always telling me what I did wrong. Like he knows it all. I *have* a coach. *He* tells me how I played. I don't need my father to do it, too."

His father's attitude toward girls bothered Kevin as well.

"He's always bugging me. He pushed me toward some girl in a restaurant the other day, whispering 'hot stuff' in my ear. I was *so* pissed, and *so* embarrassed. I could have killed him for that."
"What happened?" I asked.
"Nothin'. Absolutely nothin'. I didn't say anything to her—and I gotta admit, she *was* cute. And I didn't have the balls to say anything to him, either."
"Takes 'balls?' What happens if you *do* say something to him?"
"I never do. I'm sure he knows I'm pissed. He doesn't care. He just gets a kick out of it or something. Or he really thinks I *should* go after her."

This was a significant point in Kevin's treatment. He began to talk about his father's attitude toward women, his feeling both pushed and upstaged by his father when it came to girls, and his own shyness and timidity when he felt drawn to a girl. He also started to address the tremendous difficulty he had confronting his father. His talking about not having "the balls" to say anything to his father opened up the issue of how he felt about being male, and a young man (as opposed to a boy).

Theses were difficult sessions for Kevin. He felt embarrassed, even mortified at times, about his wanting to remain a boy, rather than entering the world of men. He saw how his reluctance to be the young man he actually appeared to be was connected to his wanting to hang onto having a strong father who could protect him, and how this interfered in his capacity to confront his father directly. He saw that the world of men and women together was a world he felt afraid to enter.

After about eight or nine months, the first phase of this treatment drew to a close. What had been an easygoing, open treatment relationship became more strained as Kevin started seeing his mother in somewhat more understanding and accepting ways, his father in more critical ways, and our work as somewhat more painful than he originally either imagined or experienced it to be. The subject of the relationship between his changed and changing feelings about his parents and his current difficulties with his peers began the next phase of treatment.

Treatment Process: Middle Phase

During the next year (plus) of his treatment, Kevin shifted the way he looked at the world; it went from outside in to inside out. He looked carefully at his own role in the way events in his life had happened and continued to occur. He talked much less about his parents and much more about himself and his relationships in school, both with his peers and his teachers and coaches. The primary context in which his parents came up was in relation to where he saw the origins of his own traits.

The relationship between Kevin and me also shifted. It remained strong, but there was considerably more tension. He sometimes questioned the point of coming for treatment (though he never missed a session and was regularly on time), and said at times that he "hoped that this was going to do something for him" or he'd "really be pissed off." My tendency was to respond to him directly and frankly: to talk to him about how and why treatment could and did help, and to point out that he had already seen how he had changed since he began talking with me and felt good about the changes he had made. I would then address what might be some of the other reasons for his raising these questions now, such as the nature of his difficulty in dealing with what we had been discussing most recently (e. g., his fear of embarrassment).

This phase of treatment was ushered in, in some respects, by the beginning of a new school year. In his first phase of treatment, Kevin had started in a new school. It was a private school in New York City, and more rigorous than his previous (public) school in Oregon. The school required that he repeat tenth grade. Kevin was embarrassed by this in some respects, but relieved in others. He did not want his schoolmates to know he was 17 (when they were 16), but (with me) was openly relieved at the prospect of having a chance to do his tenth grade year again. He had gotten mediocre grades in what he regarded as a "second-rate" school in Oregon, and wanted to see if he could improve in a better school. He initially said that if he were surrounded by kids who cared about school, he would too (an example of what we came to call his "outside in" approach to life).

He did, in fact, get better grades in school (he had a B average, as compared to a C the year before), but was well aware that some of his classes had been repeat classes from the previous year, which made the classwork easier. He also was aware that eleventh grade was a pivotal year for high school students, in terms of college plans, and that his new "inside out" approach to life was moving him in the direction of confronting his own real thoughts and feelings about the future.

His peers were quite caught up in thinking about college applications, and the best high school classes to take for college preparation. Kevin felt highly ambivalent about going to college. He knew that this set him apart from his schoolmates and wondered why he felt the way he did. We began to make connections between his wish to remain a boy and his anger at and disappointment in his parents and their "personal agendas." He realized that he felt robbed of a stable childhood, having been shuttled back and forth between the two coasts. He came to see that he shied away from competing with his father in any way, which eliminated many areas in which he could be exercising his capabilities. Perhaps most importantly, he began to see how the many ways he had sabotaged himself were ways of (passively) expressing the anger and disappointment he felt toward his parents, particularly his father. He felt that it was his father who wanted him to go to college; Kevin did not know whether he had ever decided for himself whether he wanted to go. He only saw it as something that he was going to do because his father wanted him to do it, or he was not going to do it because his father wanted him to do it. "How did I make him this important? It's like my whole life revolves around him, rather than me."

Kevin began to scrutinize himself. As a result, at times he became far more self-conscious, but he also seemed to become stronger and more self-possessed. He was beginning to get a sense of knowing himself.

"I can't stand these zits. What are they from? I never used to have them. At least I don't think I did. But I never even looked, so how would I know? You know, otherwise I think I look okay. I like this haircut. And I've been lifting every morning and I definitely can see the difference."

It wasn't only Kevin who was looking at Kevin. He also began to notice that others, especially girls, were looking at him. He was self-conscious, but intrigued by the prospect that they might be interested in him. "I know Susie was looking at me. You know, not just looking but checking me out. And she's cute, you know? I mean, I could get into that, you know?"

"Kevin, that's a lot of 'you knows' all in one paragraph. Something going on here about what you do or don't know about girls, boy-girl stuff, that kind of thing?" I asked.

"That's a tough one. I know and I don't know. I know I'm supposed to be cool and all that, but the truth is, I think I have some hang-ups about all this stuff. My father is such a stud—at least, that's what he makes himself out to be. But lots of women dig him, so maybe he is. But what does that have to do with me? I don't know. All I know is, when I like a girl, I can't talk to her. I feel like I'm tongue-tied. Maybe it's one of those things where I'm comparing myself to my father. He's such a talker. But I don't think that's all that's going on. I think . . . I can't believe I'm even saying this to you. But if I don't tell you, who the hell am I going to tell? I think I'm really scared shitless to have sex." Kevin looked down at the floor.

"So you think that talking to someone you like immediately gets connected to having sex?"

"Well, you know, one thing leads to another and all that."

"Got any idea what you're scared *of* in having sex?"

Kevin fell silent. I waited a few minutes, then asked, "Can you say what just crossed your mind?"

Kevin clearly felt awkward and uncomfortable. He looked as if he were about to cry and was trying to fight it off.

"I know this is right out of the books or something, but I thought about that time when I walked in on my mother and Pete [his mother's second husband]. I know I told you they

were holding each other, but I really think they were having sex.
I try to block out the whole thing, but that's what I thought
about when you asked whatever you asked me before. What did
you ask, anyway?"

"I asked if you had any idea what you were scared *of* in
having sex."

"Guess something's going on with that thing with my
mother and Pete. I know I was completely freaked out at the
time. I mean, I didn't think my mother ever had sex with him.
I was only 12 for Chrissakes. I didn't want to know about it, I
sure as hell didn't want to see them at it. It disgusted me
completely. It still does, in fact. He's such an asshole."

"Are you disgusted when you think of sex, altogether?"

"Well, I know I've got this thing about which girls will do it
and which won't. I don't want to think that a girl I'd like would
do it—which I know is screwed up. A guy my age is supposed to
want to have sex, right?"

The many issues for Kevin about what he wanted, whether it was
acceptable for him to have wants, sexual and otherwise, became the
major topics of his treatment at this time. Discussions ranged from
sex, to scholastic and athletic accomplishments, to relationships with
friends, to dating girls. Kevin was extremely engaged in treatment.
He often bounded in, and right away began with comments like
this:

"I'm 5′8″, 128 pounds. I want to be 6′, 150 pounds. That's my
ideal. I've been working my ass off in cross country. Coach says
I've peeled a full 20 seconds off in the last two months. He's
totally impressed. He's not the only one. I think it's going to my
head. I almost got myself to say something to Jessica today. Do
you believe it? *Jessica.* She is *so* gorgeous. Hey—do you think
this means something? I've been having this same daydream
over and over again. I'm in Madison Square Garden. It's the last
few seconds of the game. We're down by one. I steal the ball and
haul it down from midcourt, go up for the lay-up . . . and I
score. The clock goes off. The crowd goes wild. I love it."

Kevin felt better and better about himself. The improved self-esteem developed in concert with an increasing awareness of his thoughts, feelings, and fantasies. As a consequence, he was building up his courage to ask out a girl; someone he thought was quiet and pretty and "who seemed kind and thoughtful." He said he thought that he had seen her looking at him, and this was boosting his resolve. The day he managed to talk with her for the first time, he was exuberant.

> "I did it! Do you believe it? I actually talked to Stacey for a good ten minutes after school today. We walked out together. I waited with her for the bus. Maybe I'll call her tonight. What a trip!"

His pride filled the room.

Stacey was the first of several girls he talked to, dated, and with whom he had some sexual contact. There was one girl in particular, Margaret, to whom he became very attached. This opened up a whole other set of issues for Kevin about commitment and closeness.

> "I dunno, Doc. This Margaret thing, it isn't like all the others. She's really something else. She's different. She thinks about things. And her life has been tough. She's also gorgeous, ya know. She's 5′ 8″, thin. She's really got a great body. Her skin is the color of coffee. Her mother's black, her father's a WASP, like my father. Though he doesn't treat her mother too well. A little like my mother's deal. Though he screws around . . . I don't think Pete does that. And she's an incredible athlete. She's beautiful to watch. She does hurdles better than any guy I've ever seen. She's got grace, real grace. And she works really hard in school. She wants to do as well as she can. Not like me, kind of getting by, barely using what I've got. Even afraid to know what I've got and what I don't. Makes me think about what's important . . . where I'm going, all that stuff. Plus she's not as into sex as some of the other girls. It's gotta mean something."

Kevin was troubled by his relationship with Margaret. He realized that he was afraid of getting hurt, or of hurting her. He seemed to have the conviction that male–female relationships inevitably led to someone getting hurt.

"Look. My mother got hurt by my father, and sure got hurt by Pete. My father never stays in any relationship very long, so he's probably afraid of getting hurt."

"So is that it?" I asked. "Don't you think it's possible that there are other ways that people can be in relationships?"

"I don't know. Maybe. Takes work, I guess. You've got to look out for the other person *and* yourself, I guess."

"So what do you think? Does that seem like something that's possible for *you?*" I persisted, knowing it challenged some of Kevin's preconceptions.

"I don't know. Gotta think about it." And he became quiet.

I waited. I knew that these were very complicated issues for Kevin. For him even to imagine being different from both of his parents pressed his sense of separateness, as well as his capacity to be individuated. It seemed important at that moment to do so, but it clearly posed a risk for him.

The session that day ended before Kevin had responded. For the first time, he arrived quite late (fifteen minutes) to his next appointment.

"Sorry I'm late," he said as he walked in. I didn't say anything. "You mad or what? I couldn't help it. I had to talk to my computer teacher after school."

"Hey. I didn't say a thing!"

"Well, I know you shrinks. Everything's gotta mean something. So you probably think I came late because of what we were talking about last time. But that was no big deal. . . . In fact, I've been thinking that I really don't need this any more. I'm fine. I mean, why *do* I have to come, anyway? The court only required six months. It's definitely been way more than that. And I'm okay. I'm fine."

"It's a good thing I didn't say anything. I can't imagine

what you would have said if I had! This is all on the basis of what
you figured I was thinking."

Kevin was silent. He looked angry for a moment, then
broke out in a big grin. "Got you, didn't I? Thought I was outta
here, right?"

"Actually, what I thought was that I probably said something last time that really rocked your boat . . . and I wasn't
sure it was so smart of me to do it."

"I don't know what happened. I know I was upset, and that
hasn't happened in a long time. I was kind of pissed, kind of
sad. I thought about not coming today. Then I couldn't figure
why I felt that way. It bothered me that I didn't understand the
whole thing."

"We touched on some sensitive stuff, you know? For you to
really think about being your own person, different from your
mother *and* your father. Someone who is as he wants to be, not
as he thinks other people want or expect him to be. It's new.
Different."

"Maybe I'm not ready for this," he said, looking down in
front of him. "Maybe," I responded. "But I kind of thought you
were at least ready to think about it."

"Yeah, maybe."

The next few weeks were difficult ones. Kevin was more open
about his ambivalence about independence, but it left him feeling
somewhat more embarrassed than he had been in quite some time.
Outside the treatment, he was feeling very good. His relationship
with Margaret was strong, and he was doing reasonably well in
school—scholastically, athletically, and socially. He also was getting
along with both his father and mother.

"Look," he said to me during this time. "This is the only place
I don't feel good. So why am I coming, anyway? If it wasn't for
this, I'd be batting 1.000."

"That's a tough one, Kevin," I responded. "I figure that the
reason it's hard to come here is that there are some things that
you actually have to deal with that you feel are best dealt with

here. And they're not easy things, you know, they're things like figuring out exactly who you are, independent of your parents and friends. Who you want to be. What you want to do with yourself come next year. These things will be around for you to deal with whether you come here or not."

"Yeah, yeah, okay. I know. But I *am* doing all right."

"You're not going to get any argument from me about that."

And so it went. The push–pull character of the treatment remained, as Kevin continued to try to sort out what kind of person he was and wanted to be. In the consulting room, his spirits went up and down. Outside treatment, he stayed on a relatively even keel. Then one day toward the end of his junior year of high school, Kevin came in and said:

"I'm not going to college. I'm just not ready. I don't care what anybody else thinks, either. Including you. Or my father."

"Something happen?" I asked in a gentle, but matter-of-fact tone of voice.

"I slept through my final this morning. I can't believe it. I can't believe that I still have to screw everything up. What good is all this therapy or anything else? I'm just too screwed up to get anything right. My father was so furious at me. He really screamed. Said that I was just a loser. I'd never come to anything. He was sick and tired of paying for me to come here when it didn't do anything, anyway. Made me feel like shit. But he's right. I *am* a loser. And I never will come to anything. I might as well just give it up. Forget school. Forget this. Let him save his goddamned money." He got up and started pacing around the room.

"What good *is* this? Why *did* I sleep through the thing? I certainly *thought* I set the clock right. But I put it on 'PM' instead of 'AM.' I was so tired, by the time I went to bed, that I couldn't see straight. I just can't believe this. And I was ready for the thing. I studied my ass off for it."

"Which one was this?" I asked.

"Chemistry."

"You were going into this final with about a B, right?"

"Yeah."

"So, certainly, Mr. T. [teacher] knows you're serious about the class."

"True. I mean, I went from a C– to a B. He knows I've been working really hard in there."

"He also knows you're not a loser."

"Maybe if I go talk to him and tell him what happened, he'll still give me a chance to take it."

"You never know unless you give it a shot."

Kevin *did* go in the next morning and talk to the teacher. The teacher asked him if he had heard anything about the exam (he hadn't), then permitted Kevin to take it on the spot. Kevin was enormously relieved, and pleased that he had gone into speak with Mr. T. He actually ended up doing better in school at the end of his junior year than he had ever done before. He was on the honor roll, having achieved a B or B+ average. His father's "knew you could do it" fell on somewhat deaf ears.

"He's full of it. You know what he said to me? He said that he was just trying to get me off my ass by yelling at me the way he did the day I slept through the chem final. Do you believe that? He's always got a quick answer. I felt bad enough that day without his telling me I'd never come to anything."

That summer brought a hiatus in the treatment. With some trepidation, Kevin went off to Oregon for two-and-a-half months. He planned both to have a job and to fulfill the two hundred hours of community service that had been the other requirement of his court proceeding from the department store break-in incident of the year before.

"So, Doc, ya think I'll be okay?" he asked at the end of our last session before the break.

"This is going to be one of those typical answers, Kevin,

because it isn't *really* up to me, you know? So . . . what do *you* think?"

"I could just be a smartass about this. But what the hell. I think I'll be okay. Even without you. *And* Margaret. Even *with* Billy around. But hey, will ya miss me, or what?"

"I don't know, Kevin. At the risk of being a repetitive bore . . . what do *you* think?" I asked with a smile.

"Yeah, you'll miss me. I know you like me. I can tell these things."

"Psychic?" I responded.

"Nah. I just pay attention now. Must have learned something from someone."

Treatment Process: Final Phase

When Kevin returned after the summer break, he was in good spirits. At one point, he had confronted Pete about mistreating his mother; at another, he had told Billy that he thought Billy had to "get himself together or he'd ruin his life." He had fulfilled his community service obligation, and made enough money in his job to get the stereo he had his heart set on buying.

"It was cool. I feel okay about the whole thing. I mean, I really missed Margaret . . . but I handled it. I talked to her almost every night. My mother's gonna freak out over the phone bill. But I even told her ahead of time, *and* I gave her some money for it. And hey, I almost wrote *you* a letter. Okay, I never got it together. But I thought about it. Hope you had a good summer. Did you?"

"Yes. Thanks for asking. I *did* think about you. And I certainly wondered how things were going for you. I'm glad all went well."

"Well, you know, as well you could expect. Pete is still an asshole. Billy is still immature. But my mother was good. I felt like it was the first time I had really talked to her in a long time. She's all right, my mother. And she definitely loves me. Nothing wrong with that. She was really proud of me for making honor roll." His face flushed.

"Sounds like you were really able to be yourself out there," I responded.

"Guess so."

The summer in Oregon worked out better for Kevin than he had imagined was possible. Being back in New York, however, meant that he was expected to go full steam ahead in the college application process. This was not easy for him. He remained unsure about whether he even wanted to go to college.

"I really don't know what the big deal is. I don't mean I'll never go. I just don't feel like going now."

"What would you do instead?" I asked.

"I'll get a job or something. I don't know. What's the difference?" he responded, with some irritation in his voice.

"This subject really seems to bother you. What's up, do you know?" I asked.

"I'm just not like other kids, that's all. Even Margaret doesn't get it. Maybe especially. She can't wait to go. I'm just not into it."

Kevin *did* know more than he was saying. One of the unmentioned problems was that Kevin was unsure about whether he could get into a college that he wanted to attend. His grades had improved dramatically, but his scores on standardized tests ranged from average to below average. Things changed dramatically in December of his senior year.

"The track coach from [a midwestern college he was interested in] was in town today. He told my coach he was impressed with me. Can you believe that? He said my scores were okay enough to get in there, with track and my grades. Maybe I better get those applications out. I can't believe it, but I actually have a chance to get in after all."

"So all this time, you think you've been worried about getting in?" I asked, with a smile.

"You knew that, didn't you?" he said, with a big grin.

"Thought it was possible. But why do you think you didn't bring it up?" I asked.

"Do I have to bring up everything? It was bad enough bombing the tests in the first place." Kevin looked uncomfortable.

"Well, we've got to deal with the facts, you know? We are who we are, and all that." I said this seriously, as I looked directly at him.

"Maybe there are things I don't want to face about myself." He looked pensive.

I waited a few minutes, then asked, "Something in particular you have in mind?"

Kevin looked at me with his jaw set. He seemed sad but determined to let me know what he had in mind.

"There was this party in Oregon. I got really smashed. I don't even remember what I drank, how much. But I *do* know that there was this girl at the party who was all over me. She was, you know, kind of a slut type. Anyway, I woke up with her. We were both naked. I don't even know *what* happened. I mean, I guess I assume we did it. But I don't know for sure. Here, Margaret and I have been talking and talking about it—and *not* done it, because we both acknowledge it means something to us. And I go out there and just have sex with this girl. At least, I assume I did. And without using anything, as far as I know. Man, the whole thing is just lousy. And I feel lousy about it. I haven't told Margaret. I feel like I did something that she would never forgive me for. I don't even forgive myself for it. It's like I'm still a different person when I go out there. And then I felt bad that I didn't even tell you. You made that comment about really being myself out there, and I just couldn't tell you. I *was* mostly myself." He fell silent.

"You think maybe this is you, too? That you're not all one way or another? That you like to party *and* you like to be serious, for example?"

"I don't know. Maybe. I never really thought about it that way," he replied in a low voice. "I think I'm still hung up on being the good boy or the bad boy, and all that stuff."

The next few weeks were hard ones in Kevin's treatment. He came late a number of times, and he missed a session altogether for the first time. The message he left was telling: "Hey, Doc. I'm not gonna make it there today. I've got something to do with my friends that can't wait. I'll see ya next week."

Kevin's attention was shifting again. He no longer seemed to need to be the "good boy" in his treatment that he had been all along. For the first time in the two years he had been in treatment, for instance, he was making a clear statement that his activities with his friends took precedence. He was also struggling with how much to let both of us know more about who he actually was. He was beginning to seem like the 19-year-old he had just become. I was not surprised when he came in and said:

"I don't want to hurt your feelings or anything, but I'm thinking that I've had enough of this therapy thing. I feel okay. It was fine being away over the summer. Obviously, I've been getting along in the last few weeks coming here a lot less. And I don't like having to think about coming, when I've got other things I want to do. You know, with my friends. With Margaret. Whaddya think?" he asked somewhat nervously.

"I'm glad you brought it up," I responded. "I certainly noticed that you were busier with your friends and Margaret than you used to be, and that you seemed to feel less like coming here. . . . But what's this about hurting my feelings?"

"Well, I don't want you to feel insulted or anything if I am not into this anymore."

"That would almost make it seem like I had one of those personal agendas we used to talk about. Strange as it may seem, I think it's great if you feel like this is something that's not as useful for you anymore."

"So you think I'll be okay without it?" Kevin was grinning, but seemed genuine in asking the question.

"What's 'okay?'" I asked.

"Well, you know, I won't flip out or anything," he responded.

"To be honest, I never thought of you as someone who had flipped out in the first place," I said.

"Yeah, I guess that's true. But I *am* used to coming here. And you're okay . . . if I stop, can I give you a call or something if I want to come in or talk to you?" he asked somewhat anxiously.

"What do *you* think? Of course!" I said.

"Well, I don't know. I figured you'd say it was okay, but I wasn't a hundred percent."

"Sounds like you've been thinking about this for awhile," I noted.

"Yeah, definitely."

"So what did you have in mind for when we'd end?" I asked.

"Well, like today, I guess."

"This is one of those things that it might be good to live with for a bit before we make a final decision. What do you think about a few more visits, so we can sum up things and think some about the future?"

He agreed. We planned to meet for two more weeks, four more visits. As it turned out, Kevin only came to two of the appointments. The first one he came late, the next two he missed altogether. He came on time to the last appointment.

The sheer emotional intensity of the ending process was hard for Kevin to tolerate, which he acknowledged in our last session. He said that he would miss me, that he sometimes felt that he didn't know what he had gotten out of coming, but that he had the feeling it was more than he could understand at this point in his life.

"So, I guess this is it," he said, somewhat sadly, as the session came to a close.

"Guess so," I responded, feeling filled with emotion myself, keenly aware of how much I would miss him.

"So, thanks. I'll be in touch," he said as he extended his hand for a handshake.

"Take care," I responded, as we shook hands.

"Yeah, you too," he said softly, as he left the room.

I never heard from Kevin again. I did get a note from his father with the last check, saying that he had gotten into the two colleges to which he had managed to send applications (his way of putting it), and that he would most likely be going to one of them.

DISCUSSION

When Kevin began treatment, his physiological development was that of a middle adolescent, but his psychological development was that of an early adolescent. He knew he was no longer in childhood, but he had never given up the strong desire to be there. He did not want to be his age or at his point in life.

Kevin had an abundance of anger and disappointment toward his parents that he had been unable to confront. This was particularly the case in relation to his father. In maintaining the idealized version of his father that he initially presented in treatment, he was fending off the deidealization process that is so necessary to early adolescent development.

Underlying the anger and disappointment (especially toward his father, but certainly toward both parents), was a storehouse of unconscious guilt. This guilt led him to get involved in situations that resulted in his getting in trouble. The anger and disappointment (about which he was not initially conscious) motivated the guilt, which he attenuated through actions that led him to be punished. This, for example, is what drove him to break into the department store.

His strongly fending off awareness of these negative feelings about his parents made Kevin's aggression relatively unavailable to him in other ways. He tended to express it passively, thus he was unable to excel in school or sports. It also made taking the initiative in social relationships quite difficult.

His attachment and attention were so strongly caught up in his parents and their lives that he had little energy available for the pursuit of his own friendships, girlfriends, or overall sexual and/or narcissistic development. He had focused very little on what kind of man he wanted to be, for instance, or even what it meant to him to be male. His father dominated his image of manhood. The comparison between themselves and their friends so typical of early adolescents, and so necessary for their development, was and had been absent in Kevin's life.

The first phase of treatment primarily focused on these early adolescent issues. We talked about who his parents actually were and had been, when and how he had difficulty pursuing people or experiences that he was interested in, and what it had been like shuttling back and forth between the two coasts. Kevin began to get a sense of the ways in which he had found his childhood troubling, including his parents' "personal agendas," and how, in his mind's eye, their lives had come to take precedence over his own. This aided him in putting his childhood behind him and becoming more focused on his own needs and wants in the present.

Kevin was very struck and moved by my consistent attention to and interest in *his* feelings, thoughts, and fantasies. He was unaccustomed to having an adult deal with him in this manner, and very appreciative of it. It aided him in both attending to and valuing his inner life. While he entered treatment with virtually an exclusive focus on what others around him thought, he was able in the context of treatment to begin to think about what *he* observed, thought, and felt.

By the end of the first phase of treatment, he was squarely involved in the middle adolescent developmental process. His attention was on himself and his friends, more than on his parents and their lives. He was thinking about his own sexuality, including the difficulties in thinking about himself as a man, and as a sexual person. He began to enjoy his own body and capacities in a way and to a degree that had not been available to him before.

In this context, regressive, dependent feelings became more troublesome for Kevin. He resented his reliance on his parents, and my role in his life came into question. His need for me and/or treatment became a problematic issue. His peers were talking about going off to college, while Kevin was struggling with whether he could manage to define his life for himself. He simply did not feel he had enough faith in himself to consider going to college.

Much of the second phase of treatment involved the shift from looking at everyone around him to define who he was to looking within and at himself to define who he was. It was in this phase that he became psychologically the middle adolescent that he was physiologically.

There was, for example, a dramatic shift in his narcissism. This was illustrated by his Madison Square Garden fantasy, awareness of girls looking at him, and interest in his own appearance and performance. While the first phase of treatment was dominated by Kevin's talking about his parents and childhood, the second phase brought with it a focus on Kevin's inner life and social life. This was a change from a predominant focus on separation issues to a predominant focus on individuation issues. This is a critical characteristic of the move from early to middle adolescence.

As a middle adolescent, Kevin felt more solidly rooted in the social world (rather than the world of his family). His relationship with Margaret was especially important in this context, for it made him far more aware of how *he* wanted to be in a relationship and how that differed from the ways his parents had been in their relationships. It also brought up the issues about sexuality that are crucial for middle adolescents to examine.

In the final phase of treatment, though still a middle adolescent in most ways, Kevin demonstrated the first hints of late adolescent development. He brought up issues related to commitment, for instance, in his relationship with Margaret. He showed empathy and mature understanding of her and his mother. At moments, he even showed that he had a real sense of how I felt and thought about him. He also had clearly began to define a sense of who he wanted to be, that is, a mature ego ideal.

This treatment clearly served to aid Kevin in his journey through the adolescent process. Developmentally speaking, when he ended he was solidly his age. He would go off to college just beginning his late adolescent development, as would be the case for most of his peers. He had regained his footing, and was, therefore, back on the path that he had lost in the early stages of his adolescence.

He seemed to have arrived at adolescence unprepared for the vast transformations that are part of this developmental period. He simply did not have sufficient energy available to undergo these changes. The degree of self-involvement and preoccupation of both of his parents during Kevin's early years precluded their attending to him in the ways and with the intensity that he needed for adequate narcissistic and instinctual development to occur.

His attention was turned outward, toward his parents, at precisely the moment when what he most needed was to turn his attention inward. His focus was on staying at home, when what he needed was to proceed out into the world. Thus, the main thrust of the treatment was to support his capacity to look inside as he moved outside the home.

10

Going Through the Motions: A Late Adolescent's Wish to Wait

Gather up the fragments that remain, that nothing be lost.
John 6:12

The integration of the varied aspects of genitality, such as puberty, gender, sexuality, and a mature ego ideal, is the main and most difficult component of the late adolescent consolidation of identity. Celia, the patient described in this chapter, came to treatment at the age of 21 appearing to have negotiated much of this consolidation process. It soon became clear, however, that she was going through the motions of a late adolescent life, but still had to contend with significant early and middle adolescent issues in order to feel that she was solidly grounded in her chronological age and apparent stage in life. She did not know how to proceed in her development; indeed, she did not wish to proceed. The beginning of her late adolescence had been interrupted; it took a number of years of treatment for the process of her development to be reinitiated.

What is presented here is a ten-year psychoanalysis of a young woman who suffered multiple early physical traumata. As is usually the case in circumstances with such traumata, her treatment involved repeated reenactments of those early experiences, painstaking reconstructive work, and an intense and highly conflicted transference neurosis. Her early traumata interfered significantly in Celia's adolescent development. This case discussion primarily will focus upon how the analytic work served as a catalyst for important aspects of her late adolescent consolidation, particularly those that involved her genitality.

THE TREATMENT

When Celia began treatment, she was an exceptionally bright graduate student in a Ph.D. program. She was fair-skinned, of average height and weight, always neatly groomed, and quite pretty. She looked somewhat younger than her age.

Her presenting problems were bulimia and feelings of intense fearfulness with her contemporaries, both female and male. For the first month, the treatment was a face-to-face psychotherapy three times a week. The patient then began to use the couch and moved into a four-sessions-a-week analysis.

Celia suffered from a traumatic neurosis, characterized by episodes of intense anxiety, dissociation, and sleep disturbance. She was also severely hearing-impaired in both ears.

History

Celia was the oldest of three children. She had two brothers; one was two-and-a-half years younger, the other, eight years younger. Her parents were in their early twenties when she was born.

She was told that her mother's pregnancy and delivery were normal. When she was 5 weeks old, however, she began having difficulty breathing, turned blue, vomited constantly, and was rushed to the hospital. At 2 months of age, a tracheostomy was performed. The trache (artificial tube inserted through the neck to assist breathing) stayed in place until she was nearly 5 years old.

The initial problem was the presence of a hemangioma, a blood cyst, in her throat. The cyst prevented normal breathing in the infant-sized throat; the trache was removed when her throat could safely accommodate the lump. Before it was clear that the cyst was a hemangioma (which is irreducible and inoperable), radiation treatment and surgery were attempted. The trache was held in place by a collar. Inside her throat, the presence of the trache caused an accumulation of mucus, which had to be suctioned at regular intervals throughout the day. This was carried out by her mother. First, her mother created suction in a tube that was attached to the trache by sucking on it herself; later, she used a suctioning machine. When she was being suctioned, Celia was made to remain as still as possible. During that time, her food had to be soft, thus much of it was pureed. There were also multiple hospitalizations, examinations, probes, and pictures.

Soon after the trache was removed, Celia developed first one case of scarlet fever, then another. Once recovered, she began kindergarten. It was her kindergarten teacher who detected her hearing impairment. Once it was detected and diagnosed, her hearing impairment was treated by giving Celia hearing aids. Enunciation difficulties, which had arisen because of the hearing impairment, were also treated at this time.

The fact that Celia had learned to speak sufficiently well before her hearing impairment was detected is evidence of her enormous innate cognitive and adaptive qualities, for she had to find ways to accommodate both the trache and the hearing problem. In this bit of history is also evidence of a rather high degree of denial in the family environment. It was a *teacher* who discovered the severe hearing impairment that was probably present from birth and most certainly affected her speech development. It is possible that the hearing impairment developed as a result of the radiation therapy she received or the scarlet fever she contracted, however, the fact that the older of her two brothers had the same type of hearing impairment suggests that Celia's problem was congenital.

Despite an initial misreading of her capacities, which led to her placement in a slow first-grade class, Celia's intellectual abilities showed through from an early age. She always did extremely well in school, something which was given high priority in her family. She also was very athletic and tended to play with boys. This was in stark contrast to the older of her two brothers, who was thin, unathletic, musically talented, and sensitive. The obvious masculine/feminine stereotypes figured importantly in Celia's self-image. She thought of herself as more of a boy than her brother; her brother was thought of by both her and the rest of the family as feminine and girlish.

This older brother was always being encouraged to eat so that he would look stronger, more masculine. Celia, on the other hand, a somewhat pudgy child, was discouraged from eating. Limits were constantly set on the amount of bread and the number of sweets she could eat. The whole eating process was highly regulated in her household; both her mother and father were extremely concerned about their appearances and the way their children looked.

She described her mother as very tailored, very weight-conscious, and somewhat prim. There were no discussions of sex or bodily changes and little physical affection. Celia was given books to read about reproduction and menstruation.

Her father, on the other hand, was more physically available, in the sense of affectionate, although physically present much less. He was a consultant who always worked long hours. He also was described as athletic, super-rational, and argumentative.

Celia was captivated by her father as a little girl. She would sit in the bathroom while he shaved each morning and watch him as he got dressed to go to work. Her mother, who was quite modest, would lock the bedroom door as she got dressed in the morning. Celia was not permitted to be with her.

At night, her mother would give Celia a perfunctory peck on the cheek. Her father would lie down in bed next to her and play a game in which he would make believe that it was *his* bed and that she was invading it.

During her mother's pregnancy with her second brother, Celia's first brother became particularly thin. There was a great deal of attention paid to making him eat more so that he would "fatten up." Her rivalry with her brother and fascination with her mother's pregnancy led to a preoccupation with the Hansel and Gretel story and her first secret eating experiences. She would sneak the bread and candy that she was forbidden to eat and her brother encouraged to eat. After her mother delivered her younger brother, Celia developed tonsillitis. Soon after, she had a tonsillectomy.

When she reached puberty, Celia began feeling somewhat isolated and anxious. The boys who had played with her as youngsters were no longer so interested in her; the girls with whom Celia had previously had very little contact rarely included her in after-school activities. In an effort to gain their attention, she invited a group of the girls over and made the older of her two brothers strip and exhibit himself in front of them.

With the advent of puberty, the fact of Celia's femaleness was more apparent to her than it had been in childhood. She had a good deal of trouble integrating this. Speaking about the exhibiting incident with her brother brought into focus aspects of Celia's response to the growing awareness of herself as female. She felt a sense of loss, humiliation, shame, envy, and rage.

To add to the anxiety she was experiencing with her peers were some tensions at home between her father and mother about his extensive traveling. This was a first. Celia's parents had fought very little in front of her before this time.

Celia finally made her first close female friend at the end of ninth grade. The friend was a dancer; she was tall, slim, and graceful. In an attempt to be closer to her friend by looking more like her, Celia went on a diet and lost 30 pounds. Her parents were very pleased, they commented frequently about how pretty she looked. It was the first time they had attended to her appearance with such apparent pleasure.

A year later, her father spent a number of months on the West Coast while the rest of the family remained in the suburbs of Washington, D.C. (where they had always lived). When he returned, he told the family that he was going to have to be out there for the following year, and he wanted all of them to join him.

Celia was deeply upset. She was in her junior year of high school, at the head of her class. Finally, she was more comfortable socially. And now she was told that she would have to move away for her last year of high school, a year she was looking forward to with great anticipation. She was to be the school valedictorian, she fully expected that some of the boys she had been talking to on a regular basis would ask her out on dates, and she was secure in her friendship with her best friend. The idea of moving made her feel absolutely frantic.

Her mother and brothers were not enthusiastic about moving, but were not about to fight with her father. He was far more outspoken and opinionated than any of them, and they did not want to argue with him. Celia often described her mother as someone who almost never expressed an opinion or a feeling. Her mother may well have been depressed on and off throughout Celia's childhood.

After a good deal of *sturm und drang*, Celia's family did move to the West Coast for her senior year of high school. It was during this year that Celia's clear bulimic pattern began. She binged secretly on sweets and bread, in particular, and made attempts to "get rid of it" by taking laxatives and running excessively. She did, however, steadily gain weight. She felt desperate, unattractive, out of control, and unhappy. She was often exhausted, stayed home from school a good deal, and felt terribly isolated. She described trying to tell her mother what was going on, but feeling unable to. In her own words, "I couldn't tell her, but I tried to show her—tried to make her see me." She reported having had frequent visits to physicians. She knew at the time that she wanted them to realize that something was very wrong.

It was a transition point for Celia. For the first time in her life, she had a major conflict with her idealized father. Her father had, to some degree, become the nurturing "mother" figure whom she felt she had missed in her relationship with her actual mother. The rage that welled up inside her was channeled into the compulsive, self-destructive, even violent bingeing and purging.

The year was a tremendously painful one. It was followed by four years in a highly competitive East Coast college where her bingeing and purging continued, as well as her struggles with her peers. She made a few friends in college, did well academically, and had a number of sexual experiences. These sexual experiences did not include either intercourse or much pleasure. When involved sexually with a man, Celia would become numb, dissociated. She often attempted to overcome her anxiety by drinking alcohol. She was flirtatious and flamboyant in party situations and gave the appearance of being more sexually experienced than she was. She led many friends to believe that she was quite sexually active, even though her actual experiences were rather limited in number and in physical activity. She went to see a therapist in the college counseling center for a year during this period.

Treatment Process

Celia began treatment by talking about her compulsive eating and the ways she "got rid of it" by drinking excessive amounts of coffee and taking laxatives, which gave her diarrhea. She spoke of feeling strange, animal-like, because of this. It was very difficult for her to describe exactly what she ate, how and when.

Once again, as a first-year graduate student, she was feeling alienated in school: unknown and unrecognized. In the first few weeks of treatment, she said that she had a great deal she wanted to talk about but that she felt very self-conscious. She could not help but watch me carefully for any reactions I might be having, particularly as she described her binges. She seemed anxious, frightened, and needy.

When she talked about her early medical history, Celia was affectless, almost mechanical in movement and speech. She did not mention her substantial hearing impairment (a 75 percent loss without her hearing aids and a 40 percent loss with them) until I introduced the possibility of her using the couch. At that time, she said she thought it might be easier to talk if she weren't looking at me, but she was concerned that she would have difficulty hearing me (even if she were wearing her hearing aids). It was with a sense of great humiliation that she then told me of her hearing impairment, and the history of its detection and treatment. Her family's emphasis was on its "not mattering." She was "just like everybody else." Celia said that she never felt like everybody else but always did what she could to *appear* to be like everybody else by hiding her hearing aids and choosing her words carefully, to avoid words that were hard for her to pronounce. (Her enunciation difficulties had led me to speculate that Celia might have a hearing impairment.)

On the couch, Celia remained extremely tense. She spoke more freely, but in a monotone. She described numerous fantasies with vivid physical images: blood pouring, cutting, piles of feces, hot metal coming into her. They reminded her of her preoccupation as an early adolescent with the Holocaust: the skinny children, the human experimentation, the death, chaos, torture, and injustice. She became very frightened and started calling me at night and over weekends with great frequency. Her messages on the answering machine were panicky: she could hardly breathe, she felt choked, she felt so lonely it hurt. She was far more expressive of her need and wish for me on the answering machine than she was in the office.

The treatment was off to a stormy start. The transference was intense and preoedipal in nature. I was primarily the mother and doctors who were necessary for her survival and who required that she keep herself as still as possible while being suctioned or examined. The fact that there were sessions, with regulated beginnings and ends, and a couch to lie on—all of it was used in the service of repeated reenactments from her early years. The couch was the doctor's examining table, the bed she would lie on while she was being suctioned or undergoing some medical procedure. The regulation of the sessions felt like the countless experiences of relying on doctors and her mother for regulation of her bodily systems. The doctors and mother seemed to form a composite image (representing those who had been responsible for her survival) in one version of this early transference. The formation of composite images was an important and repeated phenomenon in the treatment.

The blood, the feces, the cutting, the Holocaust: one by one, we sorted and sifted out what it felt like to be that infant and young child with repeated experiences of being filled up with mucus which had to be suctioned so that she could breathe and speak, filled up with pureed food which led to softened feces that were difficult to hold in, a body that was examined and experimented on, and so on.

This first phase of treatment lasted for about two years. It was a period with an enormous amount of reenactment. Over and over again, the physical traumata of her early years were reexperienced. My interpretations were largely aimed at reconstructing these events and the analysis of the massive denial, repression, suppression, and isolation she used to keep herself from being constantly overwhelmed. In time, as she spoke of these early experiences, her affect became integrated with the content of the memories.

It was a very difficult period in the treatment. Celia had frightening images, urges, and feelings. She suffered with sleeplessness and general anxiety, and felt compelled to binge, purge, drink, call me repeatedly, and sob endlessly at night. All of it seemed to come at once. She was multisymptomatic and in a great deal of pain. Sorting it out, piece by piece, was painstakingly slow for her.

The sense of crisis was an important part of it all, the sense of crisis which she had had to repress over and over again as a child. It was crisis evoked by both external and internal danger. Externally, there were all the medical procedures; internally, there was an enormous amount of repressed rage and fear.

I felt confused, ineffectual, and fearful at this time in the treatment. It was very difficult to understand what was happening. I suspect I was experiencing some of Celia's repressed reactions, as well as the reactions of her parents and doctors. Countertransferentially, I had to struggle with frustration about the repetitive phone calls, helplessness in my attempt to lessen her general anxiety, and fear with regard to the possible danger to her physical well-being because of the excessive use of laxatives and caffeine in her purging.

A thread emerged at this time which helped to bring this beginning phase to a close and permitted a consolidation of the transference neurosis. It was a thread of understanding related to the difference between Celia's behavior toward me in the office and her behavior toward me in her messages on the answering machine. In the office, she almost never addressed me directly, except to ask: "What can I do about these images? How can I make them stop? Why does it hurt so much at night?" On the answering machine, she would leave messages saying that she loved me, needed me, couldn't stand being without me. She would plead, "Couldn't I help her? Wouldn't I help her? Why didn't I *do* something?!"

The answering machine was a critical component of the treatment experience. It mediated the relationship between us, it permitted there to be a connection, much like the suctioning tube that allowed a connection to her mother, the hearing aids a connection to the world of sound. These mechanical devices were hidden, as she kept a part of her connection with me hidden. Interpreting this led to a phase in which she saw me as cold, mechanistic, and distant. This first was seen as a maternal transference, then it became clear that I was the prosthesis, the mechanical device. She used me, I did something for her, but there was no real human connection between us. She used the sessions to empty herself of feelings and thoughts which permitted her to function in the world outside the office. What was inside her was like so much waste of which she had to rid herself: mucus, feces, other bodily substances.

She remembered wanting to be messy, wet and gooey, particularly at night. She would have to urinate, and thrill in holding it in, and then letting just a little leak out. She recalled being wet, and touching herself to soothe the pain of being alone after her father left. She remembered calling out to her parents, saying that she needed to be cleaned up, or being in the bathroom and asking to be wiped.

This allowed the interpretation of the sexualization of the medical procedures: the ways in which she derived pleasure and relief from being filled up and emptied out, the warmth and wetness of the mucus, the feces, and the substances which flowed from her vaginally. The almost overwhelming excitement at night of being with her father emerged and was related to the desperate need she felt for me while at home in the evenings. Once again, she spoke of being filled up with feelings, urges, and the need to let them out to me.

This was then contrasted with her desire to take in every bit of me she could—in essence, to binge on me. She had a dream in which she was with her therapist from college. In the dream, the therapist says she is going to tell Celia about her life "in order to ease the pressure." She will say where she is from, who her husband is, what her religion is. Celia goes out from the therapist's office angry and tells the head of the college clinic what has happened.

Tearfully, Celia spoke of feeling empty every time she left our sessions. She would go out and buy bagels and candy bars, eat them all on the way home, and feel that she was doing something terribly wrong. When I suggested that there might be something she felt was terribly wrong that she wanted from me, she became very quiet. Then she said, "You know, don't you?" I responded by saying, "Perhaps there is something *you* know that you feel is terribly wrong?" Celia cried, "I'm sorry. I'm so sorry—I just can't stand not knowing about you."

She then spoke about having seen me on the street with someone she assumed was my husband, following us, seeing us go into a building, then looking in the telephone book. She figured out that the building we had gone into was my apartment building. This gave Celia the opportunity to talk about wanting to know private things about me, wanting to steal the knowledge and hide it, if it weren't freely given. She described her rage at not being given free access to me and my life and her jealousy. She said that what she *did* know about me made her feel very powerful. Once the taking-in process was identified as one which made her powerful, it became possible to see a phallic element in her bingeing, as well as a jealous, enraged one. When she left the sessions and ate, she felt that she had taken the authority and control away from me and put it into her own hands. She *took* what she had been deprived of by me: me as mother, me as father, and me as mother and father together. The putting in of the food was a masculine identification; the receiving of the food, a feminine identification; its ingestion, an oral-sadistic component.

It then became necessary "to get rid of it," get rid of the fantasied forbidden knowledge and the satisfaction of the forbidden urges. In fantasy, she had found a way to be included in the parental bedroom drama. The jealousy and rage was toward me as her oedipal opponent and preoedipal supplier: the mother who could have Celia's father to herself, and the mother who not only performed her nurturing, life-sustaining function in a controlled and distant manner, but seemed almost to be draining Celia in the suctioning process, rather than offering her supplies. She was the father who rejected Celia to be with her mother, and the father who supplied her with affection. She was the father and mother who were together, thus excluding her.

Celia felt powerless, empty, and alone in response to not getting what she wanted from me. Her ritualized bingeing and purging managed to contain reactions that spanned all the childhood psychosexual stages: the *oedipal*, in the intense jealousy, exclusion and identification; the *phallic*, in the way she could shore herself up and take control through the putting in of the food; the *anal*, in the massive control over bodily processes that she felt she had to exercise; and the *oral*, in the sense of necessity she felt to have contact with me after she had binged and purged. The preoccupation with these prohibited her from progressing into the adolescent psychosexual stage of genitality. Each of these childhood psychosexual stages was tinged with crisis, the effect of the cumulative physical traumata.

This middle period of the analysis involved much interpretation along these lines. Both the adhesiveness of her libido and the enormous quantity of aggression that she had to bind in her life made Celia's transference neurosis a particularly charged and chaotic one. In the oedipal transference, the positive oedipal was intensified by her father's nocturnal bed games; the negative oedipal by the suctioning process, which left Celia feeling drained and needy of her mother's love and attention.

This process was complicated by Celia's tendency to feel disbelieved and misread. This stemmed from a number of sources. Certainly, she felt that there was a general lack of understanding of the importance of her inner experience shown both by her parents and the doctors who treated her. Celia did not remember anyone ever explaining the various medical procedures to her, nor was she ever forewarned about an upcoming medical procedure. For example, she was not told beforehand that the trache, which had been attached to her for all of her conscious life, was going to be removed. It was as if no one realized that she would have thoughts, feelings, and fantasies about such an experience. That Celia was placed in a slow learner's class in school, that she had hearing impairments, and that people had difficulty understanding her speech, all contributed to her tendencies to feel disbelieved and misread as well.

Her parents' attempt to normalize her experience both for themselves and Celia, to make it seem as if she were "just like everybody else," served to help in Celia's external adjustment, in school for instance, but it created a whole hypercathected, inner private world for her. This was a world filled with rage, torture, fear, and impotence. Letting someone into that world, showing both herself and someone else what that inner drama looked like, was very difficult for her.

As the meaning of her ritualized bingeing, purging, and calling became more evident, it diminished. More and more of her expressions of love and rage were brought into the treatment sessions themselves. Her fear that these expressions of strong feeling would overwhelm me, that I would, in essence, feel that I had binged on her, been overfilled by her, and then need to rid myself of her, was articulated, as well as how this fear had infiltrated all of her close relationships.

The calling became infrequent and the purging almost stopped. The purging, which was her most dangerous symptom, was analyzed in the context of the denial of her physicality, her physical vulnerability, and the difficulty she had in developing regulatory mechanisms for her bodily processes. Her rage at being intruded upon in so many ways also had to be addressed. When she felt compelled to rid herself of what she had overeaten, Celia went running to burn up the calories.

The bingeing became periodic rather than daily. There was much interpretation of the meaning of her multiple physical losses: the collar, the trache, the suctioned mucus, the removed tonsils, even the softened feces. Her attempts at filling her throat with food so that she could feel the phallic lump, thus feeling powerful and whole rather than punctured and mutilated, were shown to occur as various castration fantasies, as well as more general fantasies of the loss of bodily integrity, emerged. An oral-sadistic component also was interpreted: a component which evolved from a preoedipal primal scene fantasy and a fantasy in which a frustrated and enraged Celia bit off her father's or her older brother's penis-breast during fellatio.

She was at a point in her graduate education when she was teaching and working on her dissertation. In the teaching, she became bent on dazzling both me and the students with her brilliance. In the context of so much injury, her intellect had become invested with phallic-narcissistic significance. What emerged at this time, however, was also a new desire to be not only brilliant, but beautiful. She wanted her students and me to be impressed with both how she looked and what she said. On the days when she came to sessions before teaching, she was often well dressed. At these times, she walked into the office in a slower, more deliberate manner. She then carefully placed herself on the couch. The integration of many aspects of her physicality into her constellation of self-representations preceded this development in the treatment. Once the importance and meaning of her physical development in both its normal and unusual aspects was established, Celia was able to make the most of it, an adaptiveness which served her well throughout her life. She went back for speech therapy to improve her enunciation, to an audiologist to try out a new kind of hearing aid to improve her hearing capacity, began to wear contact lenses, and bought quite a number of new clothes.

The experience of teaching evoked many memories of her early relationship with her younger brother. She had spent long hours teaching him various games and skills when they were children, both to help him in his personal habits and to help him learn school skills. Just as this early relationship had stirred up a competitive entanglement with her mother, so did her current teaching stir up positive oedipal competition with me. The interpretation of various aspects of her femininity and the teaching also reawakened a strong maternality in Celia, something she had felt in her relationship with her younger brother and now felt toward her students.

When these changes occurred, in her fourth year of treatment, she began to masturbate. She said at the time that it was the first time in her life that she had done so. This masturbation appeared to be in the service of performing some maternal function on her own behalf, that is, providing self-comfort and release of tension. It also was in the service of getting to know her body and its reactions, particularly genitally, as is the case for many masturbatory experiences during adolescence. A compulsive component quickly developed, however, which remained for some time.

The typical masturbatory situation involved Celia's beginning to read for her dissertation, becoming aroused, and, in her words, having to "do something about it . . . The tension is so great. I just have to do it. It's like I'm getting rid of something. Almost like a part of my body. I get all filled up—and then I just have to do something to get rid of the filled-up feeling." There was a clear parallel with her prior compulsive bingeing and purging.

At some point in the masturbatory process, as she got more excited, Celia went into a dissociative state that was similar to that into which she entered in her sexual encounters with men. She had an orgasm, but was most often numb when it occurred. The repeated medical procedures, all of which were performed without anaesthesia (except the tonsillectomy), played a role in this overdetermined phenomenon. She went into her inner world and stayed still, the adaptive mechanism she must have utilized in her early life. She then hung on to the omnipotent composite fantasy figure that existed in that inner world, for to be aware of the other person throughout a sexual encounter is to be aware of her femaleness and her partner's maleness.

In the masturbatory situation, the reading represented plunging into her inner world and the world of forbidden knowledge. Her repetitive conscious fantasy while masturbating was that either I was or she was being fed by a man. In my case, it was my husband. As the female of the fantasy was being fed, her belly would get bigger and bigger, rounder and rounder, and the male would touch it. This was interpreted in a number of ways. It was a fantasy of oral impregnation, particularly harking back to her mother's pregnancy with Celia's second brother. It was a fantasy of body as phallus, in which the putting in of the food was a way of making the body/phallus erect, a fantasy that illustrated the importance of touching and physical acceptance. It also was a fantasy demonstrating the strength of her wish to be privy to the primal scene.

During this period, she became very interested in pursuing a relationship with a fellow with whom she had become friendly in her graduate program. They began to see a good deal of each other, but then he withdrew from her. While they were seeing and talking to each other with some frequency, her masturbatory activity nearly ceased.

She had a dream at this time in which her department moved and she lost her mail box. She spoke of the movement that she felt had occurred in her and her awareness of change. She said she had felt scared in the dream about losing her mailbox, then laughed and said: "I wonder how you spell that word, 'mail.'" I interpreted the wish and fear in both holding onto and losing her "male-box," the composite, all-powerful male/femaleness, her fear of these changes and the sense of loss which accompanied them. "Yes," she said, "I know what you mean. And you know what the biggest fear of all is right now? That if I continue to change and grow, that if I have a boyfriend, have intercourse, have a degree, I'll lose you."

The fact that Celia made some reference to her own growth was a real change; the fact that she linked it to losing me is indicative of the continuing relative lack of differentiation in her object relations. She simply could not fathom that there was room for both of us in the world. To give you a flavor of what it was like to be with her at this time in the treatment, which was toward the end of the middle phase—in the sixth year—I will report a bit of process. These were sessions which took place soon after we had returned from the August vacation.

The First Session

Patient: [comes in smiling]. The courses went really well yesterday—
            I'm really excited about the teaching. [She goes on to talk
            about two writing courses she is teaching, the literature she is
            using to teach them, and interactions with the students. In
            this context, she says several times that she is never quite sure
            that the students "get" what she is saying, that she can

"connect" with them, that there isn't "static" in the communication between her and the students, etc.]

Analyst: Perhaps there is some way you are generalizing from your
impaired auditory capacity to your capacity to "hear"
people in a broader context.

Patient: I think that's true. I never believe I am hearing people.
Maybe I don't even think that they can hear me.

Analyst: It has always been hard for you to believe that I hear you.

Patient: I never think you *believe* me. My parents never believe me.
[She goes on to detail several recent exchanges with her
parents in which they questioned her judgment and her
honesty—whether she had done something she was supposed to do or not, whether she really did something that
she had said she was going to do, whether she should do
something other than what she said she was going to do.]

Analyst: There's a good deal about what's *actually* happened.

Patient: And always stuff about whether I have done it or not. They
never think I have done what I was supposed to do. I guess
I never think I have, either. I never think *you* think I have,
either.

The Second Session

Patient: [seems annoyed]. I'm sick of these confrontations. One of
the students keeps challenging me—everything I say is to
be questioned. Why can't he just listen to me!? He reminds
me of that student last spring—the one I ended up having
to go to the Dean about. I hate feeling pushed. I always feel
like they're saying I'm not doing enough—not saying
enough, being enough. [Patient goes on to talk about all
the ways that she feels like she is being pushed by her
parents, her students.]

Analyst: Feel pushed by me?

Patient: Guess so . . . sometimes I want to scream out, "What do
you want from me?"

Analyst: A way of pushing me away?

Patient: Well, I never know when I'm doing enough for you. I

always feel like you want me to say more, do more. I feel
like I always have to push. I'm sick of pushing. Always
more, more, more. And, then, you know what happens, of
course. I push and push, then feel depleted.

Analyst: And think about bingeing?

Patient: I started to last night. I wanted to call you. I felt so tired.
You know, it really *is* like the difference between eating and
bingeing—not knowing when I've had enough is like not
knowing when I've done enough. And as soon as I feel like
I have been pushed, or I have to push, I feel like eating.

Analyst: Or feel like you want more and more of me?

Patient: I never feel like I have enough of you. In some ways, I
never feel like normal eating is enough, either. Normal
eating leaves me feeling like something is missing.

The Third Session

Patient: [seems to avoid looking at me as she enters the room]. I
feel like I want to eat all day long. It's really like an
addiction. . . . You know, I know we both had come from
teaching yesterday. It just seems so stupid. I wanted to talk
about it directly. These secrets are so stupid. I have such a
thing about knowing where you are when I'm not here. I
loved knowing you were teaching when I was teaching. I
thought about you doing it. [She goes on to talk about how
she knows that I teach, where I teach; she has known for a
long time. She loves that we teach in the same university.
Even though she knows why I don't tell her things like this
about myself, that she feels like I'm keeping secrets.]

Analyst: So perhaps it's not the food so much as it's me that you
want to devour! It certainly seems that you feel like I have
been holding back from telling you things.

Patient: Well, you *do* hold back, don't you? I guess this time you
could say I was holding back. Maybe you didn't even know
that I knew that you were teaching then. I forgot that I
never told you I knew. And then I get into this whole thing
about doing what you do—maybe even being like you—

and think you don't say anything about it because you
don't consider yourself to be in the same category as me or
something.

Analyst: Knowing things about me or doing something I do allows
you to feel close to me; if this remains secret, you feel
rejected?

Patient: I feel rejected so much of the time. I feel like you don't
really want to be close to me. [Patient cries.]

It was extremely difficult for Celia to express directly her anger
and frustration with me. It was not until this time in the treatment
that the anger started to emerge with more overt clarity. She was
upset with me for not taking charge of her more directly: she said
that she wanted to be completely out of control, make a mess, be
anything but normal. She was acutely aware of her desires to be
passive, and all of this took place as she began to acknowledge
feeling more real in most contexts of her life.

This prompted a fuller discussion of the pressures she felt to be
"normal" growing up. Her parents' emphasis on her being "just like
everybody else" rose to the surface. At this time, she met a young
man in her department with whom there was reciprocal interest.
The "normality" of this was both exciting and frightening to her.

The relationship progressed to the point of sexual intimacy. In
the physical relationship, Celia felt more than she ever had before.
Within a few months, she had her first experience of sexual
intercourse. She was able to remain aroused and engaged in the
experience, but was unable to reach orgasm during intercourse. She
did permit her partner to bring her to orgasm through manual
stimulation.

This was a turning point in both her life and in her analysis.
The romantic relationship progressed to a mutual decision of
marriage. Celia was thrilled: she felt she truly loved Benjamin, she
looked forward to having a life with him, and she began to feel that
much had been accomplished in her analysis. She also began to
question who I was to her and who I would be in the future. For the
first time, she started to talk about what it would be like not to be in

analysis. This heralded the termination process, which took place over the next three years.

Planning for her wedding prompted a serious look at whether she wanted to invite me, and what her relationship with her parents was like both in the present and in the past. She acknowledged missing the very needy part of herself, and having real longings to revert to calling me frequently, bingeing and purging, and being angry at her parents for not being as emotionally present as she had wished them to be. She struggled with these longings, sometimes giving in to them, sometimes remaining able to observe them without enacting them. She became determined to keep the wedding an event that felt like it belonged to her, rather than to her parents, and ultimately decided that she would be more comfortable and tuned in to what was going on if she did not ask me to come.

She had a wonderful time at her wedding, but said that she was aware that she was losing some connection to me. She sensed that her comment from a few years ago was coming back to haunt her, that is, that having a boyfriend and so on would mean losing me.

Although Celia was making real progress in the area of her personal relationships, she continued to have enormous difficulties working on her dissertation. She felt that I was holding back from telling her why this was the case. She resented her own normality, once again, and wanted to demonstrate that she still needed me by showing how troubled she was: she accumulated credit card debt by buying expensive makeup, which angered her new (rather frugal) husband; she spent hours at home trying to read for her dissertation and write, and found herself distracted by old fantasies and desires to masturbate; and she began abusing a drug she was given to regulate her thyroid activity (after a thyroidectomy that was prompted by the detection of precancerous cells that probably resulted from her exposure to radiation as an infant, when there was an attempt made to reduce her hemangioma through radiation treatment).

Celia succeeded in raising the level of intensity in the treatment to the point of crisis by her abuse of the thyroxin. The drug itself raised her metabolism, which created the appearance of tremendous anxiety in her and, certainly, the real experience of anxiety in me. She was putting herself in a life-threatening situation that served as counterpoint to her otherwise more and more "normal" life. While I focused on the drug abuse, she started being more open with her husband about her expenditures and making progress with writing her dissertation. Toward the end of the eighth year of her treatment, she also achieved orgasm during sexual intercourse.

Interpreting her wish to speed up and gloss over her feelings about ending with me and moving on in her life was effective in helping Celia re-regulate her use of the thyroxin. She had a dream in which she was having heart surgery, that strings were being cut in her heart, and that I was there along with her parents. She started to cry in the session that she reported the dream, knowing that there were "strings," connections, being severed between us and between her parents and her. We were no longer really playing the same roles in her life, and it was hard for her to conceive of alternative relationships.

We set an ending date for a year and a half from that time. This was a period filled with questions like "How was she supposed to feel? How could what she feels be 'normal?' What should she *do* with her feelings?" It was a moving time, in which Celia struggled more and more to see me as a real person and to be a real person with me.

One day I coughed several times in her session. At first, she did not say anything, then she hesitatingly asked if I was okay. It was the first time in all the years of treatment that she directly addressed me in this way. Both of us acknowledged this, then Celia said that she worried about bursting the bubble in which she felt we had functioned for so many years—a bubble in which I had no real needs or wants, and one in which she was the only one who was needy or wanting. The bubble was precious to her, but left her feeling small, smaller than she was now actually feeling. She then spoke of feeling proud about the dissertation work she had been doing, which advisors had told her was brilliant, proud of her ability to be open with Benjamin, and extremely excited about the possibility of getting pregnant—a subject she and Benjamin had been discussing a great deal.

Celia did become pregnant in the next few months, defended her dissertation, and applied for academic jobs. During this time, her husband was offered a job in another city. When it began to look like both the baby and her particular field of interest were reducing the likelihood of her getting her own job, along with the ever-narrowing field of choices left open to her by virtue of where her husband was going to be, she began talking about changing fields and becoming a psychoanalyst. She pressed me about whether I thought this was something she could actually do. I interpreted her wish to be like me as a way of keeping me in her life and her abiding curiosity about what was going on inside her, but did not respond to her wish to have me give her permission.

The ensuing months were intermixed with her fears about childbirth, which we dealt with as both related to the actual upcoming event and her termination, her anticipation of moving away from family, friends, and me, and the ending of her analysis. In this time, she had a dream in which she was unsure about whether she had an appointment with me or not. In reaction to the dream, she brought up questions about what kind of contact we might have in the future: whether I would respond if she wrote to me, whether I would see her or talk to her over the telephone, and so forth. She said that she felt quite ready to end the analysis but did not want to lose touch with me. She felt sad, overwhelmed, aware that she would miss me terribly, and a nagging sense of lack of completion. The nagging sense of lack of completion was connected to her lifelong sense of being physically unlike other people, that is, incomplete, and a fantasy of possible perfection, which she related to the overidealized version of me that she carried for many years of her treatment.

She gave birth to a baby boy a couple of months before her termination date. She was thrilled, but anxious about breastfeeding, and then quite frightened by the pediatrician's discovery that the baby had a congenital heart defect, which, ironically, could result in his not being able to adequately oxygenate his blood, thus turning blue. What would have to happen to remedy his medical condition was unclear at this time, but she did know that surgery was inevitable.

Just before the ending date, Celia had a dream in which she did not have enough gym to graduate. Her fears of lack of bodily integrity, lack of sufficient strength to deal with her baby's problems, not having had enough of me—all poured out. And yet she also noted that she felt fortunate to have had the chance to look at her own early medical experiences in the way that we had together.

The last session was very moving for both of us. Close to the end, she said she did not know what to say; I noted that she really did not have to know, that sometimes feeling was enough. She said that she was sad, but that she had come to see this as the ending of a chapter—in her life and, she hoped, in our relationship with one another. As she stood up to leave, she said, "Thank you very much." I told her to "Take good care," and she responded, "You, too." I was keenly aware of the greater sense of reciprocity that now existed between us.

DISCUSSION

The discussion of this case clearly could take many routes. The profound and repeated early traumata and their effects on the treatment, the etiology and treatment of her eating disorder, the nature of her object relations, her identifications, and the transference–countertransference relationship, are but a few of myriad possibilities. This discussion however, will focus on the effect of her treatment—particularly in its early stages—on Celia's adolescent development. It took a number of years to integrate her pubertal changes, gender, sexuality, mature ego ideal, and mature ethnocultural identity so that she could feel more comfortable at her chronological age.

Celia's symptomatology emerged at the end of her middle adolescence, the beginning of her late adolescence. When her family had to move to the West Coast because of her father's professional obligations, Celia had not yet internalized and stabilized her middle adolescent changes enough to be able to maintain them in the face of such dramatic change. In making the move, she had to leave behind a whole adolescent life that was in full swing. Indeed, she had struggled to be at this point in her life: she had risen to the top of her school academically and, for the first time, had a well-developed social life. The extraordinary interference in this recently earned status, developmentally speaking, was more than Celia's somewhat fragile psychic structure could bear. It was at this time that her bulimia began. It remained, and a series of other disturbances evolved over the next few years, until she sought out treatment.

To achieve late adolescent genitality and identity consolidation, Celia's early experiences of her body had to be recalled, examined, and understood. She needed to bring her current resources to bear on comprehending the nature of her physicality, both in the past and in the present. Her early traumatic experiences had left her developmentally paralyzed; Celia had not been able to leave behind the overwhelming bodily experiences of this time. She thus had been unable to contend comfortably with the significant changes of puberty and early adolescence, the middle adolescent considerations related to gender and sexuality, and, certainly, the overall integration of genitality and identity that late adolescence entailed.

Celia needed and wished to wait to begin the adolescent process, and was merely going through the motions of living an adolescent life when she entered treatment. Before she could proceed, she had to come to terms with three major aspects of her childhood: her more sexually ambiguous body, the physical comforting of her parents, and the fending off of her awareness of her parents' exclusive relationship with each other. Each of these had implications for each of the subphases of adolescence. Once they were more thoroughly explored and integrated, Celia was able to begin a young adult process of development and stabilize it.

In order for Celia to become fully aware of her womanly body, she needed to rework the nature and meaning of the countless physical intrusions and appendages of her childhood. The trache, the bandages, the hearing aids, the glasses, all seemed to dominate her picture of her physical self. These were all added on to her actual body, all put in or on, then removed. Her bingeing and purging were adolescent re-creations of some of these childhood experiences, as well as attempts at reworking them. Thus, as is often the case with patients suffering from traumatic neuroses, the beginning of Celia's analysis was rife with reenactments of the traumata of her infancy and young childhood, both in and outside the treatment. Indeed, the focus of the early part of the analysis was on bringing the reenactments into the consulting room. Interpreting the role of the answering machine in her treatment was critical in this regard.

Revisiting these early experiences in treatment permitted Celia to leave them behind, thus opening up a capacity to focus on how her body actually was in childhood and what it became in puberty. Discussing the incident in which she exhibited her brother's genitalia to her friends brought Celia in touch with what she had, what she lacked, and how these issues dovetailed with the physical traumata of her early years. At this time in the analysis, Celia began to become more curious about her own genitalia. This was the period in which her conscious masturbation began. She explored the features of her body more freely, both its parts and its responses. Her genital phase had begun.

It was during this period in her treatment that Celia recalled the very charged "goodnights" with her father in bed next to her. She realized that she felt excited by his presence, but resentful of her mother's absence. She spoke of wanting him with her through the night, wanting to join her parents in their bedroom, and wanting to interrupt them when they were together. This was a time in her analysis when she called me frequently at night and over weekends. I was able to use my very strong feelings of frustration from the repeated intrusions to understand the depth of Celia's early longings and disappointments.

Interpreting the connections between the feelings and experiences of her childhood and her wishes to have me more in her life and to be more in my life began to ease her between-session anxiety considerably. This opened up the possibility of her having a real, intimate relationship with a male, an important aspect of middle adolescence.

The memories, images, and fantasies of this time raised many questions for Celia about her femaleness. The most significant of these questions were how womanly she felt, how sexy she felt, how comfortable she was with being a woman, and what she saw as the social implications of being a woman. These are central issues in both middle adolescence and the late adolescent consolidation of genitality.

The intensity of the sexually ambiguous fantasies that dominated the early part of her analysis diminished enormously in this period of Celia's treatment. Seeing herself as interested in dating, perhaps meeting a man with whom she could become seriously involved, was a major shift in her sense of herself. Once she saw herself more clearly as female, with a woman's specific body parts and physical responses, she developed a desire to present herself in a more clearly female fashion. Her manner of dress changed from one that masked her body to one that showed its contours. She began to be proud of how she looked.

Where once she was preoccupied with her body, her bingeing and purging, her social anxiety, and missing me, her focus now turned to how she was perceived by the people she met and toward whom she gravitated, both with regard to friendships and potential romantic interests. There was clear growth in her capacity to see herself as a woman, rather than as a boy, a girl, or some male/female composite.

This permitted her to be able to relate comfortably to a man. The possibility of becoming interested in and involved with Benjamin then opened up. Ultimately, she was able to commit herself to being in an ongoing relationship with him, an important aspect of her maturing ego ideal and important in the development of her overall late adolescent genitality. Defining herself professionally, and accepting and acting on the fact of her hearing impairment (by buying better hearing aids, for example) contributed to the maturation of her ethnocultural identity. She began to see herself as an academic, and as someone who, like many others, had a significant hearing loss. Each of these placed her in ethnocultural groups. Meaningful consolidation of identity as a late adolescent and young adult had taken place.

Her teaching brought back memories of early and strong maternal feelings in her relationship with her younger brother. These memories ushered in thoughts about her relationship with her mother, who until this time had been consistently presented as distant, even mechanical. She described many hours of creative play with her mother, including many shared art and writing projects. This led to the late adolescent integration of oedipal identifications, which permitted Celia to have a clearer sense of herself as adult.

Celia's genitality and sense of identity had moved beyond those of the late adolescent phase of development. Celia had used the analysis, particularly in its early and middle stages, to examine and reexperience her early traumata so that she could feel the many intense feelings of that time and move into both middle and late adolescence more securely. The resources she now brought to bear both on understanding and experiencing the feelings of that time were strong enough that she was not again overwhelmed. She no longer wished to wait for her adolescence to begin. Rather than go through the motions of adolescent development, Celia could now see herself and experience life as a late adolescent.

Once securely in her late adolescence, Celia was able to look forward and backward with greater clarity. This enabled her to move into young adulthood, which is where she was when her analysis ended. Adolescence became a phase of the past, not one she was waiting to experience fully.

Developmental Considerations

11

Developmental Disruptions:
Transcultural Movement, Divorce,
Death, Infirmity, and Adoption

The ever-whirling wheel of change; the which all mortal things doth sway.

Edmund Spenser, *The Faerie Queene*, VII, 6, 1

Adolescents are keenly aware of the world around them. They turn
to their sociocultural contexts for stimulation and nourishment at a
time when their developmental needs inhibit them from turning to
their families. Adolescents' sensitivities to the outside world are
heightened both by their cognitive development and their emotional needs. They can perceive the world with more clarity and
complexity, and for purposes of differentiation, they must do so.
When events occur that dramatically change their physical or social
worlds, such as a move from a culture of origin, a divorce in their
families, or the death of a loved one, there are profound effects on
development.

There also are ongoing life circumstances that have particular
implications for adolescent development. Two that often result in

adolescents' seeking treatment are being chronically ill or having been adopted. In both instances, aspects of normal identity formation are disrupted.

Each of these circumstances will be discussed in terms of its implications for adolescent development and identity formation. In each instance, a clinical illustration will be included to aid in seeing how normal development may be disrupted. These illustrations are but one example of the vast range of themes and variations that might be presented in any of the conditions discussed. They are not meant to be inclusive; they are meant to be illustrations of how the conditions may impact on a given adolescent's life. The various experiences under consideration do not necessarily result in psychopathology. Disruption in normal development occurs, but a particular person's history before the experience is crucial to whether the experience is likely to cause pathology that requires psychotherapeutic treatment.

TRANSCULTURAL MOVEMENT AND ADOLESCENT DEVELOPMENT

What happens when adolescents, who are so attuned to and reliant on their sociocultural contexts, are thrust into dramatically different school and community environments? Eva Hoffman's (1989) moving personal account of emigrating from Cracow, Poland, to Vancouver, Canada, at the age of 13 to escape the rising tide of anti-Semitism gives us an apt example:

This morning, in the rinky-dink wooden barracks where the classes are held, we've acquired new names. All it takes is a brief conference. . . . Mine—"Ewa"—is easy to change into its near equivalent in English, "Eva." My sister's name—"Alina"— poses more of a problem, but after a moment's thought . . . [they] decide that "Elaine" is close enough. My sister and I hang our heads wordlessly under this careless baptism. The teacher then introduces us to the class, mispronouncing our last name—"Wydra"—in a way we've never heard before. We make our way back to the bench at the back of the room; nothing much has happened, except a small, seismic, mental shift. The twist in our names takes them a tiny distance from us—but it's a gap into which the infinite hobgoblin of abstraction enters. Our Polish names didn't refer to us; they were as surely us as our eyes or hands. These new appellations, which we ourselves can't yet pronounce, are not us. They are identification tags, disembodied signs pointing to objects that happen to be my sister and myself. [p. 105]

This beautifully describes the profound effect that transcultural moves during adolescence can have on identity formation; they can create a disjunction between an internally derived sense of identity experience and the aspect of identity that is imposed from the outside, that is, the cultural world. When the sociocultural context shifts, it becomes far more difficult for ethnocultural identity to coalesce.

Adolescents and others who make transcultural moves mourn their cultures of origin, for the loss of a culture is similar to the loss of a loved one. "Bit by bit, the mental representations of people, places, and various kinds of symbols associated with the culture are brought to mind" (Levy-Warren 1987, p. 305). This mourning for the culture of origin may come into conflict with adolescent identity formation.

At precisely the developmental moment when the cultural world ascends in importance, those adolescents who move from their cultures of origin experience a profound sense of alienation from their prior foundations of identity. Their inside worlds and their outer worlds cannot easily join together to form the ethnocultural identities that permit them to feel the sense of autonomy that is part and parcel of this developmental phase.

To permit the maturation of both the ego ideal and ethnocultural identity, adolescents take in nourishment from the sociocultural world. This nourishment is in the form of representations of the varied ways that people define themselves and act with each other. Transcultural moves during this maturation process put adolescents in the position of having highly variable sociocultural images to integrate. If these representations are extremely discrepant, integration is correspondingly difficult. In these instances, trauma may ensue. At the very least, adolescents who make transcultural moves have to integrate their parents' views, those of friends from their cultures of origin, and those of contemporaries in their new cultures.

Adolescents need to take in representations from their cultures and form outside attachments in order to separate from their families of origin. When this process of cultural nourishment is disrupted, separation and individuation become more difficult. The maturing psychic structure is in flux, thus in an unstable, weakened state, and yet much must be accomplished. The potential for trauma is great. The traumatic effect is felt in both the formation of adolescents' ethnocultural identities and their ego ideals.

Elena

Dr. and Mrs. Sanchez were extremely distressed. Their 16-year-old daughter, Elena, was ignoring her curfew, dating a boy they did not like or trust, being insolent with both them and her grandparents, and ignoring her schoolwork.

> "We don't know what has happened to her. She was always such a sweet, well-behaved girl. There is such a change since we came to this country. She would never have acted this way if we had stayed in Colombia. Perhaps we should have stayed," her mother said sadly.
>
> "But that was out of the question," her father broke in. "We simply could not remain there."
>
> "But she never wanted to come, Carlos. She asked to stay with my sister. Perhaps we should have let her. She was already in high school."
>
> "Out of the question. We stay together as a family. Her brother didn't complain. Why does she always have to be so difficult?"

Elena had no interest in coming for psychotherapy, according to her parents. I recommended to them that they tell her that they had come to speak to me, and that I had said that I felt that I could not understand the situation unless I also heard Elena's point of view.

"So what did my parents tell you?" the slim, attractive, dark-haired, dark-complected Elena asked.

"They said that they were concerned about the hours you were keeping, the boy you were seeing, your schoolwork, and the way you were acting with the adults in your family."

"That about sums it up. They hate me, basically."

"What's it like for you to be with them?"

"Horrible. They are so 'old country.' I didn't want to come here in the first place, I missed everything about home for what felt like an eternity. And now that I'm settled in here, they don't like me. Why'd they make me come in the first place? I wanted to stay with my cousins."

"When did you actually come?"

"We moved the summer before last. I was 14½. I came here just before tenth grade. It was really something, let me tell you. The kids at this school were different and cliquey. I didn't have any friends for what felt like months . . . well, that's not exactly true. It was weird. At first, the Hispanic kids were friendly to me. They treated me like one of them. But you know, I was really different from them. These kids were from the islands—you know, Puerto Rico, the Dominican Republic. Colombia is a completely different world. And also, I don't know how to say this . . . but my father's a doctor. We had a lot of money in Colombia. I mean, we're more average here. But there, well . . . it was a different story."

"You've used the word 'different' several times to describe your situation. Sounds like you felt unlike the kids here in a number of ways."

"I guess I still feel different. Maybe I always will. I mean, now my friends are more similar to me in terms of parents' money and education and stuff, but they're not Latin. Being Latin means something, too. There's just no way of fitting in."

"And at home? Do you feel like you fit in with your family, or do you feel different there, too?"

"It's the worst there. They act like they hate me; they won't let me do what the other kids do. It's like they think we're still at home."

"So, does 'home' still feel like Colombia?"

"Funny that I said that. It doesn't really feel like that to me, but I know it does to my parents and grandparents. My brother feels more like me, I think. He's like my ally at home." Elena suddenly looked down and became quiet. We sat for a few moments in silence.

"You seemed so sad just now. What's going on?"

Elena looked up at me, her eyes welling with tears. "I've never talked about any of this with anyone, you know. I really miss home, miss my friends there, miss everything. When we went back to visit this past summer, I thought my heart was going to break. I just feel so confused. Sometimes, I can't concentrate in school at all. I'm daydreaming about things from Colombia. My boyfriend thinks I'm crazy or something. I can't talk to my mother, because she starts to cry. I can't talk to my father, because . . . well, I never could. He just doesn't understand anything that has to do with emotions."

Elena missed Colombia, felt alienated from the adults in her family, out of place in school, and going through the motions of being part of her peer group, rather than really feeling connected to it. She did not feel that she "belonged" anywhere, or with anyone. She decided to come back to speak with me.

At first, Elena wanted to talk about how to deal with her parents. Ultimately, she wanted to sort out who she felt she was, who she wanted to be, how she felt about Colombia, and how she felt about the United States. Discussing these issues in treatment permitted her to mourn Colombia, and to begin to define both her ego ideal and her ethnocultural identity.

Her difficulties concentrating in school, which derived in large part from fending off a mourning process for her culture of origin and a paralysis in her separation process, were resolved when both processes were set in motion. The interpretation of her transference in treatment aided her in resolving separation issues with her family; the description of her experiences in Colombia were crucial to initiating and resolving her mourning for her culture of origin.

Transcultural movement shakes the roots of identity. When this reverberation takes place at a time when these roots are still forming, as is the case in childhood, or re-forming, as is the case in adolescence, identity formation itself may be disrupted. As adolescents separate from their families of origin and build autonomous identities, their sociocultural worlds provide them with the sustenance necessary to build upon the identities of childhood. This nourishment is provided through attachments, alternative ideas about how the world works, and groups to which the adolescents can belong and with whom they can identify. When the sociocultural context dramatically changes, constancy of replenishment is disrupted. These adolescents may then be thrust back into their families at just the time when they need to move outward into their peer groups.

The subphase in which the transcultural movement occurs is relevant to consider. Early adolescent moves are most likely to affect the separation process; middle adolescent, the relationships with peers that are so important in the maturation of ethnocultural identity and the individuation process; and late adolescent, the maturation of the ego ideal and refinement of adult oedipal identifications. In each instance, there will undoubtedly be reverberations throughout adolescence; the areas noted are simply those that are most likely to be disrupted.

The potential for trauma resulting from adolescent transcultural movement is great. Adolescents' psychic structures are already weakened by the influx of impulses and their relative lack of stable means for dealing with these impulses. Assimilating the internal cognitive, emotional, and sexual changes requires a turn toward the social world. When that social world itself changes, the adolescent is thrust back upon personal resources that are themselves in a diminished state. It is difficult for the adolescent simultaneously to mourn childhood, mourn the culture of origin, separate from the family of origin, and individuate.

Especially because she was at the brink of moving from early into middle adolescence when her transcultural movement took place, Elena is an example of an adolescent struggling to accomplish these tasks. She became overwhelmed in her attempt. She got lost in the processes of identity formation and mourning, and used her treatment to bolster her capacities to resolve them.

Treatment was effective because it aided her in affectively recalling her experiences in Colombia, looking more carefully at her parents and herself, and defining herself as someone who was of both her culture of origin and her new culture. In essence, then, it supported her in mourning both her culture and family of childhood, and in defining her mature ego ideal and ethnocultural identity. She especially needed support in defining her mature ego ideal and ethnocultural identity because of the disruptive effect of moving while these processes were in their nascent stages.

When treating patients who have made transcultural moves during adolescence, it is crucial to be aware of the profound effects such a move may have on the maturation of ethnocultural identity and the ego ideal. The move disrupts the emotional replenishment provided by adolescents' sociocultural contexts, thus making maturation far more difficult. Attending to these issues in treatment facilitates the necessary processes of mourning, separation, and individuation, and frees adolescent patients to make the life choices necessary to establish places in the adult world of their new countries.

DIVORCE AND ADOLESCENT DEVELOPMENT

Separation requires that adolescents' parents be stationary targets. Adolescents must be able to see who their parents are more realistically, using the cognitive and emotional resources currently available to them. This sharpened focus is what permits adolescents to deidealize their parents, thereby freeing them to construct ego ideals that are based upon what is actually possible.

If parents are moving targets, that is, the way they present themselves seems ever-changing, it is more difficult for adolescent children to get a clear picture of their parents. Undergoing a divorce often creates such circumstances: how parents present themselves and what their relations are with each other often show their adolescent children very different aspects of them than their children previously had seen.

The identificatory and mourning processes are inevitably disrupted. The growth and maturation of adolescents' views of and attachments to their parents cannot progress in an even manner. Feelings of disloyalty and betrayal, rage and disappointment, and surprise and discomfort abound. Adolescents may feel compelled to choose one parent or the other, or just as compelled not to choose either parent. In any case, their capacity to focus on themselves in the shift of narcissism that is part of normal development is diminished. They may thus be left without the necessary resources for proceeding in the separation and individuation processes required in adolescent development.

The work of Judith Wallerstein and her colleagues (1980, 1989) on the effect of divorce on children emphasizes the importance of developmental level at the time of the divorce, as well as the changing meaning of the divorce over time. A divorce occurring during adolescence may freeze that child in ways of dealing with life circumstances that make later development more difficult. Kirsten Dahl (1993) describes a case of a prepubertal girl whose parents underwent a divorce when she was 8 years old. The pathological effects of this divorce did not surface until four years later, when puberty set in and the girl was overwhelmed by attempting to use defenses erected at a much younger age. The case illustration that follows demonstrates a similar process: Daniel's parents divorced when he was 11, but evidence of his being overwhelmed did not emerge until he was faced with the resolution of the issues of late adolescence and the entrance into adult life. The divorce left him with highly conflicted adult identifications and an unrealistic ego ideal; both of these made the prospect of becoming an adult daunting.

Daniel

"I don't know where I'm at," Daniel said in response to my inquiring about what brought him to see me. "I'm 23 years old, supposedly in the prime of my life, but miserable, undecided, moody, and removed from everybody and everything. I really don't know how to proceed. I was hoping you could give me some direction. I need a mentor."

"I certainly don't think it makes sense for me simply to tell you what to do, because that just glosses over the problem you're having in making up your own mind. Maybe we can find out what keeps you from knowing what you want your own direction to be, and free you up to make your own choices."

"That would be great. Is it really possible?"

"Let's see what we can do if we work at it together. You strike me as someone who has probably already given some thought to all this, so why don't you tell me your own thoughts about the roots of your difficulties?"

"Well, you're right about that . . . I feel like it's all I've been thinking about for years. I feel like I have been going through the motions of my life, but not living it for almost as long as I can remember. Well, that's not quite true . . . it really started when my parents got divorced when I was 11. They told me at the end of the summer, just after I had come home from a few weeks at a sports camp. I couldn't believe it. Believe me, they had never fought or anything. This announcement came completely out of the blue. We were such a polite family. Even when I think about it right now, I can't get over it."

"How did you react at the time?"

"Like the good boy I always was. I acted like I understood. I didn't rock the boat."

"Did you even know what you actually thought and felt?"

"Don't think so. Except that there was this one incident in school."

"And what was that?"

"I refused to do an assignment. I said that I thought it was stupid. A waste of time. Very unlike me."

"Do you remember what the assignment was?"

"Never thought about it until right now, but it definitely was relevant. I was supposed to write something about either what my father or what my mother did. You know, interview one of them about what they actually did at work. Guess I didn't want to deal with it."

"Maybe it involved a choice you didn't feel comfortable making."

"You mean, him or her?"

"That's what I was thinking. What do you think?"

"That's been an issue all along. Each of them still bad-mouths the other. I constantly feel like I have to mollify him or mollify her. I can never let either of them know what I'm actually thinking. And certainly not what I'm feeling. Of course, half the time I don't even know what I'm feeling."

"Perhaps there's a relationship between feeling forced to choose, forced to remain silent, and your difficulties knowing what you want for yourself at this point in your life."

"Hadn't thought about that. Maybe. . . . So is this what therapy is like?"

"Certainly, an aspect of it."

Daniel lived with his mother in the apartment of his childhood during the school week, and saw his father for dinner once a week and stayed with him over alternate weekends. He felt very close and similar to his mother, and different and distant from his father. His relationships with both of them, however, remained agreeable throughout his adolescence. As he put it, he "didn't want to rock the boat." This was at some psychic cost. Though he was highly competent in school, in all respects he felt increasingly separate from his peers. He said that even those that he ostensibly was close to, including female and male friends and females he was dating, seemed not to "really" know him.

"I don't think I knew myself. . . . maybe that's still the problem."

Daniel was traumatized by his parents' announcement that they were going to divorce. The versions of his parents that were internally represented remained fundamentally those of his parents of childhood. He was unable to deidealize them and to obtain more realistic assessments of who they were, critical components of the differentiation process of adolescence. To keep them in this childhood conceptualization, and to keep the affects associated with the divorce and the adolescent developmental process at bay, he unconsciously utilized more and more of his psychic resources. Ultimately, he was not left with enough psychic energy to continue to traverse the steep paths of the adolescent journey.

Treatment aided him in revisiting this trauma, and his representations of his parents of childhood and those of his adolescence. Reexperiencing those feelings and relationships in the transference permitted a mourning process to occur that had been stopped in its early stages.

"I think of you as my guru, you know. I'm relying on you to lead me on a path to true manhood."

"This assumes that someone else knows better than you what your personal path should or will be."

"I certainly hope so. I sure as hell don't know where I'm going. I feel lost without a guide."

"Maybe there's no such thing. Maybe each of us determines our own path."

"How come other people can do it, then, but I can't?"

"How do *you* answer that question?"

"I have no faith in myself. I feel like everything I have ever accomplished was a sham . . . an experience of going through the motions, but not really getting anywhere."

"Sounds like a baby/bathwater problem. . . . you have accomplished what you have accomplished. That can't be taken from you; but it seems as if you didn't feel that it was for you."

"I got stuck in trying to please Mommy and Daddy, trying to make them love me," Daniel said, with great sarcasm in his tone.

"You make that sound like some kind of criminal act."

"Well, it kept me from ever knowing what the hell I wanted for myself."

"And now?"

Daniel's voice sounded husky, as if he was fighting off tears. "It's as if I still can't believe what's happened. I mean, he's remarried and has another kid, and she's remarried. And me? I'm still living as if it's twelve goddamned years ago, agonizing over losing my idyllic childhood . . . which wasn't so idyllic, after all. I've just been trying to remember it that way."

In an article about object loss and mourning during adolescence, Laufer (1966) notes that interferences in normal mourning keep affects originally connected to the lost parental objects in an unchanged state, thus requiring layers of additional defenses to be erected to keep the affects repressed. He describes the impairment of ego functioning that ensues, as well as the distortions in the relationship to the self and outside world.

His article is about actual loss through death, but it applies equally to object loss that results from such experiences as divorce, especially when the divorce is as unexpected as Daniel's parents' was to him. Prior idealizations, as are present with representations of parents of childhood, remained in place, thus making it extremely difficult for him to form the adult identifications necessary for the maturation of the ego ideal.

His difficulties in making decisions for himself stemmed from having highly unrealistic expectations for adult life. These, in turn, arose from his never having mourned the parents of his childhood, thereby deidealizing them and leaving him free to get to know his parents as an adolescent—with the more mature resources available to him at that time. Knowing them more fully as an adolescent would have permitted Daniel to form adult identifications with his parents, thus more fully preparing him to proceed into adult life.

His incapacity for responding adequately to his parents' divorce as a young adolescent robbed him of energy that would have been available for forming the kinds of relationships with his peers that make the adolescent passage easier to negotiate. Thus, he was left feeling at some remove from his contemporaries, unable to derive the support from them that comes from shared experience.

When the parents of adolescents decide to divorce, adolescents must focus on who their parents are, what the parents' relationship is to each other, and what each parent's relationship is to the adolescent. This comes at a time when adolescents need to be focusing inward, for purposes of individuation, or outward at peers and adults who are not their parents, for purposes of separation and the maturation of the ego ideal. These differentiation processes can easily be obstructed when adolescents feel compelled to reengage with their parents' needs and wishes, which often accompanies a divorce.

When the divorce occurs during early adolescence, as was the case for Daniel, it may become more difficult to revise childhood conceptions of parents. When deidealizing the parents of childhood takes place in the context of an intact family, adolescents can leave the parents of childhood with the sense that the overall family structure will be a foundation for revised relationships with the parents. When divorces occur at this juncture, the process is far more difficult. The relationships in the family of childhood *and* its structure must now change; the early adolescent is faced with establishing new relationships within the family *and* becoming accustomed to a new way of living with parents who are now living apart from each other. Early adolescents may feel that they do not have the personal resources available to accomplish both the change in the relationships and the change in the family structure.

Middle adolescent divorces pose somewhat different issues. At a time when adolescents usually focus on the comparison between their internal parents and the parents they see in the real world, in an effort to refine the parental representations in keeping with the cognitive and emotional resources currently available, they instead place a greater emphasis on their external parents. When divorce leads middle adolescents to focus on their parents' needs and wishes, it is far more difficult for them to be aware of which images of their parents derive from childhood and which from the present. It is the childhood representations that must be left behind in early and middle adolescence, as clarity of vision about who the parents actually are (in comparison to who they are wished or expected to be) develops during middle adolescence.

Middle adolescents' greater involvement with their contemporaries is one of the mechanisms through which the refinement of parental representations occurs. Divorce interferes with this involvement with peers when middle adolescents feel that they have to be more involved with their divorcing parents (than with their peers).

Late adolescent divorce creates an impediment to development when it interferes in the adolescents' capacity to be self-focused and to form adequate adult identifications with parents. In this subphase, divorce can keep the adolescent riveted to parents and family life when personal goals and plans for the future must be established.

Divorce is not necessarily a situation that results in adolescent psychopathology, but it is one that creates particular difficulties for development. The adolescent, rather than being the agent of change in forging new relationships in the family, may either be caught up in adjusting to changes imposed by alterations in the parents' lives or become the object of conflict as the parents' alterations are sorted out. It is important for clinicians to consider these particular difficulties, especially with respect to the subphase of the adolescent in treatment, and how this life situation can interfere in the adolescent's progressive movement through the developmental process.

DEATH AND ADOLESCENT DEVELOPMENT

The permanent loss of someone dear is never easy to face, but its occurrence during adolescence is especially difficult. Adolescence is a time when the level of symbolic loss is high, thus making literal loss all the more complicated to endure. The most important figurative losses are those of the parents of childhood and the family relationships, in general, of childhood. If one of the figurative losses is confused by becoming a literal loss, development is disrupted. The impact of this disruption may not result in immediate psychopathology, or even eventual psychopathology, but the experience certainly will leave its mark.

Adolescence is a period of development in which personal limits of all kinds are established. The limits of intellectual ability, athletic prowess, physical size, or artistic talent are but a few of the many examples of these limits. In confronting limits, adolescents are symbolically contending with their mortality. Indeed, many adolescents become preoccupied with death—the reality of it, the meaning of it—in normal development.

If they also are challenged by contending with the actual death of someone they love, coping capacities are stretched to their limits. They must symbolically mourn the various aspects of childhood that they are leaving behind by engaging in the adolescent developmental process simultaneously with engaging in a mourning process for someone who is both symbolically and actually lost to them. Many adolescents are stymied by this highly complex and emotionally laden task.

The extraordinary amount of psychic energy expended in accomplishing this task may not have apparent consequences in the adolescent's present life, but may well show up in the future. Such was the case for Robert, who came to treatment at the age of 27, alternatively despondent, lonely, and filled with rage.

Robert

"The last guy I saw made me lie on the couch and come three times a week. Then he never said anything. Lot of good that did. Are you one of those Freudian types like him?" Robert glared at me as he spoke.

"I was trained to be a Freudian psychoanalyst. I don't really think that's related to how much I do or do not say . . . but I have a feeling that your anger is not just about Freudianism or silence . . . and your anger isn't just anger."

Robert seemed taken aback. His countenance changed to one of sadness. "I think you'll find that I'm one of those people

who has more bark than chew, or whatever the expression is."
He became quiet and looked out the window.

He remained silent for a number of minutes, and seemed
to become more and more sad.

"You seem so sad and far away right now."

"Yeah. I get this way." Robert's voice had an angry edge.

"And the anger seems so much like it covers over that
sadness."

Robert continued by discussing his current life, which he
felt was devoid of meaning. He was an attorney who worked for
a civil rights organization, a "do-gooder," as he sarcastically put
it, "who can do no good with problems so big that no one
person can make a dent." He felt frustrated in his job, and
unable to advocate on his own behalf.

"It's fine if I'm fighting for someone else's rights, but not
my own." He said that the women in his office were "bitches"
and the men "unapproachable."

His difficulty with aggression was immediately apparent; his
very significant problems with love and attachment emerged as the
session continued.

"I've got nobody in my life I care about. I can't even decide
whether I'm straight or gay. I've been with men and been with
women; when I'm with one, I fantasize about the other.
Although I think I fantasize about men more when I'm with
women than I do women when I'm with men. I don't just
fantasize, either—when I'm going out with a woman, I usually
have anonymous sex with a man. Don't worry, I practice safe
sex. Anyway, when I'm with a man . . . that doesn't really
describe things accurately. I've only had one real relationship
with a man, the rest has all been one shot deals. But when I was
with him, I thought I really should be with a woman—but I
didn't have strong desires to be, and I didn't fantasize about
being with one." Robert sounded earnest when he spoke of his
sexual and dating life. The edge was out of his voice and he
made direct eye contact.

"So, it sounds like you inevitably feel dissatisfied—whether you're involved with a man or you're involved with a woman. No choice feels quite right."

"You have a problem with it?" he retorted.

"There's that bark, again. Perhaps this gives us some idea why you said that your bark was worse than your chew before. Sounded like you had a sense that the way the expression came out wasn't quite the usual. You said 'chew' instead of 'bite.' Maybe chewing things over is what's a problem. You have a tendency to bark or bite rather than chew."

"Very clever. Bet you think you're smart."

"Is it possible for you to say whether what I said made some sense to you?"

Robert grinned. Indeed, his eyes even twinkled as he said: "I like this. I don't intimidate you—and you're going to make me think about all this stuff that I've just been pissed off, confused, or depressed about for as long as I can remember."

Robert was not an easy person to engage in real self-examination, nor was he someone who expressed any appreciation for achieving insight, but he was someone who responded well to what he felt was the truth. Many months later, after meeting three times per week, he was still critical about my capacities as a therapist—but admiring of my tenacity in trying to truly understand his inner experience.

"You may not be too smart, but you certainly have endurance," he noted with a quick smile.

"We all have to use what we've got," I responded.

"Sometimes, I really wonder what it is that I've got," he said, ruefully.

"Have you always?"

"I think I went into automatic when my father died. You know, I had always done well in school . . . and I just continued to do well. I didn't think about it. I certainly didn't think that it meant anything, either. Even going to an Ivy League school and getting into a top ten law school. It all seemed like just so much bullshit."

Robert's father had died of pancreatic cancer when he was 15. The cancer was detected, his father fell quite ill, and died—all in the space of four months. Robert, his two older sisters, and their mother were all shocked by the experience. There was little open grieving, little talking. Each family member was left to contend with the death alone.

Robert did not mention the untimely death of his father until he had seen me for ten sessions. He initially wanted to speak only of the present, an illustration of the defensive posture that he had assumed from the time of the death itself. In a sense, he had attempted to kill off this overwhelming past. The psychic energy expended in doing this mounted to such a degree that he could not take pleasure in his daily life, and he robbed himself of the potential resources for making necessary life choices, particularly in the realm of his sexuality.

"You know, I never really knew my father. He was so aloof when I was a kid, and then he was gone. And my mother and sister just won't talk about him. Or can't. I don't know what it is. And I'm mad at him . . . for not being around more when I was young, and then just dying. It makes me feel terrible to say this . . . but I hate him for it. I feel really gypped. He wasn't one of those fathers who coached the Little League—he was too busy doing his gardening over the weekends, and didn't get home until late at night during the week. And, then, dammit . . . he had to die." Robert's voice broke. He was trying to be angry, but his profound sense of loss broke through.

Robert had never been able to mourn fully for his father, and thus felt caught in the struggles of middle adolescence, the period of development most interfered with by his father's death. Not successfully resolving the issues of that subphase made late adolescence extremely difficult for him to negotiate. He then entered young adulthood highly compromised. His constitutional strengths were significant, so that he was able to perform the tasks of his daily life with a high degree of competence. What was lacking was a real enjoyment of his capacities and enough psychic energy to make the important decisions of his personal life, especially in the domain of his attachments.

Robert's mother had always been dominant in his life, particularly because his father was so emotionally and physically absent. Neither of his parents was affectionate. The timing of his father's death, in combination with these factors (and others), left Robert particularly vulnerable to conflicts in the realms of sexuality and gender identification.

Robert's absent father never became a real figure with whom he could adequately identify; his dominant mother was the more aggressive figure, and their relationship with each other was one that Robert never saw with the eyes of a sexually involved adolescent. He never had a physically intimate relationship with a contemporary before his father died; thus, his knowledge of physical intimacy was exclusively an autoerotic and cognitive one.

One consequence of his father's never becoming a real figure was that many of Robert's images of him remained in an unconscious, overidealized state. His longings for this powerful paternal figure's affectionate connection were palpable, as were his fears of maternal intrusion and engulfment—made all the more frightening by his not having had a strong paternal presence to protect him. The women's world in which he was left when his father died was one that Robert found to be claustrophobic.

Robert was more able to mobilize aggression in his relations with women than men. His adolescent and young adult relationships with the female members of his family were highly conflicted; nonetheless, the fact that he had these relationships permitted him to revise and rework his prior representations. His separation from them was only partially resolved, but there was more progress in those relationships than there was in the relationship with his father.

In "The Waning of the Oedipus Complex," Loewald (1979) describes the necessity for the oedipal child to commit parricide in fantasy. The same holds true for adolescents, in the context of their oedipal issues and in the context of separating from their families of origin. This fantasied murder frees adolescents from their prior conceptions so that they can come to know their family members in the present. They use their aggression in this process, that is, they symbolically kill off the parents of childhood so that they may come to know the parents of adolescence and adulthood.

The actual death of a parent or other close family member interferes with the unfolding of this complex process. It makes it far more difficult for the adolescent to utilize aggression adequately in the service of further oedipal resolution and separation. Adolescents who lose close family members are often left with strong conflicts around the exercise of aggression, particularly in the context of using it to further their own interests.

The fact that Robert lost his father during middle adolescence had a lasting impact on the formation of his gender and sexual development. He had enormous difficulty seeing himself as someone who could be in a relationship that was intimate in both emotional and sexual terms. To him, it felt like a choice to be with one person was inevitably a choice to destroy another. One of the primary functions of his treatment was to untie the knotted elements of this fantasy, intertwined as it was with early and adolescent oedipal issues, separation issues, issues of mourning for the symbolic and real loss of childhood, and mourning for the actual and symbolic loss of his father.

The death of an adolescent's close family member is inevitably a circumstance that complicates the already complex indentificatory process. A death infuses the identificatory process with anger, guilt, and sadness. Questions arise about the viability and continuity of relationships, thus creating conflicts in intimate relations. Treatment of those who have suffered family losses must take these important adolescent developmental factors into account.

INFIRMITY AND ADOLESCENT DEVELOPMENT

At times, adolescents are rendered physically incapacitated as a result of accident, surgery, or illness. In such instances, there can be profound effects on their shifts of narcissism, and their sense of bodily integrity and ownership. Moves toward greater independence may be interrupted by their need to be in the care of the adults around them; moves toward developing greater competence in using new capacities may be impeded by their being temporarily immobilized.

These kinds of physical experiences are largely temporary disruptions in the developmental process. Usually, at worst, they nudge adolescents off track and psychotherapeutic intervention may be called for to aid them in reestablishing their developmental equilibrium. Most often, however, these adolescents undergo temporary periods of developmental slowdown, to which they often respond on their own and with the help of family and friends. These experiences may result in awakening adolescents to their own vulnerabilities, thus leading them to be somewhat more self-protective than the average adolescent. They come to realize early in the developmental process that their bodies have limits that must be respected.

In the most dramatic instances, when adolescents face life-threatening circumstances, the impact may be more profound. The psychic scars tend to run deep and include not only an awareness of their own limitations and mortality, but also either a general fearfulness and passivity or its direct opposite, a counterphobic impulsivity, that is, a strong need to take action, even in situations when acquiescence or receptiveness may be more sensible. For instance, a counterphobic adolescent could break a glass and step on a piece of it, and instead of waiting to have a physician make sure that all the shards were carefully removed, the adolescent might pull out the glass or cut into the foot. The idea of waiting to be cared for is abhorrent to this adolescent. Action must be taken.

These reactions to the experience of facing death may become characterological, depending upon the timing of the experience. When these experiences occur in middle adolescence, when there is the greatest flux in character development, there is the greatest likelihood of characterological change. In early adolescence, development is often disrupted, but character formation is so much in its formative stages that it is unusual for it to be affected. In late adolescence, character formation is usually far enough along that this kind of experience is less damaging.

The developmental process of adolescents with chronic illnesses, however, is quite distinct from those who have bouts with illness, accidents, or surgeries. Those with chronic illnesses often have lived all their conscious lives feeling different from their peers, a factor that takes on much greater significance during adolescence, when relations with peers are crucial to the separation and individuation processes. The fact of their illness often forces them to be more wary of physical risks and less able to participate in various adolescent activities. The activities they have to be more careful about range from athletic endeavors to party exploits. In any case, they may feel estranged, excluded, or enraged as a result.

Jeannie

Jeannie's parents were frantic. She was 16, dating, going to parties, staying out late. . . .

"It's all very normal, we know," said her father.

"But she could kill herself!" cried her mother.

Jeannie was not promiscuous, not taking drugs, not drinking excessively. She was drinking occasionally, and only in small quantities. She was hanging out with her friends, who drank soda and ate junk food, drank beer from time to time, and liked to be out listening to music until midnight.

For most parents of kids this age, what Jeannie was up to would hardly have been grounds for deep concern. She was even doing well in school and, generally, getting along with her family. The problem was, Jeannie could not safely drink alcohol or even soda, or eat sugary foods.

Jeannie had juvenile diabetes. She always had been vigilant about her insulin and eating habits throughout childhood and early adolescence. The advent of middle adolescence, however, brought forth very different attitudes and behavior. In order to maintain her popularity, which was strong, she wanted to participate in social activities with her friends. These activities, however, were potentially life-threatening for her. Coming home late meant that she was taking her insulin later than usual; while out, she was experimenting with substances (like soda, alcohol, and candy) that she had avoided her whole life because of their high sugar content.

Jeannie was adamant. "They're ridiculous! I'm the straightest kid I know. And it's *my* body. I can take care of myself. I have for years. I'm not *doing* anything!"

"What do you think makes your parents so concerned?"

"They think I'm going to screw up with the insulin or something. They forget that I've been dealing with this on my own since I was a kid. What do they think I am, stupid or something?"

"Is it just the insulin? I had the impression that they were worried about what you were eating and drinking, also."

"That's so unbelievable. I am so careful. All my friends drink much more than me—and certainly eat more junk. My friends think I'm some kind of health nut, because I have so little of that stuff."

"So your friends don't know about the diabetes?"

Jeannie's demeanor suddenly changed. She was quiet for a few moments, then said: "I don't tell too many people. Only my good friends know. I don't want people to feel sorry for me or think I'm weird or something. Which they would, you know. Nobody really understands this. I don't need anybody's pity. I can deal with this just fine."

Jeannie's "I can deal with it" refrain stood in stark contrast to the events that ensued after our first meeting. That weekend, her parents received a call from the parents of a friend of hers who was having a party. The parents told her that they thought Jeannie had passed out from drinking too much. Jeannie's parents told the friend's parents that Jeannie had diabetes and that they should call for emergency medical help. When they arrived at the friend's house, the emergency medical squad was already there. They told her that Jeannie had gone into shock, but seemed to be recovering.

My next meeting with Jeannie was a sober one. She recounted, somewhat abashedly, the story of her evening at the party in which she had gone into shock.

"I think I wanted to forget that I wasn't like the other kids. We were playing a kind of drinking game. You know, who could drink the most beer without stopping for a breath. I was determined to play . . . Jesus. It was really horrible. . . . You know, most of the kids at school think I got drunk and passed out. I'm sort of glad that that's what they think. It's better than their knowing I've got this weird illness."

"Sounds like you think having diabetes could make you some kind of outcast."

"I don't think it, I know it. Kids don't get it. They just think there's something wrong with me. And they should stay away."

"Is that what's happened when you have told people?"

Jeannie fell silent. "Not exactly. But I've hardly told anybody. I only tell my closest friends, and they wouldn't tell anybody else."

Treatment with Jeannie was far from smooth sailing. Soon after this interchange, she became somewhat depressed. She lost interest in school and went out less and less. Her parents were very concerned about her. They had never seen her so unhappy. With me, she was withdrawn and sullen.

"What's the point of this, anyway? This therapy has basically succeeded in making me feel worse and worse about myself."

"When you think back about it, what do you remember our talking about?"

"What's the difference?"

"I think that whatever it is that is making you so unhappy is related to the talking we have been doing in our sessions. So, what stands out for you from the sessions may give us a clue about the source of the unhappiness."

"Look. There's nothing you can do about it."

"What I take from your reaction is that one of the things that's bothering you is the impossibility of changing something—so either the something has already occurred, or the something is unchangeable."

"This is bullshit." Jeannie looked more upset than angry.

Jeannie's treatment had brought to consciousness the fact of her illness in the context of a new level of understanding. Unconsciously, children often see their bodies as belonging to or, at least, fundamentally in the care of, their parents. The change in bodily ownership that occurs primarily involves the adolescent taking responsibility for bodily care. This happens because adolescents come to realize such truths as they only have one body, it's theirs to care for, and it has limitations.

Middle adolescence brings with it a particular need for comparison with peers. It is the subphase in which most adolescents have attained the majority of their growth. Male adolescents, whose growth lags behind their female counterparts, catch up to and then surpass them during this subphase. The world of middle adolescence is most profoundly a world of contemporaries. They constantly look at themselves in comparison to their peers to see how they differ, how they are the same, how they are better, and how they fall short.

All adolescents have to deal with some degree of disappointment about their bodies. The bodies they may have imagined for themselves in childhood are rarely the bodies they ultimately have; the bodies they have in comparison to the bodies they observe among their peers often leave them with longings as well. The degree of disappointment, however, varies widely.

Children with chronic illnesses often have the fantasy that they will grow out of their illnesses. Jeannie, for example, told me that when she was told she had juvenile diabetes, she did not know what "juvenile" meant. When she asked, and was told that it meant "childhood," she assumed that she would not have diabetes when she was no longer a child.

The profound sadness that she began to manifest was about the loss of this fantasy of recovery and the acute and painful awareness of the reality of her illness, how it limited her life, and her impotence in relation to it. She looked around at her friends and felt very different from them. She yearned to have a body that did not limit her involvement in the social and physical activities they shared.

Beneath her sadness there was an enormous amount of rage—at

her body, at her parents, and, ultimately, at me for not being able to cure her. She also was angry at her parents for giving her the illness. She was highly conflicted about this rage, believing it was unfair for her to feel it. The rage, thus, was defended against and was initially only evident in snippets of the exchanges with me.

The experience of being physically incapacitated has particular meaning during adolescence. In terms of overall impact, subphase plays an important role. Early adolescent physical incapacitation may keep the dependencies of childhood alive for longer than might otherwise be the case; physical difficulties in late adolescence may keep adult strivings in the background and adolescent reliance on adults greater than usual. Middle adolescence often poses the greatest difficulties for those with physical problems, because it is the period in which comparison with peers is at its highest—and the need to conform is similarly high. Physical differences are noticed by the adolescents themselves, but also by their peers. Feeling different may lead these physically compromised adolescents to feel isolated, inferior, or ashamed.

Jeannie's having diabetes is a particular instance of physical difference. There are countless other instances, ranging from chronic illnesses such as Hodgkin's disease, Crohn's disease, hemophilia, or herpes, to physical disabilities such as being deaf, blind, or paralyzed. In these instances, longstanding physical differences take on meanings that they may not have had before.

Adolescents with these differences may come to be seen or to see themselves as unable to keep up with their friends, be like their friends, be really *of* their age. Their responses range from withdrawal to a kind of hyperparticipation, almost as if they need to show that they are just as able or even more able than their peers. Jeannie was trying to keep up with her friends or surpass them. She did not take into account that her actual capacities were such that even the most limited participation put her at far greater risk than her friends even if they drank more than she had.

Adolescents must redefine their physical differences in accordance with their development. The way a child views a disability is quite distinct from how that child as an adolescent views the disability. An adult view of that disability is again different. Jeannie, for example, felt that her parents were both to blame for her illness and impotent in dealing with it. As an adolescent, she was angry about how her body had failed her, how her parents had failed to protect her from having this illness, and how impotent *everyone*—she, her parents, and I—was to do anything about it. I don't know how she will feel as an adult, but I do know that it will be different from what she currently thinks and feels. The meaning of the same experience or physical factor changes as development proceeds, because cognitive and emotional experience grows over time—usually by becoming more complex—and our cognitive and emotional resources are responsible for recording and interpreting our experience of the world.

There are experiences that can be particularly difficult because of the issues and tasks of adolescent development, as is the case with adolescent transcultural movement, parental divorce, accident, injury, or a family member's death. There also are lifelong physical factors that change in meaning for the individuals who have them because of the developmental period that they are in. Those with chronic illnesses or disabilities think and feel differently about these physical factors at different points in their lives, for both cognitive and emotional reasons. Similarly, there are long-standing conditions that take on a different meaning during adolescence. Adoption is one of them.

ADOPTION AND ADOLESCENT DEVELOPMENT

The transformations in identity that occur during adolescence involve significant changes in relations with parents, internally and externally. The internal representations of parents change from those of the parents of childhood to (primarily) those of the parents of adolescence. The parents themselves are seen more realistically for who they are and what they can offer to the adolescent. The kinds of needs that adolescents manifest toward their parents derive from their internal representations of the parents.

Parental representations change over time, as has been described elsewhere in this book. In brief, early adolescents must shift over-idealized images of their parents based upon their needs to rely on their parents for self-definition and for sustenance, emotionally and physically. Middle adolescents must readjust their views of their parents to account for the parents' true characteristics, in preparation for getting to know themselves and further refine their ego ideals on the basis of what is realistic to expect of people in the world and of themselves. They (mostly) shift their attention from a focus on what their parents want and expect of them, to what their friends and they themselves want and expect of them. It is not that middle adolescents do not care about what their parents' wishes are, it is simply that these wishes do not predominate in middle adolescents' lives the way they might have in early adolescence. Late adolescence brings with it another shift in relations with parents, often a reinvolvement with parents in a transformed way. Parents are seen as adults who know and love their older adolescents, and are turned to for advice. There is a much higher degree of mutual respect and acceptance. Late adolescents' values and ideas are far more self-derived, which permits them to feel more comfortable speaking of them with their parents, regardless of whether the parents agree or not.

What I have just described is not what always happens and is not the only "normal" route of development. It is a path that is often followed, and one that reflects the continuously changing pattern of relationships within a family between parents and children. When adolescents raise the question to themselves, "What are my parents really like? Who are my parents, really?," those adolescents who are adopted often get developmentally off-kilter. Their knowledge and fantasies of their biological parents get intertwined with their knowledge and fantasies of the parents who raised them. These entanglements may become quite complicated to separate. The developmental tasks of adolescence may become more difficult; the developmental process may go somewhat awry.

The special vulnerability of adoptees has been discussed in a variety of ways. Some focus on adolescents who have problems in their sense of identity that are seen as related to adoption (Frish 1964, Kornitzer 1971, Sorosky et al. 1975). Herbert Wieder (1977,

1978a,b) stresses the heightened separation anxiety and identifica-tory conflicts of adoptees. Karen Gilmore (1995) provides a clinical example that describes the evolution of an adopted girl's gender identity disorder. She writes that the adopted girl's early separation trauma in combination with the adopted mother's strong disap-pointment over not being able to give birth formed the foundation for the girl's disorder. Paul Brinich (1980, 1990, 1995) describes the recurrent fantasies of being unwanted, the needs to test the commitment of the adoptive parents, and the conflicts, ambiva-lence, and anxiety of *both* the adoptive parents and the adopted children. Brinich (1995) notes that adoption provides a particular instance of bidirectional ambivalence in the parent–child relation-ship, but emphasizes that this ambivalence is prevalent in psycho-analytic treatment and outside of it, and in both adoptive and non-adoptive families. Having two actual sets of parents provides fertile ground for "the use of defenses such as splitting, externaliza-tion, and projection" (p. 196); however, many non-adopted children have fantasies that their parents are not actually their parents and are thus prone to the use of these defenses as well.

An extensive survey of patients over a ten-year period in a mental health clinic indicated that adoptees were slightly over-represented among child and adolescent patients, but under-represented among adult patients (Brinich and Brinich 1982). This more recent account is in contrast to the long-held view that adoptees are at significantly greater risk of psychopathology (e.g., Bohman 1970, Kornitzer 1971, Schechter 1960, Sorosky et al. 1975), a view supported by data other than the Brinichs' that has been collected on the subject (e.g., McWhinnie 1969).

In any case, I believe that adoptees are put to a particularly strong test during adolescence. The areas of psychological risk for adoptees and the areas of psychological risk for adolescents are quite similar. They fall primarily in the areas of separation and identifi-cation. There are important implications, therefore, for the adoles-cent deidealization process and the maturation of the ego ideal.

Shari

"I know that this is considered old-fashioned these days, but I don't want my 16-year-old daughter having sex and running around on the street. That's not how we brought her up." Mr. DeSacco was agitated.

"We don't really know that she's having sex," said Mrs. DeSacco. "You're just making that assumption."

"Don't be naïve. What do you think she's doing out until all hours with that boyfriend of hers?"

Shari grew up in an urban environment. Her parents, the DeSaccos, adopted her after eight years of trying to conceive a baby. She was adopted through an agency at the age of 3 months. Before the adoption, she lived with one foster family for two-and-a-half months. She had stayed with her biological mother for her first two weeks of life. She was the only child in her adoptive family. She had been told of her adoption at the age of 7, in response to her questioning her mother about why she did not look like either of her parents.

The DeSaccos were a Catholic, upper-middle-class family. They lived in a homogeneous neighborhood with single-family homes. Shari attended a small, Catholic private school not far from where she lived. They consulted me for advice about how to respond to Shari's recent behavior, which included staying out late, ignoring their wishes to let them know where she was going and when she would be home, and seeming less motivated in school. They were concerned that she might be having sex, drinking, and/or using drugs.

In meeting and talking with Mr. and Mrs. DeSacco, it was unclear to me whether their concerns primarily were based upon actual observations of or intuitions about Shari, or fantasies related to their own unconscious conflicts. I suggested that I meet with them again, but that they ask Shari to come along with them to our next meeting. They had already told her that they were seeking professional advice, for the fighting in the family had reached a level that was intolerable.

When the DeSacco family arrived, the first thing I noticed was the stark contrast in appearance between Shari and her parents. Both Mr. and Mrs. DeSacco were pleasant-looking people who were short, slightly overweight, of light complexion, and conservatively dressed. Shari was very striking: tall, slender, dark, and wearing a tight-fitting, black short skirt and a red halter top.

All three family members looked at me as they sat down and said nothing. It seemed clear that I was expected to speak.

I looked directly at Shari and said, "I met with your parents two weeks ago. They said they were concerned about you and about the fact that there was so much fighting going on these days among the three of you at home. I thought that it made the most sense for us to discuss this all together, because you probably had a view of what was happening that was different from theirs."

"I don't understand why they don't trust me." Shari sounded genuinely hurt. Her voice and manner were not quite what I expected upon first seeing her. She was relatively soft-spoken and seemed a bit shy. Her appearance had suggested to me that she might be more sure of herself. She then turned toward her parents and said, "What *is* it you think I'm doing?"

Mr. and Mrs. DeSacco looked extremely uncomfortable. Mrs. DeSacco looked at her husband. "I think *you* should say something."

"I don't like all this staying out at night. I think you're too young to be coming home so late."

Shari's eyes filled with tears. "I feel like you're accusing me of something. You're thinking something you're not saying. And it's always there, in your eyes, in your voice. Why don't you just say it?"

Mr. DeSacco's voice went up several decibels and his face darkened. "Well, are you having sex with him or not?"

"Mr. DeSacco are you aware of how angry, even accusatory, you sound right now?"

Shari's father's face changed immediately. He looked more distressed than angry. Shari looked at me, then looked at him, then cast her eyes downward. When she spoke, she spoke very quietly: "I can't believe this is happening."

The situation in the DeSacco family was a complicated one. Shari's father was too suspicious, from both his own fantasies about Shari and his reactions to her actual behavior. Her mother was oversolicitous and overprotective, as she had been from the day Shari was brought into the household. These reactions derived as much from her feelings about her own infertility as they did about anything related to Shari's behavior. Shari was struggling with a disparate mix of feeling both too worried about her parents' wishes and reactions and quite estranged from them.

I decided that there were so many issues to sort out that it made sense to meet regularly with the family as a whole and each individual separately. For the first three months of treatment, I saw the family every two weeks, Shari in the intervening weeks, and each parent once a month.

Each of her parents had a number of issues in relation to Shari. Her father, for example, worried about her origins: her biological mother had gotten pregnant as a teenager and was not married at the time. He was concerned that there might be "bad genes." Mrs. DeSacco had always worried that Shari might ultimately reject her for not being her "real" mother. She also had fears about not being maternal enough, based upon her inability to give birth. These are but a few examples of the many ways that her parents brought their own issues to bear on the way they responded to Shari.

Shari had her own problems. She felt different from her parents and their friends, as well as her schoolmates—both because of her looks and because she was adopted. She also felt very afraid of venturing out into the social world of her contemporaries. She had strong fears of abandonment and rejection. These stemmed in part from her having been adopted and, therefore, left by her biological parents (and her foster parents). She also had little sense of her own competence in the world, partially because of her adoptive mother's overprotectiveness. Her adoptive father's apparent suspicion left her questioning her own motivations and behavior.

One result of all this was that Shari attached herself to her boyfriend in a way that was overdependent. She shifted many of her strong feelings of connection to her parents over to him and their relationship. He became responsible for defining her values and goals, both in their relationship and in school. His ideas were quite different from those of her parents.

Shari was not having sexual intercourse with her boyfriend at the time the family began consulting with me, but she wanted her parents to think that she was. "I'm sick of the looks I get from them. Let them think I'm doing it. What then? They'll kick me out? Sometimes I think he would. I don't think Mom would. But, who knows?"

Things got worse before they got better. After three months, I began seeing Shari six times a month and her parents each once a month. We met as a family on an as-needed basis. The "need" came up because of blow-ups between Shari and her parents, primarily about Shari's staying out too late (according to her parents) and her apparent indifference about her schoolwork.

"What's the difference? It's my life. If I want to do well in school, fine; if I don't, that's my problem, isn't it?"

"Do you really regard it as a problem?" I asked.

Shari looked thoughtful. "I guess I do. I mean, I know Joseph [her boyfriend] doesn't think it's important, but he grew up really differently. The truth is, I just don't feel like what we're learning in school is all that interesting a lot of the time. And I really love Joseph, you know, so what he thinks means a lot to me."

Shari's involvement with Joseph was highly influenced by her fantasies about her biological father and mother. She romanticized their relationship; she had decided that they must have really been in love, for they violated all the taboos of their time. She had recently asked and received information about her biological parents. What she found out was that they had been from different ethnic and religious backgrounds: her mother was an Italian

Catholic; her father, Greek Orthodox. Her father was a number of years older than her mother; her mother was 16 when Shari was born.

Joseph was three years older than Shari, and from a different class and ethnic background. Though he too was Catholic, he came from a Polish working-class family. He had dropped out of school after high school, and was now working in a relative's construction company learning to be a carpenter. He was a somewhat angry, disaffected, 20-year-old when he began dating Shari.

About a year into the relationship, which was about six months into treatment, Shari got pregnant. Joseph wanted to get married. Mr. DeSacco was alternately threatening to kill Joseph and throw Shari out. Mrs. DeSacco was frightened that her husband would act on his threats, and extremely worried for Shari. She first told her mother about the pregnancy, then told me.

"I don't know what to do," Shari said to me. "I don't really think I'm ready to be a mother. And I don't want to get married. I can't believe the way my father is acting, but then again I can. And my mother? I think she's going to have a heart attack or something. She's just so nervous all the time. And I've pretty much given up on school. I just can't do everything."

"What's 'everything?'"

"Deal with everybody. It feels like everybody in my life wants something else."

"And you?"

"I want to go away. Far, far away. Maybe I can think more clearly if I'm not here."

Much to her father's and Joseph's dismay, but with her mother's support, Shari had an abortion a few weeks later. She was upset about it, but was able to use the experience in her treatment to deepen her understanding of her own motivations, fantasies, and complex family issues. She decided to break up with Joseph, and began to concentrate more on her studies. She stayed in treatment until the winter of her senior year of high school, having begun in the summer after her sophomore year. When ending treatment, she told me that she wanted to do the rest of the year on her own. She wanted to know that she was ready to go off (alone) to college.

This treatment structure reflected the mix of issues presented by the DeSacco family. Shari had her full share of conflicts related to separation, abandonment, rejection, and knowing/not knowing. Her parents presented their own issues, however, which highly influenced Shari's progression through adolescence (and, previously, through childhood). Her father suffered with fears and wishes related to sexuality, for instance, while her mother was beset with conflicts related to her inability to bear children and her own fears of rejection and abandonment. Dealing with some of Shari's parents' issues was necessary to relieve part of the tension that Shari was experiencing in her family.

Shari's own conflicts stemmed from a number of sources. Issues surrounding her adoption were a prominent derivative, although not the only one. Her father's views about Shari's social life, for example, generally were strongly held and "old-fashioned"; Shari correspondingly had strong, mixed views about her own behavior. Her father was highly dominant in his relationship with Shari's mother, a problem-filled model that Shari used in her relationship with Joseph. Her mother's permissiveness impeded Shari's development of a way to discipline or regulate herself, which interfered in Shari's capacity to do homework, study for exams, or learn how to drink in social situations without overdoing it.

The conflicts arising from her adoption, however, were mostly in the areas of separation, ego development, and identity formation. Shari had difficulty separating from her adoptive parents, for instance, in large part because of conflicts related to fantasies of her biological parents. She enacted a romanticized, over-idealized fantasy about her biological parents in her relationship with Joseph. Her wishes to know her adoptive parents better, an important aspect of the separation and individuation processes of adolescence, were interfered with by her wishes both to know and not to know about her biological parents. The confluence of these concerns undermined her interest in school, a place where the wish to know is critical.

Shari's relationship with me was a strong one, but not as strong as is often the case with adolescents of her age. While many middle and late adolescents talk a good deal about their friends, Shari rarely did. Her focus was primarily on her family (both adoptive and biological) and Joseph. It was as if there just were not enough room among her self and object representations for anyone else.

Directly confronting her adoptive parents (or me) bordered on an impossibility. Shari simply was too afraid of rejection. Instead, she acted out in the transference and enacted in life, converting conflicted wishes and fears into actions (a tendency that Wieder highlights in his paper [1978b] on working analytically with adoptees). The most prominent example of this action-taking was Shari's getting pregnant as a teenager at almost the same age as her biological mother had given birth to her.

Through her use of the treatment and the easing of her parents' pressure, Shari was able to achieve a greater degree of separation and individuation. She left treatment, however, in a manner that was reflective of her ongoing problems with separation and her still middle adolescent manner of dealing with endings (as described in Chapter 6). At the time she left, she knew she had real difficulties in life that were greater than her peers, but felt she had to deal with these without me in order to feel independent. Wanting to feel as independent as possible before going off to college, she acted out a conflict about depending upon me and doing things on her own, rather than talking about it. Nevertheless, Shari has chosen to stay in contact with me. I have heard from her by phone and letter, and seen her in person intermittently for a number of years. She clearly has continued her development on her own.

There are many different kinds of adoption and many situations that affect adolescents in ways that may be similar to adoption. Adoptions during adolescence or later childhood, for example, are quite different from those that take place during infancy. They present special and continuous conflicts about abandonment and rejection (that Brinich discusses in his paper [1980] on the potential effect of adoption on the development of self and object representations). Adoption of a baby or child from a very different racial or ethnic background poses particular issues related to sameness and difference that reverberate throughout development, particularly in relation to the maturing of ethnocultural identity. When (or even if) to tell a child about the fact of adoption or the particular circumstances of adoption is a difficult issue similar to that faced by parents who have given birth to a child through the assistance of donated sperm or eggs. Each of these instances highlights an issue that Shari and her parents faced; each increases the pressures generally accompanying adolescent development.

There is an extensive literature on adoption. This section of the chapter is not meant to be an exhaustive review of this literature. Each of the articles cited pursues the topic more thoroughly. Adoption is included in this chapter because knowledge of being adopted often influences the way an adolescent and that adolescent's family experience the developmental process. Among the many complex developmental issues that may arise for an adolescent adoptee, the two that I would like to discuss further are separation and the adolescent's use of action.

There is an entanglement for adopted adolescents in the deidealization process that is so crucial to separation. The entanglement results from having two sets of parents, one relatively known, the other relatively or completely unknown. This leads to a difference in the impact of fantasy and reality in the object representations of both sets of parents.

Idealization tends to be stronger with unknown biological parents, because their images are more infused and confused with the child's wishes. Adolescence is usually a time when these wishes are sifted out on the basis of the adolescent's increased cognitive and emotional capacity to look realistically at parents. The absence of the biological parents often poses problems with deidealization which, in turn, result in problems in realistic identifications. These may lead to difficulties in the maturing of the ego ideal. If the maturation of the ego ideal cannot progress, adult identifications are highly unrealistic as well. These could well lead to character problems or depression. This is a possible pathological scenario; it need not occur, but it sometimes does.

Adolescents have a propensity to take action, rooted in the relationship among the intrapsychic structures at this time. The lack of a strong enough ego to contain the burst of sexual and aggressive impulses generated by hormonal surges makes them at greater risk to take actions to reduce tension that, both before and after this period of development, simply thinking, feeling, or repressing might have sufficed to reduce.

Adolescent adoptees may be at greater risk to take action than other adolescents. Their wish to know their biological parents makes the fantasies that might otherwise have been repressed more difficult to keep out of consciousness. As a result, adopted adolescents may feel compelled to enact the (unconscious) fantasies. It is a compromise: they show their knowledge of their unconscious fantasies by their actions, but keep the full awareness of the fantasies safely out of consciousness by acting instead of thinking or feeling. This is what happened to Shari; it is a common phenomenon among the adopted adolescents about whom I have clinical knowledge.

DISCUSSION

The topics presented in this chapter are wide-ranging. What they share is that the experiences described exert a special impact on adolescent development. Whether the impact leads to pathology is a matter of individual evaluation. The circumstances discussed exert special pressures on the adolescents and their families; an individual adolescent's potential for psychopathology depends upon the particular configuration of constitutional endowment, social and economic pressure, and parental psychopathology.

These experiences pose problems in the mourning for the parents of childhood, the deidealization process, the adolescent oedipal identifications, the maturation of the ego ideal, and the maturation of ethnocultural identity. These are basic aspects of the separation and identity formation processes of this time. While there are differences among these experiences, each of them brings pressure to bear upon adolescents and their families that make remaining within a normal range of behavior more difficult. Effective treatment aims at facilitating these aspects of the developmental process through an awareness of these experiences as potential areas of concern.

Epilogue: The Journey Continues—
Adolescence and Adult Life

When all is said and done, what impact does adolescence have on a lifetime? We have a stronger sense of "I," an immediate sense of who we are that feels stable and continuous. This ongoing sense of ourselves is largely what constitutes character: our customary ways of being in the world. An element of character is our mature ego ideal, the place within us that houses our beliefs, values, and dreams. Knowing who we are and feeling a sense of "I" permits us to be able to enjoy intimate, reciprocal relationships with others. In addition, we see ourselves as belonging not only in our families, but also in the larger ethnocultural world: we have formed an ethnocultural identity. All of this emerges from that wonderfully energetic, creative period called adolescence.

Yet the adolescent journey does not end, nor development

cease, as adolescents enter adulthood. The process of coming to terms with the issues of adolescence continues into adult life, and adult life itself offers us challenges. For some it may simply be a truism, but I want to note that individuals continue to grow and change throughout life. What is established in early and later childhood, and adolescence, is a significant foundation, but life inevitably presents demands and changes that must be incorporated into one's sense of self. These later life experiences alter one's appearance, one's inner state, and one's general sense of history and time. Our own histories often seem to get revised by later experiences as well.

Having adolescent children and grandchildren, for example, clearly has an effect on how we view our own lives as adolescents. Sometimes there is simply a shift from feeling as we did ourselves as adolescents to feeling sympathetically connected to our parents; other times, experiences that may have felt humiliating or frightening seem—in retrospect—to have been formative, character-building moments in our lives. A parent of adolescents related such an experience to me recently.

> When I was a kid, I was driving my father's car to a school dance. I had a beer in the car—guess I wanted to be in good spirits, so to speak, at the dance. Anyway, I reached down to pick it up from the floor—and in that split second that I looked down, I drove the car off the road into a wooden fence in front of someone's house. It was horrible. The car was totaled, the fence badly damaged. I mean, I was okay . . . although, at the time, I even remember wishing I had been hurt. I was so scared. And ashamed. I also didn't know what my father would do—but I sure as hell didn't want to find out, either. He actually was terrific about it. He made me work to pay him back for the damage to the car and the fence. I felt extremely guilty at the time.
>
> I didn't think about it for many years until recently. I think it's because my kids have become teenagers. When I look back at it now, I think mostly about how my father acted. I try to be that kind of father to my kids. But for years, I was focused on

how I kind of got away with something. I never admitted what I had been reaching down for, for instance. I always said I had been turning the radio to another station. I took the beer out of the car and tossed it into the woods before the police came. It weighed on me for years. The whole thing seems very different when I look at it now, though.

Adult life engenders reverberations with adolescence not only when adults have adolescent children, but also because there are life experiences that seem almost to be a next step in development after adolescence. Postpartum women, for instance, must face the fact that life without the responsibilities of parenthood has now passed, a change that reflects back to leaving childhood and adolescence behind. If these major transitions of the past have been difficult, women who have just given birth may find this new transition in their lives to be difficult as well.

Adult women in menopause contend with the other side of what pubertal girls confront: while pubertal girls are first coming to terms with the capacity to carry and bear a child, menopausal women are contending with the realization that their childbearing years are coming to an end. The fact that there may be a coincidence of events—that is, that menopausal women may have female adolescent children—may highly influence the experience for both. Each may have competitive or sad feelings toward the other, for instance, and mothers may wish to live vicariously through their daughters.

The adult aging process itself is the reverse of the growth process of adolescence. What adolescents are developing, in the way of size, strength, coordination, and cognitive complexity, aging adults, to varying degrees, must face losing. Contact with adolescents often leaves adults who are self-conscious about their aging process feeling waves of nostalgia for the days when they were ascending, not descending, the developmental curve.

Middle-aged parents also must contend with feelings of competitiveness and envy in relation to their adolescent children. They may feel that many of their important life choices have been made, while their sons and daughters are first beginning to make these choices as they enter young adulthood. They may long for the opportunities that they see their children having in today's world. The intense friendships that adolescents enjoy and their strong feelings about the worlds of politics, literature, or music, may leave parents feeling both quite nostalgic and quite envious.

These are but a few of the ways that adults, as individuals, contend with issues in everyday life that set off reverberations of adolescent development. The adult world, as a society, also responds to adolescence, in the ways any particular culture in a specific historical moment regards adolescents. Cultural views and values, in turn, shape the experience of adolescents entering that adult world.

What leaving home may mean to adolescents and their families, for example, depends a great deal upon the family's historical, cultural, and economic circumstances. In a traditional, closely knit society, the process of developing an autonomous identity may not involve great physical separation or economic independence. Even in contemporary American society, families who offer continuing economic support to the next generation present a different set of real-world choices than families who require their children to become economically autonomous. The children of first generation immigrants, especially those whose families' primary ethnocultural identities remain rooted in their original cultures, may have much further to travel in leaving home than those in the third or fourth generation.

The processes of forming a mature ego ideal and ethnocultural identity can also be strongly influenced by historical context. When values in the larger society are in flux, the individual process of questioning received values and finding a place in the world can become a mirror in which the larger society reflects on its own values. This can be experienced as hopeful, or frightening, as demonstrated by the continuing ambivalence toward the sixties in this country. It can be a source of idealistic change, as in the participation of northern white adolescents in the civil rights movement, or of nihilistic violence, as in the actions of adolescent skinheads. A stance that permits adolescents to question and is open-minded toward that questioning, without exploiting the malleability implicit in that period, benefits both the larger society and the adolescents.

The romanticizing of adolescence by American society, however, does our adolescents a disservice. The portrayal of adolescent life as sensuous, glamorous, and exciting, as exemplified just now in Calvin Klein underwear advertisements, increases the sense of disconnection adolescents experience within themselves and with the world at large. The romanticized version of adolescence is quite far removed from adolescents' experience of it. In fact, the emphasis our society places on youth and youthfulness does all of us a disservice. It creates difficulties for the elderly, who are often separated from the rest of society, and makes aging a source of fear and even despair at times.

The particular problem this poses for adolescents is that it diminishes a source of hope. If the youth of our society were able to envision a future filled with promise, their inner instability could be counterbalanced by their anticipation of future stability, strength, and creativity. The denigration of aging and over-idealization of youth has the opposite effect.

This over-idealization also contributes to a sense of unreality that many adolescents feel. What they see and feel in their lives and the lives of their peers is often markedly different from the glamour with which adolescence is portrayed in the mass media. Turning to their parents to achieve greater clarity about these contradictions and confusions is often ineffective, for even parents tend to describe adolescence in ways that leave their adolescent children feeling nonplussed.

Parents' memories of adolescence are filled with images of tremendous activity, intensity, passion, strength, deviance—or even delinquency—and sometimes turmoil. There is often a wistfulness in their tone as they speak of this time. This quality mystifies their adolescent children. The look that passes over a parent's face as lost youth is recalled is an unfamiliar one to the child, who may feel puzzled about the parent's real feelings about this period of life.

The parents' memories of adolescence are typically accompanied by feelings of both relief and loss. The relief comes from the vague recollection of instability. The loss results from the sense of depleted energy and imagination, where the loss of imagination is real and, indeed, necessary to become an adult. The increasing capacity to perceive and understand the complexity of inner and outer reality results in a subordination of fantasy; cultural, intellectual, and interpersonal connections begin to dominate as fantasy connections are left behind.

These connections made with the world at large, the real understanding that adolescents achieve through these connections, moves them to develop a greater sense of responsibility—to their own generation and the generations that follow. Especially in the context of some sense of disconnection with their parents, it becomes important for adolescents to see themselves as the next generation and to begin to plan for it. As a result, they are not quiet members of society. They are often the upstarts, the instigators, who continuously ask questions, raise problems and concerns, and challenge the rest of us to think about what we are doing, why we are doing it, and what the potential impact of what we are doing might be. We might otherwise take all too much for granted or, perhaps, out of some kind of inertia, simply become riveted to the status quo.

We need to wonder with them about the ramifications that the possibilities of nuclear or environmental destruction, or AIDS, have for this feeling of connection with the future. The parental generation, which grew up at the end of World War II, through the Korean War, into the Vietnam War, grew up with a *decreasing* sense of the government as a moral and protective force. This was quite consonant with the deidealization process of the parental generation that normally takes place during adolescence, and verified by the increasing capacity of adolescents to perceive and understand what was going on in the sociopolitical world.

The existence of the real possibility of nuclear destruction, extraordinary competition in the workplace, growing holes in the ozone layer, or the proliferation of incurable disease may actually undermine the desire to understand the sociopolitical world. Understanding the enormity and horror of these issues is so daunting. It is an extraordinarily heavy burden for the younger generation. The adolescents portrayed in the movie *Kids* demonstrate one possible reaction to this burden. These teenagers stay firmly within their own social worlds. Anesthetized by sex, drugs, and music, they protect themselves from the larger truths of the world around them.

Adolescence is, by its nature, a time when limitations, symbolic deaths, and explosiveness are prominent developmental issues, as well as uncontrollability and the necessity to control. A recent conversation with a young woman comes to mind: she said that she knew this sounded a bit odd, but she felt a funny kind of relief because of AIDS. She said that it provided her with an external source of control over her sexual impulses at a time when she had very little faith in her own self-control. There has always been something—pregnancy and venereal disease preceded AIDS—that adolescents turn to in this fashion. The world of today offers this kind of support, but also very little solace. The potential for total destruction is great, and the romanticizing of youth over-emphasizes the here and now for our adolescents and ourselves.

On the other hand, we are also living in a world that offers expanding roles and opportunities for both women and men, and people of diverse backgrounds, in the personal, familial, and socioeconomic realms. There is clearly growing acceptance of different living and working arrangements, interpersonal styles, and worldviews. Some kinds of overt and subtle discrimination are diminishing, while others are being struggled against. The world in which adolescents live is one that is clearly in the process of change, not one that is stagnating. That, too, is consonant with adolescence, and part of the legacy that we are left with from that period of our lives. The memory of change and a sense of greater resolution from it . . . these are aspects of the adolescent journey that are a source of true inspiration throughout life.

References

Adams-Silvan, A. (1995). Personal communication.

Adatto, C. P. (1958). Ego integration observed in the analysis of late adolescents. *International Journal of Psycho-Analysis* 39:172–177.

———(1991). Late adolescence to early adulthood. In *The Course of Life, vol. IV, Adolescence*, ed. S. Greenspan and G. Pollock, pp. 357–375. Madison, CT: International Universities Press.

Aichhorn, A. (1925). *Wayward Youth*. New York: Viking.

Allen, M. P. (1989). *Transformations: Crossdressers and Those Who Love Them*. New York: Dutton.

Ausubel, D. (1954). *Theory and Problems of Adolescent Development*. New York: Grune & Stratton.

Ausubel, D., and Ausubel, P. (1966). Cognitive development in adolescence. *Review of Educational Research* 36:403–413.

Bach, S. (1994). *The Language of Perversion and the Language of Love.* Northvale, NJ: Jason Aronson.

Baittle, B., and Offer, D. (1971). On the nature of adolescent rebellion. *Adolescent Psychiatry* 1:139–160.

Bell, A. (1964). The significance of the scrotal sac and testicles for the prepuberty male. *Psychoanalytic Quarterly* 34:182–206.

Bem, S. L. (1993). *The Lenses of Gender: Transforming the Debate on Sexual Inequality.* New Haven, CT: Yale University Press.

Benjamin, J. (1988). *The Bonds of Love: Psychoanalysis, Feminism, and the Problem of Domination.* New York: Pantheon.

Beres, D. (1958). Vicissitudes of superego functions and superego precursors in childhood. In *Psychoanalytic Study of the Child* 13:324–351. New York: International Universities Press.

———(1961). Character formation. In *Adolescents: Psychoanalytic Approach to Problems and Therapy*, ed. S. Lorand and H. Schneer, pp. 1–9. New York: Hoeber.

Bernfeld, S. (1938). Types of adolescence. *Psychoanalytic Quarterly* 7:243–312.

Bernstein, D. (1979). Female identity synthesis. In *Career and Motherhood: Struggles for a New Society*, ed. A. Roland and B. Harris, pp. 103–123. New York: Human Sciences.

———(1990). Female genital anxieties, conflicts, and typical mastery modes. *International Journal of Psycho-Analysis* 71:151–165.

Blos, P. (1962). *On Adolescence: A Psychoanalytic Interpretation.* New York: Free Press.

———(1963). The concept of acting out in relation to the adolescent process. *Journal of the American Academy of Psychiatry* 2:118–143.

———(1967). The second individuation process of adolescence. *Psychoanalytic Study of the Child* 22:162–186. New York: International Universities Press.

———(1968). Character formation in adolescence. *Psychoanalytic Study of the Child* 23:245–263. New York: International Universities Press.

———(1972). The functions of the ego ideal in adolescence. *Psychoanalytic Study of the Child* 27:93–97. New York: Quadrangle Books.

———(1974). The genealogy of the ego ideal. *Psychoanalytic Study of the Child* 29:43–88. New Haven, CT: Yale University Press.

——— (1991). The role of the early father in male adolescent development. In *The Course of Life, vol. IV: Adolescence*, ed. S. I. Greenspan
and G. H. Pollock, pp. 1–16. Madison, CT: International Universities Press.

Blum, H., ed. (1976). Female psychology: contemporary psychoanalytic
issues. *Journal of the American Psychoanalytic Association, (suppl.)*
24. New York: International Universities Press.

Bohman, M. (1970). *Adopted Children and Their Families*. Stockholm:
Proprius.

Boris, H. (1984). The problem of anorexia nervosa. *International Journal
of Psycho-Analysis* 65:315–322.

Borowitz, G. H. (1973). The capacity to masturbate alone in adolescence.
Adolescent Psychiatry 3:130–143.

Breuer, J., and Freud, S. (1895). Case histories, case 4: Katharina (Freud).
Standard Edition 2:125–134.

Brinich, P. (1980). Some potential effects of adoption on self and object
representations. *Psychoanalytic Study of the Child* 35:107–133.
New Haven, CT: Yale University Press.

——— (1990). Adoption from the inside out: a psychoanalytic perspective. In *The Psychology of Adoption*, ed. D. Brodzinsky and M.
Schechter, pp. 42–61. New York: Oxford University Press.

——— (1995). Psychoanalytic perspectives on adoption and ambivalence. *Psychoanalytic Psychology* 12:181–199.

Brinich, P. M., and Brinich, E. B. (1982). Adoption and adaptation.
Journal of Nervous and Mental Disease 170:489–493.

Brooks-Gunn, J., and Ruble, D. N. (1986). Men's and women's attitudes
and beliefs about the menstrual cycle. *Sex Roles* 14:287–299.

Brooks-Gunn, J., and Warren, M. P. (1985). Measuring physical status and
timing in early adolescence: a developmental perspective. *Journal of
Youth and Adolescence* 14:163–189.

Bruch, H. (1978). *The Golden Cage: The Enigma of Anorexia Nervosa*.
Cambridge, MA: Harvard University Press.

Chasseguet-Smirgel, J., ed. (1970). *Female Sexuality: New Psychoanalytic Views*. Ann Arbor, MI: University of Michigan Press.

Chodorow, N. (1978). *The Reproduction of Mothering: Psychoanalysis
and the Sociology of Gender*. Berkeley, CA: University of California
Press.

————(1989). *Feminism and Psychoanalytic Theory*. New Haven, CT: Yale University Press.

Clower, V. L. (1975). Significance and masturbation in female sexual development and function. In *Masturbation*, ed. I. M. Marcus and J. J. Francis, pp. 107–143. New York: International Universities Press.

Coles, R., and Stokes, G. (1985). *Sex and the American Teenager*. New York: Harper Colophon.

Dahl, E. K. (1993). The impact of divorce on a preadolescent girl. *Psychoanalytic Study of the Child* 48:193–207. New Haven, CT: Yale University Press.

Dalsimer, K. (1986). *Female Adolescence: Psychoanalytic Reflections on Literature*. New Haven, CT: Yale University Press.

Deutsch, H. (1944). *The Psychology of Women*. New York: Grune & Stratton.

————(1967). *Selected Problems of Adolescence*. New York: International Universities Press.

Diagnostic and Statistical Manual of Mental Disorders (1978). 3rd ed. Washington, DC: American Psychiatric Association.

Dinnerstein, D. (1976). *The Mermaid and the Minotaur*. New York: Harper.

Douvan, E., and Adelson, J. (1966). *The Adolescent Experience*. New York: Wiley.

Dyk, P. H., Christopherson, C. R., and Miller, B. C. (1991). Adolescent sexuality. In *Family Research: A Sixty-year Review 1930–1990, vol. 1*, ed. S. J. Bahr, pp. 25–63. New York: Lexington Books.

Eisert, D. C., and Kahle, L. R. (1986). The development of social attributions: an integration of probability and logic. *Human Development* 29:61–81.

Eissler, K. R. (1950). Ego-psychological implications in the psychoanalytic treatment of delinquency. In *Psychoanalytic Study of the Child* 5:97–121. New York: International Universities Press.

————(1958). Notes on problems of technique in the psychoanalytic treatment of adolescents. In *Psychoanalytic Study of the Child* 13:223–254. New York: International Universities Press.

Elkin, F., and Westley, W. A. (1955). The myth of the adolescent peer culture. *American Sociological Review* 20:680–684.

Epstein, J., and McPartland, J. (1976). The effects of open school organization on student outcomes. *American Educational Research Journal* 113:15–30.

Erikson, E. (1950). *Childhood and Society.* New York: Norton.

———(1956). The problem of ego identity. *Journal of the American Psychoanalytic Association* 4:56–121.

———(1959). Identity and the life cycle. *Psychological Issues* 1:680–684.

———(1968). *Identity, Youth, and Crisis.* New York: Norton.

Esman, A. H. (1975a). Consolidation of the ego ideal in contemporary adolescence. In *The Psychology of Adolescence*, pp. 211–218. New York: International Universities Press.

——— ed. (1975b). *The Psychology of Adolescence.* New York: International Universities Press.

——— ed. (1983). *The Psychiatric Treatment of Adolescents.* New York: International Universities Press.

———(1990). *Adolescence and Culture.* New York: Columbia University Press.

Evans, R. (1976). Development of the treatment alliance in the analysis of an adolescent boy. *Psychoanalytic Study of the Child* 31:193–224. New Haven, CT: Yale University Press.

Fast, I. (1984). *Gender Identity: A Differentiation Model.* Hillsdale, NJ: Lawrence Erlbaum.

Feinberg, L. (1993). *Stone Butch Blues.* Ithaca, NY: Firebrand Books.

Fischer, R. (1991). Pubescence: a psychoanalytic study of one girl's experience of puberty. *Psychoanalytic Inquiry* 11:457–479.

Ford, C., and Beach, F. (1951). *Patterns of Sexual Behavior.* New York: Harper & Row.

Fraiberg, S. (1955). Some considerations in the introduction to therapy in puberty. In *Psychoanalytic Study of the Child* 10:264–286. New York: International Universities Press.

———(1969). Libidinal object constancy and mental representation. *Psychoanalytic Study of the Child* 24:9–47. New York: International Universities Press.

Francis, J. J., and Marcus, I. M. (1975). Masturbation: a developmental view. In *Masturbation*, pp. 9–51. New York: International Universities Press.

Frank, A. (1947). *The Diary of a Young Girl.* New York: Pocket Books, 1953.

Freud, A. (1936a). Instinctual anxiety during puberty. In *The Writings of Anna Freud. Vol. II: The Ego and the Mechanisms of Defense*. New York: International Universities Press.

———(1936b). The ego and id at puberty. In *The Writings of Anna Freud. Vol. II: The Ego and the Mechanisms of Defense*. New York: International Universities Press.

———(1952). The mutual influences in the development of ego and id: introduction to the discussion. In *The Writings of Anna Freud. Vol. IV*, pp. 230–244. New York: International Universities Press.

———(1958). Adolescence. *Psychoanalytic Study of the Child* 13:255–278. New York: International Universities Press.

———(1965). *The Writings of Anna Freud. Vol. VI: Normality and Pathology in Childhood*. New York: International Universities Press.

Freud, S. (1905a). The transformations of puberty. *Standard Edition* 7:207–243.

———(1905b). Fragment of a case of hysteria. *Standard Edition* 7:3–122.

———(1914). On narcissism: an introduction. *Standard Edition* 14:69–81.

———(1917). Mourning and melancholia. *Standard Edition* 14:237–258.

———(1920). Psychogenesis of a case of homosexuality in a woman. *Standard Edition* 18:145–172.

———(1923). The ego and the id. *Standard Edition* 19:30–66.

———(1925). Some psychical consequences of the anatomical distinction between the sexes. *Standard Edition* 19:243–258.

———(1931). Female sexuality. *Standard Edition* 21:223–243.

———(1933). The dissection of the psychical personality, lecture XXXI, new introductory lectures on psychoanalysis. *Standard Edition* 22:57–80.

———(1940). An outline of psychoanalysis. *Standard Edition* 23:144–207.

Friedenberg, E. G. (1959). *The Vanishing Adolescent*. Boston: Beacon.

Frisch, R. E. (1983). Fatness, puberty, and fertility: the effects of nutrition and physical training on menarche and ovulation. In *Girls at Puberty*, ed. J. Brooks-Gunn and A. C. Petersen, pp. 29–49. New York: Plenum.

Frish, M. (1964). Identity problems and confused conception of the genetic ego in adopted children during adolescence. *Acta Paediatrica Psychiatria* 21:6–11.

Furman, E. (1973). A contribution to assessing the role of infantile separation-individuation in adolescent development. *Psychoanalytic Study of the Child* 28:193–207. New Haven, CT: Yale University Press.

Galenson, E., and Roiphe, H. (1976). Some suggested revisions concerning female development. *Journal of the American Psychoanalytic Association (suppl.)* 24:29–57.

Garai, J. E., and Scheinfeld, A. (1968). Sex differences in mental and behavioral traits. *Genetic Psychology Monographs* 77:169–299.

Geleerd, E. R. (1957). Some aspects of psychoanalytic technique in adolescence. *Psychoanalytic Study of the Child* 12:263–283. New York: International Universities Press.

———(1961). Some aspects of ego vicissitudes in adolescence. *Journal of the American Psychoanalytic Association* 9:394–405.

———(1964). Adolescence and adaptive regression. *Bulletin of the Menninger Clinic* 28:302–308.

Gesell, A. L., Ilg, F. L., and Ames, L. B. (1956). *Youth: The Years from Ten to Sixteen.* New York: Harper & Row.

Gilligan, C. (1982). *In a Different Voice: Psychological Theory and Women's Development.* Cambridge, MA: Harvard University Press.

———(1989). Preface. In *Making Connections: The Relational Worlds of Adolescent Girls at Emma Willard School*, ed. C. Gilligan, N. P. Lyons, and T. J. Hanmer, pp. 6–27. Cambridge, MA: Harvard University Press.

Gilmore, K. (1995). Gender identity disorder in a girl: insights from adoption. *Journal of the American Psychoanalytic Association* 43(1):39–59.

Gitelson, M. (1948). Character synthesis and the psychotherapeutic problem in adolescence. *American Journal of Orthopsychiatry* 18:422–431.

Glenn, J. (1978). Freud's adolescent patients: Katharina, Dora, and the "homosexual woman." In *Freud and His Patients.* ed. M. Kanzer and J. Glenn, pp. 23–47. New York: Jason Aronson.

Green, R. (1974). *Sexual Identity Conflict in Children and Adults.* New York: Basic Books.

Greenacre, P. (1958). Early physical determinants in the development of the sense of identity. *Journal of the American Psychoanalytic Association* 6:612–627.

Group for the Advancement of Psychiatry. (1968). *Normal Adolescence: Its Dynamics and Impact.* New York: Scribner's.

Hall, G. S. (1904). *Adolescence: Its Psychology and its Relation to Physiology, Anthropology, Sociology, Sex, Crime, Religion and Education.* New York: Appleton.

Hall, R. (1928). *The Well of Loneliness.* New York: Doubleday.

Hamburg, B. (1974). Early adolescence: a specific and stressful stage of the life cycle. In *Coping and Adaptation,* ed. G. Coehlho, D. A. Hamburg, and J. E. Adams, pp. 101–126. New York: Basic Books.

Hare-Mustin, R. T., and Maracek, J., eds. (1990). *Making a Difference: Psychology and the Construction of Gender.* New Haven, CT: Yale University Press.

Harley, M. (1970). On some problems of technique in the analysis of early adolescents. *Psychoanalytic Study of the Child* 25:99–121. New York: International Universities Press.

———(1971). Some reflections on identity problems in prepuberty. In *Separation-Individuation,* ed. J. B. McDevitt and C. F. Settlage, pp. 385–403. New York: International Universities Press.

Hart, M., and Sarnoff, C. (1971). The impact of menarche: a study of two stages of organization. *Journal of the American Academy of Child Psychiatry* 10:257–271.

Hartmann, H. (1939). *Ego Psychology and the Problem of Adaptation.* New York: International Universities Press.

———(1950). Comments on the psychoanalytic theory of the ego. *Psychoanalytic Study of the Child* 5:74–96. New York: International Universities Press.

Hartmann, H., Kris, E., and Loewenstein, R. M. (1951). Some psychoanalytic comments on "culture and personality." In *Psychoanalysis and Culture,* ed. G. B. Wilbur and W. Muensterberger, pp. 3–31. New York: International Universities Press.

Hass, A. (1979). *Teenage Sexuality: A Survey of Teenage Sexual Behavior.* New York: Macmillan.

Hill, J. (1973). *Some Perspectives on Adolescence in American Society.* The Office of Child Development, U.S. Department of Health,

Education and Welfare. Washington, DC: U.S. Government Printing Office.

Hill, J. P., and Lynch, M. E. (1983). The intensification of gender-related role expectations during early adolescence. In *Girls at Puberty: Biological, Psychological, and Social Perspectives*, ed. J. Brooks-Gunn and A. C. Peterson, pp. 201–228. New York: Plenum.

Hoffer, W. (1950). Development of the body ego. *Psychoanalytic Study of the Child* 5:18–23. New York: International Universities Press.

Hoffman, E. (1989). *Lost in Translation: A Life in a New Language*. New York: Penguin.

Hoffman, M. A., Ushpiz, V., and Levy-Shiff, R. (1988). Social support and self-esteem in adolescence. *Journal of Youth and Adolescence* 17:307–316.

Hogan, C. C. (1992). Sexual identifications in anorexia nervosa. In *Psychodynamic Technique in the Treatment of Eating Disorders*, ed. C. P. Wilson, C. C. Hogan, and I. L. Mintz, pp. 129–143. Northvale, NJ: Jason Aronson.

Hotaling, G. T., Atwell, S. G., and Linsky, A. S. (1978). Adolescent life changes and illness: a comparison of three models. *Journal of Youth and Adolescence* 7:393–403.

Hsu, F. L. K. (1961). Culture patterns and adolescent behavior. *International Journal of Social Psychiatry* 7:33–53.

Huston, A. C., and Alvarez, M. M. (1990). The socialization context of gender role development in early adolescence. In *From Childhood to Adolescence: A Transitional Period?* ed. R. Montemayor, G. R. Adams, and T. P. Gullotta, pp. 41–62. Newbury Park, CA: Sage.

Hyde, J. S. (1990). *Understanding Human Sexuality*. San Francisco: McGraw-Hill.

Inhelder, B., and Piaget, J. (1958). *The Growth of Logical Thinking from Childhood to Adolescence*. New York: Basic Books.

Jacobson, E. (1961). Adolescent moods and the remodelling of psychic structures in adolescence. *Psychoanalytic Study of the Child* 16:164–183. New York: International Universities Press.

——(1964). *The Self and Object World*. New York: International Universities Press.

Jones, E. (1922). Some problems of adolescence. In *Papers on Psychoanalysis*, 5th ed., pp. 389–406. London: Bailliere, Tindall, and Cox.

————(1927). The early development of female sexuality. *International Journal of Psycho-Analysis* 8:459–472.

Jones, J., and Barlow, D. (1990). Self-reported frequency of sexual urges, fantasies, and masturbatory fantasies in heterosexual males and females. *Archives of Sexual Behavior* 19:269–279.

Josselyn, I. (1952). *The Adolescent and His World.* New York: Family Services Association of America.

————(1967). The adolescent today. *Smith College Studies in Social Work* 38:1–15.

Kaplan, L. J. (1984). *Adolescence: The Farewell to Childhood.* New York: Simon and Schuster.

Kaplan, R. (1992). Another coming out manifesto disguised as a letter to my mother. In *The Erotic Impulse*, ed. D. Steinberg, pp. 71–74. New York: Putnam.

Katan, A. (1951). The role of displacement in agoraphobia. *International Journal of Psycho-Analysis* 32:41–50.

Katchadourian, H. (1977). *The Biology of Adolescence.* New York: W. H. Freeman.

Keniston, K. (1962). Social change and youth in America. *Daedalus* 91:53–74.

Kessler, S., and McKenna, W. (1978). *Gender: An Ethnomethodological Approach.* New York: Wiley.

Kestenberg, J. (1961). Menarche. In *Adolescents: Psychoanalytic Approach to Problems and Therapy*, ed. S. Lorand and H. Schneer, pp. 19–50. New York: Hoeber.

————(1968). Phase 3: puberty, growth, differentiation and consolidation. *Journal of the American Academy of Child Psychiatry* 7:108–151.

Kiell, N. (1964). *The Universal Experience of Adolescence.* New York: International Universities Press.

Kiev, A. (1972). *Transcultural Psychiatry.* Hammondsworth, England: Penguin.

Kincaid, J. (1983). *Annie John.* New York: Penguin.

Kinsey, A. C., Pomeroy, W. B., and Martin, C. E. (1948). *Sexual Behavior in the Human Male.* Philadelphia: Saunders.

Kinsey, A. C., Pomeroy, W. B., Martin, C. E., and Gebhard, P. H. (1953). *Sexual Behavior in the Human Female.* Philadelphia: Saunders.

Kleeman, J. (1971a). The establishment of core gender identity in normal girls. Part I. Introduction: the development of the ego capacity to differentiate. *Archives of Sexual Behavior* 1:103–116.

————(1971b). The establishment of core gender identity in normal girls. Part II. How meanings are conveyed between parents and child in the first three years. *Archives of Sexual Behavior* 1:117–129.

————(1976). Freud's views on early female sexuality in the light of direct child observation. *Journal of the American Psychoanalytic Association (suppl.)* 24:2–29.

Kohut, H. (1966). Forms and transformations of narcissism. *Journal of the American Psychoanalytic Association* 14:243–272.

————(1971). *The Analysis of the Self.* New York: International Universities Press.

Kornitzer, M. (1971). The adopted adolescent and the sense of identity. *Child Adoption* 66:43–48.

Lampl-de Groot, J. (1950). On masturbation and its influence on general development. *Psychoanalytic Study of the Child* 5:153–174. New York: International Universities Press.

————(1962). Ego ideal and superego. *Psychoanalytic Study of the Child* 17:48–57. New York: International Universities Press.

Laufer, M. (1966). Object loss and mourning during adolescence. *Psychoanalytic Study of the Child* 21:269–294. New York: International Universities Press.

————(1968). The body image, the function of masturbation and adolescence: problems of ownership of the body. *Psychoanalytic Study of the Child* 23:114–137. New York: International Universities Press.

————(1976). The central masturbation fantasy, the final sexual organization and adolescence. *Psychoanalytic Study of the Child* 31:297–316. New Haven, CT: Yale University Press.

Laufer, M. E. (1981). The adolescent's use of the body in object relationships and in the transference: a comparison of borderline and narcissistic modes of functioning. *Psychoanalytic Study of the Child* 36:163–180. New Haven, CT: Yale University Press.

Laufer, M., and Laufer, M. E. (1984). *Adolescence and Developmental Breakdown: A Psychoanalytic View.* New Haven, CT: Yale University Press.

Leadbetter, B. J. and Dione, J. P. (1981) The adolescent's use of formal operations thinking in solving problems related to identity formation. *Adolescence* 16:111–121.

Lerner, H. (1976). Parental mislabeling of female genitals as a determinant of penis envy and learning inhibitions in women. *Journal of the American Psychoanalytic Association (suppl.)* 24:269–283.

Levy-Warren, M. H. (1987). Moving to a new culture: cultural identity, loss, and mourning. In *The Psychology of Separation and Loss,* ed. J. Bloom-Feshbach, S. Bloom-Feshbach, and associates, pp. 300–315. San Francisco: Jossey-Bass.

———(1992). Adolescent development. In *Interface of Psychoanalysis and Psychology*, ed. J. W. Barron, M. N. Eagle, and D. L. Wolitzky, pp. 266–283. Washington, DC: American Psychological Association.

Lewin, K. (1939). Field theory in social psychology: concepts and methods. *American Journal of Sociology* 44:868–896.

———(1951). *Field Theory in Social Science.* New York: Harper & Row.

Lewis, M. (1972). State as an infant-environment interaction: an analysis of mother–infant behavior as a function of sex. *Merrill-Palmer Quarterly* 18:95–121.

Loewald, H. (1973). On internalization. *International Journal of Psycho-Analysis* 54:9–17.

———(1979). The waning of the oedipus complex. *Journal of the American Psychoanalytic Association* 27:751–775.

———(1980). *Papers on Psychoanalysis.* New Haven, CT: Yale University Press.

Mahler, M. (1968). *On Human Symbiosis and the Vicissitudes of Individuation.* New York: International Universities Press.

Mahler, M., Pine, F., and Bergman, A. (1975). *The Psychological Birth of the Human Infant.* New York: Basic Books.

Manaster, G. J., Saddler, C. D., and Wukasch, L. (1977). The ideal self and cognitive development in adolescence. *Adolescence* 7:547–558.

McWhinnie, A. M. (1969). The adopted child in adolescence. In *Adolescence: Psychosocial Perspectives*, ed. G. Caplan and S. Lebovici, pp. 133–142. New York: Basic Books.

Meeks, J. E. (1971). *The Fragile Alliance.* Baltimore: Williams & Wilkins.

Meyer, J. H. (1995). Personal communication.

Miller, J. B. (1973). *Psychoanalysis and Women*. New York: Brunner/Mazel.

———(1976). *Toward a New Psychology of Women*. Boston, MA: Beacon.

Minuchin, S., Rosman, B. L., and Baker, L. (1978). *Psychosomatic Families: Anorexia Nervosa in Context*. Cambridge, MA: Harvard University Press.

Mishne, J. M. (1986). *Clinical Work with Adolescents*. New York: Free Press.

Money, J. (1975). Ablatio penis normal male infant sex-reassigned as a girl. *Archives of Sexual Behavior* 4:65–72.

Money, J., and Ehrhardt, A. (1972). *Men and Women, Boys and Girls*. Baltimore: Johns Hopkins University Press.

Moore, W. T. (1975). Some economic functions of genital masturbation during adolescent development. In *Masturbation*, ed. I. M. Marcus and J. J. Francis, pp. 231–276. New York: International Universities Press.

Moravia, A. (1950). *Two Adolescents: The Stories of Agostino and Luca*, trans. B. de Zoete. New York: Farrar, Straus.

Moss, H. A. (1967). Sex, age, and state as determinants of mother–infant interaction. *Merrill-Palmer Quarterly* 13:19–36.

Muensterberger, W. (1968). In panel on "aspects of culture in psychoanalytic theory and practice." S. W. Jackson (reporter). *Journal of the American Psychoanalytic Association* 16:651–670.

Mussen, P., Conger, J., and Kagen, J. (1974). *Child Development and Personality*. New York: Harper & Row.

Novick, J. (1976). Termination of treatment in adolescence. *Psychoanalytic Study of the Child* 31:389–414. New York: International Universities Press.

Offer, D. (1969a). *The Psychological World of the Teenager*. New York: Basic Books.

———(1969b). Adolescent turmoil. In *The Psychology of Adolescence*, ed. A. H. Esman, pp. 141–154. New York: International Universities Press.

Offer, D., and Offer, J. (1975). *From Teenager to Young Manhood*. New York: Basic Books.

Offer, D., Ostrov, E., and Howard, K. I. (1981). *The Adolescent: A Psychological Self-Portrait.* New York: Basic Books.

Olesker, W. (1984). Sex differences in 2- and 3-year-olds: mother–child relations, peer relations, and peer play. *Psychoanalytic Psychology* 1:269–288.

———(1990). Sex differences during the early separation-individuation process: implications for gender identity formation. *Journal of the American Psychoanalytic Association* 38:325–346.

Pearson, G. H. J. (1958). *Adolescence and the Conflict of Generations.* New York: Norton.

Person, E., and Ovesey, L. (1983). Psychoanalytic theories of gender identity. *Journal of the American Academy of Psychoanalysis* 11:203–226.

Piaget, J. (1947). *The Psychology of Intelligence.* New York: Harcourt.

———(1972). Intellectual evaluation from adolescence to adulthood. *Human Development* 15:1–12.

Pine, F. (1985). *Developmental Theory and Clinical Process.* New Haven, CT: Yale University Press.

———(1986). On the development of the "borderline-to-be." *American Journal of Orthopsychiatry* 56:450–457.

Plaut, E. A., and Hutchinson, F. L. (1986). The role of puberty in female psychosexual development. *International Review of Psycho-Analysis* 13:417–432.

Rapaport, D. (1958). The theory of ego autonomy. *Bulletin of the Menninger Clinic* 22:13–35.

Reich, A. (1951a). On countertransference. *International Journal of Psycho-Analysis* 32:25–31.

———(1951b). The discussion of 1912 on masturbation and our present-day views. *Psychoanalytic Study of the Child* 6:80–91. New York: International Universities Press.

———(1960a). Further remarks on countertransference. *International Journal of Psycho-Analysis* 41:389–395.

———(1960b). Pathologic forms of self-esteem regulation. In *Psychoanalytic Contributions*, pp. 288–311. New York: International Universities Press.

Ritvo, S. (1971). Late adolescence: developmental and clinical considerations. *Psychoanalytic Study of the Child* 26:241–263. New York: Quadrangle Books.

Roiphe, H. (1968). On an early genital phase. *Psychoanalytic Study of the Child* 23:348–365. New York: International Universities Press.

Roiphe, H., and Galenson, E. (1981). *Infantile Origins of Sexual Identity.* New York: International Universities Press.

Ross, E., and Rapp, R. (1983). Sex and society: a research note from social history and anthropology. In *Powers of Desire: The Politics of Sexuality,* ed. A. Snitow, C. Stansell, and S. Thompson, pp. 51–73. New York: Monthly Review Press.

Rothblatt, M. (1995). *The Apartheid of Sex: A Manifesto on the Freedom of Gender.* New York: Crown.

Sandler, J., Holder, A., and Meers, D. (1963). The ego ideal and ideal self. *Psychoanalytic Study of the Child* 18:139–158. New York: International Universities Press.

Savin-Williams, R. C., and Weisfeld, G. E. (1989). An ethnological perspective on adolescence. In *Biology of Adolescent Behavior and Development,* ed. G. R. Adams, R. Montemayor, and T. P. Gullotta, pp. 249–274. Newbury Park, CA: Sage.

Schafer, R. (1960). The loving and beloved superego in Freud's structural theory. *Psychoanalytic Study of the Child* 15:163–188. New York: International Universities Press.

———(1967). Ideals, the ego ideal, and the ideal self. *Psychological Issues* 18/19:131–174.

———(1968). *Aspects of Internalization.* New York: International Universities Press.

———(1973). Concepts of self and identity and the experience of separation-individuation in adolescence. *Psychoanalytic Quarterly* 42:42–59.

Schechter, M. D. (1960). Observations on adopted children. *Archives of General Psychiatry* 3:21–32.

Schwartz, H. (1988). *Bulimia: Psychoanalytic Theory and Treatment.* New York: International Universities Press.

Selman, R. L. (1980). *The Growth of Interpersonal Understanding.* New York: Academic Press.

Settlage, C. (1972). Cultural values and the superego in late adolescence.

Psychoanalytic Study of the Child 27:74–92. New York: Quadrangle Books.

Sherif, C. W. (1982). Needed concepts in the study of gender identity. *Psychology of Women Quarterly* 6:375–398.

Shopper, M. (1979). The (re)discovery of the vagina and the importance of the menstrual tampon. In *Female Adolescent Development*, ed. M. Sugar, pp. 214–233. New York: Brunner/Mazel.

Silverman, D. (1987). What are little girls made of? *Psychoanalytic Psychology* 4:315–334.

Simmons, R. G., and Blyth, D. A. (1987). *Moving into Adolescence.* New York: Adine de Gruyter.

Sklansky, M. A., reporter (1972). Indications and contraindications for the psychoanalysis of adolescents. *Journal of the American Psychoanalytic Association* 20:134–144.

Sorosky, A. D., Baran, A., and Pannor, R. (1975). Identity conflicts in adoptees. *American Journal of Orthopsychiatry* 43:18–25.

Sours, J. A. (1974). The anorexia nervosa syndrome. *International Journal of Psycho-Analysis* 55:567–576.

Spiegel, L. A. (1951). A review of contributions to a psychoanalytic theory of adolescence. *Psychoanalytic Study of the Child* 6:375–393. New York: International Universities Press.

——— (1958). Comments on the psychoanalytic psychology of adolescence. *Psychoanalytic Study of the Child* 13:296–308. New York: International Universities Press.

——— (1961). Identity and adolescence. In *Adolescents: Psychoanalytic Approach to Problems and Therapy*, ed. S. Lorand and H. Schneer, pp. 10–18. New York: Hoeber.

Steingart, I. (1969). On self, character, and the development of a psychic apparatus. *Psychoanalytic Study of the Child* 24:271–303. New York: International Universities Press.

Stern, D. (1985). *The Interpersonal World of the Infant.* New York: Basic Books.

Stern, D. N., Beebe, B., Jaffe, J., and Bennett, S. L. (1977). The infant's stimulus world during social interaction. In *Studies in Mother–Infant Interaction*, pp. 177–202. New York: Academic Press.

Stokes, G. (1985). The social profile. In *Sex and the American Teenager*, ed. R. Coles and G. Stokes, pp. 31–144. New York: Harper & Row.

Stoller, R. J. (1964). A contribution to the study of gender identity. *International Journal of Psycho-Analysis* 45:220–226.

——— (1968). *Sex and Gender: The Development of Masculinity and Femininity, vol. 1.* London: Maresfield Reprints.

——— (1975). *Sex and Gender: The Transsexual Experiment, vol. 2.* New York: Jason Aronson.

——— (1985). *Presentations of Gender.* New Haven, CT: Yale University Press.

Stolz, H. R., and Stolz, L. M. (1951). *Somatic Development in Adolescence.* New York: Macmillan.

Stone, L. J., and Church, J. (1957). Pubescence, puberty, and physical development. In *The Psychology of Adolescence,* ed. A. H. Esman, pp. 75–85. New York: International Universities Press, 1975.

Sugarman, A., and Kurash, C. (1981). The body as a transitional object in bulimia. *International Journal of Eating Disorders* 1(4):57–66.

Sullivan, H. S. (1953). *The Interpersonal Theory of Psychiatry.* New York: Norton.

Tanner, J. M. (1962). *Growth at Adolescence.* Springfield, IL: Charles C Thomas.

——— (1978). *Fetus to Man: Physical Growth from Conception to Maturity.* Cambridge, MA: Harvard University Press.

Tobin-Richards, M. H., Boxer, A. M., and Peterson, A. C. (1983). The psychological significance of pubertal change: sex differences in perceptions of self during early adolescence. In *Girls at Puberty,* ed. J. Brooks-Gunn and A. C. Petersen, pp. 127–154. New York: Plenum.

Tyson, P., and Tyson, R. (1990). *Psychoanalytic Theories of Development: An Integration.* New Haven, CT: Yale University Press.

Unger, R. K. (1990). Imperfections of reality: psychology constructs gender. In *Making a Difference: Psychology and the Construction of Gender,* ed. R. T. Hare-Mustin and J. Maracek, pp. 102–149. New Haven, CT: Yale University Press.

Wallerstein, J. S., and Blakeslee, S. (1989). *Second Chances.* New York: Ticknor and Fields.

Wallerstein, J. S., Blakeslee, S., and Kelly, J. B. (1980). *Surviving the Breakup.* New York: Basic Books.

Walters, W. A. W., and Ross, M. W., eds. (1986). *Transsexualism and Sex Reassignment*. New York: Oxford University Press.

Warren, M. P. (1983). Physical and biological aspects of puberty. In *Girls at Puberty*, ed. J. Brooks-Gunn and A. C. Petersen, pp. 3–28. New York: Plenum.

Werner, H. (1957). *Comparative Psychology of Mental Development*. New York: International Universities Press.

Wieder, H. (1977). On being told of adoption. *Psychoanalytic Quarterly* 46:1–22.

——— (1978a). On when and whether to disclose about adoption. *Journal of the American Psychoanalytic Association* 26:793–811.

——— (1978b). Special problems in the psychoanalysis of adopted children. In *Child Analysis and Therapy*, ed. J. Glenn, pp. 557–577. New York: Jason Aronson.

Wilson, C. P., with the assistance of Hogan, C. C., and Mintz, I. L., eds. (1985). *Fear of Being Fat: The Treatment of Anorexia and Bulimia (revised)*. New York: Jason Aronson.

Wilson, C. P., Hogan, C. C., and Mintz, I. L., eds. (1992). *Psychodynamic Technique in the Treatment of Eating Disorders*. Northvale, NJ: Jason Aronson.

Winnicott, D. W. (1958). *Collected Papers: Through Paediatrics to Psychoanalysis*. London: Tavistock.

——— (1964). *The Child, the Family, and the Outside World*. Harmondsworth, England: Penguin.

——— (1965). *The Maturational Processes and the Facilitating Environment*. New York: International Universities Press.

——— (1967). The location of cultural experience. *International Journal of Psycho-Analysis* 48:368–372.

——— (1971). *Playing and Reality*. London: Tavistock.

Wisdom, J. (1982). Male and female. *International Journal of Psycho-Analysis* 64:159–168.

Wolff, P. H. (1959). Obeservations on newborn infants. *Psychosomatic Medicine* 21:110–118.

Wyshak, G., and Frisch, R. E. (1982). Evidence for a secular trend in age of menarche. *New England Journal of Medicine* 306:1033–1035.

Zilboorg, G. (1944). Masculine and feminine. *Psychiatry* 7:257–296.

Index

ABOUT THE AUTHOR

Dr. Marsha Levy-Warren is Associate Director of the Institute for Child, Adolescent, and Family Studies (ICAFS), Clinical Associate Professor of Psychology in the New York University Postdoctoral Program in Psychotherapy and Psychoanalysis, and a Supervising and Training Analyst at the New York Freudian Society and Psychoanalytic Training Institute. She is also a Visiting Associate Professor both in the Department of Psychology and the Program in Women's Studies at Princeton University. Dr. Levy-Warren maintains a private practice of psychotherapy and psychoanalysis with adolescents and adults in New York City. She is married and the mother of two adolescent children.